Initiation into Soul Consciousness...

The Awakening Time

by

Diana M. Olson

Initiation into Soul Consciousness: The Awakening Time

Copyright © 2003 Diana M. Olson

All rights reserved. No part of this book may be reproduced or transmitted in any form or by any means without the written consent of the publisher.

Published by Hats Off Books™
610 East Delano Street, Suite 104
Tucson, Arizona 85705 U.S.A.

ISBN: 1-58736-132-9
LCCN: 2002094804

Acknowledgments

Words cannot adequately express the sincere gratitude Derek and I wish to convey to Kalindras, Daneus, John, Robert, and the host of spiritual and cosmic guides whom we came to know and love during what can only be described as the most incredible and rewarding experiences of our lives.

We especially wish to thank all eight children who had no earthly 'conscious' choice in the selection of their parents but had to put up with us anyway whilst assisting us in our learning: Rodian, Ganis, Karl, Liana, Sara, Michelle, Jason, and Cathleen. You all deserve a medal. We wish you much light and love.

High on our list of acknowledgements, we would like to thank a wonderful teacher and kindred soul, Anny Slegten, who gave us the tools to safely explore past lives and other realities.

To Azad Jaffer we offer our profound gratitude for 'introducing' us to two incredible pale-green onyx eggs that completely changed the way we view the world.

Special thanks are extended to all of our students and friends for encouraging us with their support, even when we retreated from the scene for a while. Pierre Poignonnec and James Russell, thank you for so generously making that retreat possible.

For taking us into their hearts on the final stretch, we are deeply indebted to Elvira and Helmut Thiem, who were so generous with their wisdom, love, time, and wondrous gifts of Mother Nature's Okanagan Valley harvest.

A special thanks to my 'bosom buddy' Janet Tinnes, whose loyal friendship inspired me to 'hang in there' during trying circumstances.

To our Scottish friend—an etheric dynamo known to us in this incarnation as Tom McDowall—thank you for otherworldly insights and encouragement which kept us on track and spurred me to complete this book.

We wish to express our gratitude to Darlene Grandish, for hours voluntarily spent transcribing tapes.

Last, but by no means least, I'd like to express profound thanks to Derek, my husband, twin-flame, alter ego and partner in this joint 'awakening time' adventure, who, in his own inimitable way, showed me the true meaning of unconditional love....

Diana

Preface

When the winds of change blow sometimes it's with a rattle and a growl. Sometimes it's with a hurricane force that sweeps a body along like helpless tumbleweed. But within that relentless embrace there is a message from the universe. As soon as you allow yourself to trust and willingly enter into the experience, you will be swept upwards into new avenues of understanding. Give yourself permission to enjoy the ride.

The winds of change blew Derek into my life eleven years ago. I was a single parent working as a secretary; he was a general factotum in building and house renovations. A mutual interest in spiritualism and reincarnation brought us together, kindling an urgent desire to explore past lives and prompting us to take regression therapy training.

An inner knowing was telling us we had a specific purpose for being together, and so, like two mismatched lemmings, we threw ourselves into a chasm of mid-life career changes and matrimony.

Riding a whirlwind of learning experiences, our tempestuous relationship swept us into a 180-degree spin. An injury to Derek's hand and cutbacks at my workplace saw us both out of jobs exactly two weeks after completing training to become hypnotherapists. It seemed as if a higher energy was spurring us on to become self-employed, taking us kicking and screaming out of a rapidly disintegrating comfort zone of old ideas and beliefs. Our immediate prospects looked bleak, with insufficient funds to start a business. Yet circumstances dictated an immediate career change for both of us.

During an intense four-year time span, we battled trials of a blended family, we separated and reunited twice, and we opened our own business as hypnotherapists and teachers of metaphysics and Reiki, a method of 'hands-on healing' involving energy manipulation, which originated in Japan in the late 1800s.

During that four year 'apprenticeship,' while visiting a gem store one day, Derek placed a large onyx egg into my hand and I saw a vision from which there was no turning away. It thrust us headlong into the incredible world of rocks and crystals, automatic writing and channeling, activating psychic abilities, and inspiring us to teach others how to reach beyond their present realities. After being told I would write a book, a small quartz crystal told us of an ancient promise, a vow to meet, in this, 'The Awakening Time.'

Two years later, acting upon a deep inner calling prompting us to finish writing this book, we closed the business, gave away most of our belongings and went into virtual isolation.

This book is a narrative of our extraordinary, inextricably interwoven personal journey of a teaching and working partnership; it also includes conversations with our spiritual guides, with how-to suggestions on raising awareness and accelerating personal vibratory rates in preparation for safely communicating with higher aspects of self.

We extend greetings to all seekers of truth and hope readers of this book find within its pages many gems that will bring a gleam of understanding and enlightenment.

INTRODUCTION

'So, this is what it feels like to start a book…' I had written as I sat in front of the computer examining my thoughts, casually waiting for the inspiration and words to flow. The day began at 4:12 AM for a 5:00 AM start at the office, just like any other 'ordinary' day. 'Ordinary,' because extra-ordinary things happen on ordinary days, all the time. In fact, I'm not sure now that there ever was any real 'ordinary' day.

So much has happened that if I put everything into words nobody would believe it. Yet should I try to write it as fiction, it just might become a best seller. But fiction it's not, though I swear, sometimes fact most definitely is stranger than fiction.

Only a few days before, at a channeling workshop my husband, Derek, was giving, I had been told I was ready to begin writing a book, the first of four works, and I was introduced to Kalindras, the guide who would be with me for the duration. I had absolutely no inkling of what was ahead….

And so, like a child expectantly waiting for something wondrous to occur, I sat there in front of the computer, with fingers resting gently on the keyboard, poised, yet ready for instruction. A blank screen was staring at me, inviting words to appear. After about half an hour, I was still waiting for inspiration to flow into my mind as if directed by some magical source. By this time I was feeling a little silly. Nothing was happening, yet I waited some more.

"Give me a break," I whined to myself, and then surely enough, from somewhere inside my head ideas began flowing, but so slowly it was like coaxing fridge-cold honey from a jar. One-and-a-half hours later I had written my first page and proudly sent the document to print.

My faithful Bubble Jet began spitting out words, but only seconds later it sputtered to a halt. The dreaded 'SOFTWARE FAILURE' message flashed briefly across the monitor and then the screen went blank. Holding my breath and praying for a miracle to happen, I pressed the left mouse button and rebooted the computer. Although I was able to access my precious document, to my dismay the only words on the screen were, 'So, this is what it feels like to start a book'!

This was freaky. Was that all I'd written when I first saved my document? Hardly. I'm not in the habit of saving after typing each sentence. The most baffling thing to try and fathom was...how could those words possibly reappear when the rest of the document was lost?

I was really choked. Was this a small lesson reminding me to save the document to the computer's memory at least every few minutes? Perhaps in computer jargon it was telling me to cover my derriere, as my little dinosaur of a machine had no automatic backup feature. "Whatever that was all about, it's one lesson I won't forget in a hurry," I told myself. One lesson? Who was I kidding?

In a bizarre series of events occurring over the course of the next few weeks and months, there were more software failures, disk errors, not enough memory, and computer crashing stints than I care to admit to and for which the experts said there was no 'logical' explanation. We soon learned that 'logical,, along with 'trust' and 'lesson,' wore the same hat as 'pay attention.'

At a channeling workshop, my guide, Kalindras, suggested that 5:00 AM would be a beneficial time of day to begin work. He advised that at 7:00 AM sharp we should leave the office and return home "to nourish the physical and prepare for the work day," and segment each day so that we would have sufficient energy to carry us through our evening classes.

I eventually learned to switch off the computer at 7:00 AM sharp. Whenever I became so engrossed that I forgot, the computer would 'mysteriously' shut down. When we asked why, Kalindras explained in a very nice way that we would survive the upcoming sixteen-hour days at the office without burnout only by following a segmented schedule. We got the message; he and our other guides were just nudging us to take care of the body's physical needs so as to not overtax ourselves. Now, one thing's for sure; we pay attention whenever our guides give even the faintest suggestion of a direction or avenue to explore. Their way of bringing certain things to our attention or letting us know we're maybe overlooking a detail or two...is through the computer.

Derek and I are just a couple of ordinary seekers of truth. Sure, to many folks, our union appeared mismatched. Some predicted we'd never make it together past the six-month mark. But we knew we had been brought together for a very special purpose. That purpose became the projection of who we really are, not only opening up a new way of life, but becoming the 'open sesame' to communication with other realities, during which time our lives were turned upside down and inside out.

We trust in God and we've learned to trust our spirit guides. We listen, whilst allowing our own free will to have full rein as we explore circumstances and situations that unfold to give us a deeper understanding of what we are doing and why we are here.

Shortly after my first channeling workshop, we were introduced to more guides, crystals, and devas, and were led to two onyx eggs which affectionately became known to us as 'Intensity' and 'Sanctuary,' all to get us to use our psychic gifts, which opened the door to the realities of a whole new world.

After six months of early morning channeling sessions, we had over one hundred documents transcribed and entered onto the computer.

On February 6, 1995, I sat down with a new software manual in front of me, trying to figure out how to put everything together. I had written a book, for sure, although I hadn't followed any format or plan or outline. I'd just followed directions, one by one, and ended up with all these separate documents entered into the computer. Not exactly a book, you say? Well, with just a little juggling, I'll probably find I have two, I told myself optimistically....

Almost a year later, I was still juggling the documents and adding brief explanatory titles to each. I trimmed their numbers down to 51 as I completed the second draft, but I still had way too much material. I realized I must devote myself full-time to working on the book. At the end of December 1995, we closed our Center and left Alberta for the seclusion of a small cottage in Osoyoos, British Columbia. Devoting myself entirely to the major task of pruning and editing, and the lengthy process of sending out inquiries to publishers, it took another four months before I could say the work was done. And then there was more. I found my work had just begun!

Our book tells of what for us became "The Awakening Time." We sincerely believe this is the awakening time for everyone upon our beautiful planet, and we hope our work will help others 'see' there is more 'out there' than meets the eye as mankind embraces all that this new millennium offers.

I'm no longer a newcomer to all this metaphysical stuff. I can now honestly say I've been around the block many times and hope to do more rounds again with my three grandchildren. Although I always used to believe it was others who had all the psychic gifts, my children included (from whom, incidentally, I learned a great deal), it wasn't until I'd turned the half-century mark that my own latent abilities kicked into gear. I'm not the first one to air the view that we all have psychic abilities; we're born with them but for whatever reason, most of us push them aside when we are very young.

When I was a kid, nobody talked about such things openly. So I realize we are fortunate that we now live in an era in which it's become more acceptable to talk about vibrations and energies because of the New Age Love Affair and the once passé 'guardian angels' who have been taken out of mothballs and allowed out of the closet. Today, people are more openly seeking direction to reclaim their rightful gifts. Guardian angels have been instrumental in showing psychic phenomena in a new light. They are being given new credibility, complete with the power of protection and all the attributes of spiritual perfection, as they assist seekers of the truth to realize the value of a true friend and companion always close at hand.

These spiritual beings, guardian angels, are now receiving the recognition they so truly deserve. But, beware! Seekers of truth must learn to discern the true from the false. What do you think they would be told if they asked an imposter, a trickster (as some disembodied souls are), if it were a guardian angel or not? Do you really think it would give any answer other than the one the seeker hopes to hear? And how would these truth-seekers know the difference? They wouldn't!

These last eleven years our eyes have been opened. Our naïve opinions about life and after-life have changed. We've learned there's an ocean of imposters out there, masquerading for people desperately seeking a helping hand and who cannot tell the difference between a disembodied spirit and a high spiritual being. Do you know what happens after death to those with no beliefs or who die in fear of eternal damnation?

Most of us are blind to the truth and we're sick, weak, or lame because, by choice and imprinting, we've given our power away to other people. We have been led by our noses since we were toddlers, having been taught to place our trust in others. Now we so desperately want to put our trust in guardian angels or beings that we believe are from the spiritual realms. But, again, beware!

It would have been so easy to stay within the religion in which I was raised, but I wanted answers. And so, in my early twenties, I gradually drifted away from my church to experience life's lessons the complicated way, as most of us do. I became a searcher for the truth. And, I must admit, every day I search a little more, because the more I learn makes me realize that life is a continual learning and reassessment process. I sampled different religions along the way, discovering that the humble beginnings of most religions had been built around the teaching of prophets sent at different time periods by the Creator, our one true Source, or God, to give soul-searching man and woman direction. The origins of the various religious beliefs seemed similar, with a common thread running through all of them: telling of a creator figure, and a continued existence on another plane after death.

Because of my own imprinting, at first I found the theory of reincarnation and soul fragmenting difficult to swallow. In our society, the ego in all of us has a hard time accepting this. We all like to believe it's me, here and now, that is the only important thing on earth and when we die it's going to be me, the same, going on forever and ever in Heaven or some such eternal and celestial abode.

Other cultures accept the multi-life aspect of themselves without question, yet to our society it may seem there are not many advantages, as oftentimes those who embrace this philosophy are seen as doing little to improve their lot, because of a belief in karma.

Be that as it may; whether we believe in one life to be lived or many, it's our responsibility to ourselves to expand our own conscious awareness and spirituality, not sit back and expect some organized religion or priest or deity to do it for us. We must literally do it for ourselves.

We urge you to seek and find the truths for yourself, from within. That may not happen, though, if you rely solely upon neatly packaged and bound creeds and dogmas—they have lost much of their original content and context through the repeated interference and censorship of human egos with limited understanding and vision.

Although they may have served a wonderful purpose and provided a strong foundation, it is now time to go beyond beliefs that may be serving to keep us stuck. But there is no need to discard those beliefs. We will need them later as a yardstick to measure our progress, and at that time we may find within them new meaning.

We were all delivered onto this planet as perfect little specimens, though some of us may have chosen to learn through certain physical challenges and painful experiences in every sense of the word. Prior to this lifetime on earth, we chose the lessons we wish to learn and we set the scene for them by selecting parents or guardians who would provide the necessary background for such experiences that assist us on our own chosen path in life.

If, in our opinion, we felt we were given a bum steer, whether good or bad, it was because of the choices we made. Regardless of what may have happened in our lives, we must accept that there was a reason. It's up to us to seek out and find that reason, and learn the whys and wherefores. Then, if we feel we've learned enough from current lessons and really want to change present circumstances, our learning experiences, and broaden our outlook so we may truly see the forest and not the trees, know that we will be assisted. There are willing teachers ready to guide us through this segment in the School of Life.

But we must avoid blaming others for any disappointments in life. By perceptively raising our conscious awareness, through searching for a higher level of understanding, we may not only find 'the reason' for those disappointments or hurts, we may also find true enlightenment. There are many courses on the market designed to open one's conscious awareness, and if we trust our inner guidance, we may be directed to responsible, caring teachers. Priceless information and a shortcut to begin the journey may be found, enabling us to perhaps learn in one weekend or a few weeks the essence of what may have taken our teacher twenty years or a lifetime to learn.

There are less expensive, slower, routes to take and it is possible to do it alone, physically alone, that is. Much information has been channeled from high spiritual beings and is in book form. But in our search, we must keep an open mind and accept only information that feels right deep down inside—as a truth for self—and reject what doesn't. Whatever 'sits right' is right for us.

However, when we are ready to receive 'different' information, we may even get the message where or when we least expect it. Sometimes the sender doesn't always seem to know the difference between AM and PM, as we found out on more than one occasion. Like when we'd already been 'at it' since 3:00 AM. That day there was no getting away from it, no crawling back under the covers, no hiding under the pillow looking for more sleep.

Again, during the sleep state, Derek had been shown the truths, the secrets of the ages, as time was before time began, and as time is now. In the beginning, we were all One and time stood still. For the second consecutive morning, he was being told that now is the time for us to prepare for the task ahead. And the task is to show the way of the journey home. The way is one that has to be found and then told of or shown to others, so that they, too, if they so choose, can find their own way. And we are sure they will, because this is **The Awakening Time.**

TABLE OF CONTENTS

Chapter 1 1
'Spirit' ball; past-life regression leads to career change; 'Uncommon hypnotherapy'; strange phenomenon of entity attachment; demise of charley horses.

Chapter 2 15
Lessons of patience, tolerance; our first psychic fair; dreamcatcher; Intensity and Sanctuary; channeling workshop; a new guide; Jasmine.

Chapter 3 33
Early morning answers; red herrings; lessons; avoidance in life's dance; we're all an aspect of each other; honoring others' choices; seeking perfection in our desire to return to Source.

Chapter 4 43
Post-psychic fair; in darkness there is light; crystal cap brings a laugh; Awakening Time crystal and profound message.

Chapter 5 55
Symbology of the egg; man's need to align with nature; earth changes; 'The owl with the spotted glare'; working with onyx and crystals

Chapter 6 67
More strange happenings; lights in the sky; 'clicking' in my ear; observers and a giant eye; we create our own reality; Thanksgiving Day distraction—lessons in setting boundaries.

Chapter 7 85
Quartz Deva conversations; working with quartz; sugalite; crash course in awareness raising.

Chapter 8 97
Releasing cellular memories; healing; creating through dreams; nightmare interpreted; blame and denial; learning then letting go.

Chapter 9 .... **109**
Man out of touch; early religions; 'demons'; shutting out clairvoyance; self-worth; the creative force.

Chapter 10 .... **119**
We're given a name; a spanner in the works or a test?

Chapter 11 .... **131**
Parenting and control over 'older' souls; flying solo; family relationships; red slippers; another 'explosion'—an unresolved childhood issue.

Chapter 12 .... **143**
The Oneness; higher energies; cosmic beings and other realities; thoughts faster than light; roles and lessons.

Chapter 13 .... **153**
In training; the overall picture; simultaneous incarnations—spinning top analogy; Stanley Park; energy of renewal; divine essence within everything; the written word—panning for gold but finding gemstones.

Chapter 14 .... **169**
Questions on creation and evolution; different species; life forms from other planets; the monkey—for man to see himself within all life.

Chapter 15 .... **181**
Another rev-up?; Darginak; healing and cosmic guides; a knowing; saying grace.

Chapter 16 .... **187**
Rhythmic breathing; open-eye vs. closed-eye meditation; celibacy; words of advice; generate one's inner light.

Chapter 17 .... **203**
Releasing disembodied spirits; a column of light to attract attention; earthbound entities learning through 'osmosis.'

Chapter 18..217
How past lives affect us—degenerative disk disease gone after past life regression; first century A.D. earthenware bottle finds its way 'home'; Bros. Job and Matthew.

Epilogue..227
We do indeed create our own reality; isolation; Good Friday and the Awakening Time; learning through love.

Derek's Postscript..235

CHAPTER 1

It was 6:00 AM and I was wide awake on the Chesterfield with my hands cupping the back of my head, thinking of the new man in my life. I had a few minutes to spare before preparing to join the day's rat race. Outside, Edmonton was still locked in the grip of a typical Canadian winter. Hardly the scene to inspire any kind of 'get up and go.' I groaned, staring straight ahead at the painted concrete wall as I listened to the CHED radio newscaster forecast a high of minus 32 degrees. Then there was a brief flash of light as something like a small comet burst through the wall and hurtled towards me.

Startled, I watched the intrusion intently. I could see 'energy' forming a tail that followed the comet-like object and I could hear a high-pitched whizzing sound as I witnessed its rapid progress across the room. Silver-gray in color, it appeared to be slightly larger than a tennis ball. Instinctively, I ducked to one side, but kept the object in my line of vision. And then the thing stopped quite suddenly, hovering in mid-air about a foot away from the side of my head.

I could see the ball of energy pulsating and I turned my head slightly to get a better look. Just then the energy-ball vanished, but at that exact same moment I became aware of an intense throbbing in my forehead, just above the center of my brow. Touching my forehead, I could feel a pulsating beneath the skin, and I instantly became aware of an electrifying buzzing sensation spreading throughout my whole body, as if I had just been plugged into an electrical outlet.

I jumped to my feet and stood there momentarily, somewhat stunned by what had happened. Then I glanced around the room. Everything seemed normal...not even a mark on the wall where the strange object had burst through.

Cautiously, I placed both hands on my head, expecting to find my hair frizzled and standing on end, as in a silly comic strip. I made my way into the bathroom to take a good look at myself in the mirror. I looked normal enough for that hour of day, and there was nothing unusual about my hair. Surprisingly, I didn't feel scared. It was more like, "Then what the hell was that all about?" As if in response to my question, a strange kind of exhilaration filtered through as my imagination began to kick into high gear.

My next reaction was to call Derek, this new man in my life. Looking back, I saw how his arrival in the area had heralded more than one 'strange' event. Who was this man? Like me, one could best describe him as an eccentric. He's certainly the only person in this whole wide world who quite literally caused me to feel sparks fly the first time he touched my hand. Our relationship definitely began with a huge explosion once I allowed myself to think of him as in my square. He had energy to burn, I knew, but was it possible he could send a bolt of something like this my way? If he did, then I wanted an explanation, now. I wasted no time in finding out.

I quickly dialed his number, and as soon as he picked up the phone I blurted out, "Were you thinking of me just now?" After an affirmative response, I told him of my strange, 'electrifying' experience and asked what was going on. It wouldn't have surprised me in the least if he'd admitted responsibility for what happened. I had already learned that whenever he awoke in the mornings and began thinking of me, his early morning thoughts became my wake-up call! I had heard about 'thought forms,' too. Was there some connection?

Of course he had been thinking of me, he'd said, but what on earth made me think he was in any way responsible for such a strange occurrence? The plea of innocence was straightforward and simple, but I wasn't satisfied. I wanted an answer as to why my whole body was still buzzing like my fingers were stuck in a light socket.

Derek was intrigued by what had occurred, but he had no answers for me. Intrigued? What an under-statement, I thought, as I hung up the phone and sat puzzling over the strange phenomenon.

At a more respectable hour, I telephoned the very reverend lady who ministered to us at our church. My mentor could shed no light on the weird happening, but although she'd never heard of anything exactly like this before, she had heard mention of 'spirit balls' appearing to people.

Spirit balls? What the dickens were they? Again, my imagination ran riot. Had I been the target of flying beings from that realm we call Heaven or maybe even outer space? Perhaps a cosmic equivalent of Cupid armed with a large slingshot and energy balls instead of an arrow?

In the days that followed, I sought out people who might be able to throw some light on the subject of spirit balls, or flying balls, and I generously shared details of my strange encounter, but to no avail. Agreed, in the past I've been known to be a tad flamboyant when discussing my beliefs. This time, though, there was no mistaking what folks were thinking. Their expressions conveyed the message that I must be suffering from a mentally debilitating 'New Age plague' and therefore physical contact should be avoided at all costs.

Eventually, I got the message. I learned to keep my mouth shut, except with Derek. I was so grateful that I now had someone in my life who wouldn't scoff at what I said, or think it unusual.

I do vaguely remember eons ago asking for a man in my life with the same values, someone who would work alongside me, a spiritual person strong in his own beliefs and walking the same path. Reflecting back on the old saying from the good book, "Ask and ye shall receive," I'd like to point out that one must be very clear when asking. And very specific. If you want a companion, know that you may just attract someone, who is equal in awareness, but that person also may bring the strongest or hardest lessons into your life experience.

There were numerous occasions before I met Derek when I sat down to meditate and just knew I was on the right track. As I closed my eyes, I would see a wonderful vision of the most beautiful being; I told myself it must be the guardian angel I had longed to see as a child and I identified with the loving energy I always felt in its presence. The aura was indescribably brilliant, and quite distinctive, so I would mentally acknowledge my vision and proceed with the meditation.

One of the reasons I loved going to Sunday morning services was because I enjoyed watching the auras of the different speakers as they worked from the podium. It always intrigued me to see the auras changing color whenever each speaker began reading. But I only see auras when I'm specifically looking for them and 'unfocus' my eyes...and I'm not in the habit of doing that very often.

The day I took a look at Derek's aura, I did a double flip. We were teaching students how to see auras, so I sat Derek in front of a large black velvet banner, and then in front of a white one, using him as a subject for the lesson. There, in front of me, resplendent beneath those wonderful colors of a distinctively shaped aura, sat the vision I had seen so many times during my meditations; this was not some guardian angel, it was Derek! I was so thrilled as I realized those 'visions' had been given to me for a special reason. Obviously, this relationship of ours was destined to be more than a passing fancy. I almost kicked myself for not unfocusing my eyes earlier. Just think how much more unconditional love would be generated throughout the world if everyone could see the true beauty of everyone else arrayed in their crowning glory.

Of course, when I recounted the aura story to my eldest daughter (with her twin brother, she's half-way down the progeny line of six), she delighted in saying, "I told you so, Mom, when you first saw him, but you never listen to us kids, right?"

Admittedly, when I first noticed Derek shortly after his arrival in Edmonton, Liana had eyed him up and down, then she'd nudged me and whispered, "See that man over there, Mom? Well, he's the one you're going to spend the rest of your life with."

I'd followed her gaze. "Sorry, kid," I'd said, "he's definitely a cowboy and not my type." The guy was dressed in jeans and cowboy boots. I definitely wasn't into blue jeans. And I'd been without a man for eleven years, so at this stage in my life, I certainly didn't plan on making any changes.

Boy, was I in for a surprise! Somewhere along the line I must have eaten my words, because things moved very quickly after that. Not only did we begin working as a team during hands-on healing sessions, but also we were married within eight months.

For an entire two weeks after the 'spirit ball' experience, I felt a buzz and glow throughout my entire body, day in, day out. It took that time for me to adjust to the new energy. It wasn't as if previously I hadn't been aware of energy and vibrations. On countless occasions I'd actually taken hold of a tangible energy and felt it flowing through my hands prior to 'giving' a hands-on healing, so I was no stranger to the sensation that was now running so evidentially and strongly through my body at all times.

As the weeks went by, I became more accustomed to the heightened energy and more aware of my own sensitivity. Before, when holding my hands a few inches above a person's body during a healing session, I could feel hot or cold blasts of energy 'telling' me where the natural flow was blocked. Now, in addition, I would frequently receive 'visions' or 'messages' which I would convey to the recipient. I can't say I understood how this was happening, or why, but I did know it was not I 'doing' the healing; I was simply allowing my body to be used for energy transference at those times.

Derek had been doing past-life regressions for some time; he had a natural knack for them. And, of course, I was always right up front when he called for a volunteer. One evening, as he led me into a regression, the experience was so vivid my heart began pounding. It felt as if my heart was ready to explode right out of my chest. I thrashed around desperately trying to free myself from falling beams and debris. Choking on dust-clogged air, I was fighting to get my breath and I could feel stairs being pulled away from beneath my feet. I had entered the experience right at the point where a house was collapsing upon me during a tornado, and I was re-living the terror. Fortunately, Derek was sufficiently skilled to detach me from the scene quickly and I came out of the experience none the worse for wear or scare other than my heart feeling as if it was racing double time.

But it seemed as if the incident had a higher purpose. We recognized at that moment the importance of a regression facilitator having the appropriate expertise or training for handling such situations properly. Looking back, I can see how the stage was being set for a career change. It was definitely a cue to seek training in the use of hypnosis, prompting probably the most guided decision either of us ever made.

Almost immediately, we embarked upon the necessary courses to become hypnotherapists. Several months later, armed with a wonderful tool to bring peace and harmony to all, including ourselves, we thought we were ready to open our own business. But it didn't quite work out that easily.

For a while I was the only one bringing in an income, as Derek was between jobs when we married. His teenage son and daughter moved in with us immediately after the wedding, bringing two friends with them. The strain was soon felt upon more than our meager budget. Derek finally found work, but within a couple of months serious hand injuries sustained during an accident on the job prevented Derek's return to the construction trade. And he made a most unwilling convalescent, possibly because the male ego gets quite bruised when good work ethics have been the be-all and end-all of life, and suddenly there's no job.

During this initial period of adjustment, our relationship was tested to the limit as offspring came and went. In true blended-family style, they appeared to do a wonderful job of playing one of us off against the other. I hear that this is the norm with combined families, but how come nobody warned me before our nuptials? I felt like the old nursery rhyme woman who lived in a shoe, with so many children she didn't know what to do. But that's not quite a fair comparison. At least the old woman got to spank her kids soundly and put them to bed, but ours were too big for that. Instead, three kids were shown the door, and two, plus grandchild, moved out.

Finally, realizing our marriage would survive only if we were on our own together, Derek and I rented an apartment for just the two of us.

In the course of that first year and three months of financial stress and blended-family tests, I had shown Derek the door once, and he had voluntarily 'walked out' three times. Friends pleaded with us to settle our differences. "You work so well together," they would say, "you're meant to be together." Those words always reminded me of the vision I had seen of Derek so many times in my meditations. If we were meant to be together, then why wasn't the path smoother for us?

* * *

During our hypnotherapy training, we had come to accept that things would be triggered in our lives; this is the subconscious mind's way of drawing our attention to situations that need to be looked at, reviewed, cleaned up, and cleared out. It's as if we are continually going through a personal, internal house-cleaning process. And boy, was stuff being triggered between us! Our buttons were being pushed all the time. But if we expect to help others, we have to clean up our own act first. Fortunately, our training certainly gave us plenty of opportunity to do just that.

Canada's Hypnotism Training Institute of Alberta, in Sherwood Park, near Edmonton, was unique as a place of learning. After taking our training there to become certified clinical hypnotherapists, Derek and I were enthusiastically looking forward to taking the advanced 'Uncommon Hypnotherapy' course, under the tutelage of the Institute's Director, Ms. A. Slegten, affectionately known to her students as Anny. She has a wonderful understanding of and empathy with her students and clients alike. Also, she has considerable knowledge of things esoteric. This brilliant woman devised a method to work with people in a coma and children or adults who are unable to communicate. She adapted the technique to conduct sessions 'in absentia,' using two qualified hypnotherapists, one of whom acts as the facilitator and the other as a surrogate in place of the client, the 'surrogate' interacting with the client on a psychic level.

The technique is very effective; however, it is only for therapists who are staunch of heart, as it can be fraught with unexpected complications when the surrogate session is used for spirit-releasement or clinical depossession (modern terms for exorcism). Unless full precautions are taken, there is a risk that the facilitator or the surrogate may end up with the client's 'symptoms' and may not have a clue what hit them until much later, when they begin to feel and act differently.

We had been impressed during the training as we watched live demonstrations of the process, and we felt deeply privileged to have taken the course.

Quite literally, within hours of completing this specialized training, we received an urgent telephone call. The caller sounded quite agitated in her concern for a mutual friend's teenage son who had a mental disorder and had been admitted once again into hospital. The call was a plea for help and it sounded like it would be a perfect opportunity to test out our newly acquired skills to work in absentia.

Within minutes, the boy's mother arrived at our home, bringing a photograph of her son. She spoke of conversations her son heard inside his head, and his fears of losing his sanity.

I elected to be the facilitator and Derek took on the role of surrogate. We had barely begun setting up 'protection' for ourselves before beginning the session, when Derek felt a thudding in his chest. Naturally, he was puzzled, but I believed it was probably the excitement of our first real surrogate session. Little did we know what we'd let ourselves in for! We went ahead with the routine. Afterwards, the mother left, obviously very skeptical but nevertheless somewhat optimistic.

Within a day or so of doing the surrogate session, I realized how moody Derek had become. He was surly to some extent and acting quite out of character, but I made allowances; I assumed the moodiness was because he hadn't been bringing in an income for some time because of his injured hand and, being a person raised on hard work, idleness didn't sit well. It was a 'man thing,' I told myself.

Barely one week later, due to the economic climate, the axe really fell. I was laid off from my secretarial job. Now we were both unemployed. And there was no nest egg to fall back upon...the hypnotherapy training had exhausted our source of supply.

With major cutbacks rampant within the business sector as a result of curtailed government spending, we knew that people my age were facing greater challenges in the job market and Derek couldn't go back to his old type of work; his accident had seen to that. The atmosphere at home was so tense it felt like an undercurrent of volatile energy simmering underground, just waiting for an opportunity to erupt.

Within two weeks of doing our first surrogate session Derek's moods worsened and we had a blazing row. Bitterness and hostility rained back and forth in a verbal battle so intense that it mounted in a crescendo of unbridled fury. I was astounded! This nasty 'piece of work' wasn't the man I married. And in a fit of rage, Derek gathered up a few of his belongings and that was it, he was gone. Just like that.

I told myself that this was the best thing that could have happened. We'd had arguments before, but I had never seen him like this. I couldn't understand how someone had changed so much in such a short space of time. He'd gone from a happy, teasing, lovable rascal to this moody, despicably nasty man whom it was impossible for me to love any more. I wanted inner peace and harmony in my life at all costs and if it meant Derek cutting loose, then so be it!

But I felt uneasy. There was something about this situation that didn't sit right. Apart from Derek's moodiness, there had been very little forewarning. Sure, we'd had our challenges, trials even, but not the stuff to cause such a swift split. Derek had always been a little on the loud, excitable side, but this? No. Not rage. Something was very wrong. But what? Although I felt relieved when he left—I didn't have to put up with the moods anymore—I worried for him.

About a week later I learned that, after storming out, Derek had bought a one-way plane ticket to Vancouver. After several angry, long-distance telephone calls, the tempest seemed to subside. And with subsequent mutual apologies appropriately made and accepted, Derek asked me to join him on the West Coast. We both agreed that, without the interference of kids, our relationship just might stand a chance for survival. So, without further delay, I packed up and moved to Vancouver.

Things were intolerable; nothing was sorted out between us, there had merely been a change of scene for moods and squabbles. I felt I had been manipulated away from my children. Within six weeks, I was back in Edmonton with my kids and that was that!

One thing I've learned through this is that we all have free will. Free will to do as we choose is our God-given right, isn't it? Yes, you say? My friend, you surely jest! Think again. I'm now convinced that we have free will only so long as it fits in with the Divine Plan, and if it doesn't, we're free to do as we're told. Obviously, Derek and I weren't through with our lessons yet.

But wonders never cease. Just weeks later, a subdued knight gallant straddled his Pony for the twelve hour drive to Edmonton from Vancouver. This wasn't the angry stranger who had stormed out of my life, it was the whirlwind man I loved and had married. Now, he was back to his lovable self again, or so it seemed. He helped me pack all my belongings once more and I willingly accompanied him back to the coast.

During the journey, Derek related a strange experience he'd had on the flight to Vancouver when he'd left in a rage. He reminded me that while in the armed forces, he'd served time as a paratrooper, so he was no wimp, having jumped from airplanes many times; in fact, he said, he was as comfortable with flying as ducks are with swimming. Consequently, one hour after he had stormed onto that Vancouver flight, he realized something was very wrong.

Just as the pilot announced that the plane was approaching Vancouver at a height of twenty-eight thousand feet and was beginning the descent, Derek felt a sudden, excruciating pain shooting through his right eye-socket and neck and across his shoulders. He was immediately locked into such agony that he held onto his head for the whole of the descent, desperately trying to alleviate the pain, but no self-healing could shift the piercing torture. He was panic-stricken. Fear of death flashed through his mind with the thought that this must be the end. Yet strangely, as soon as the plane landed, the pain disappeared as fast as it had first occurred.

After listening to Derek's account of the flight, I wondered what had caused the mysterious pain. It goes without saying; I was soon to find out.

Shortly after arriving at our destination in North Vancouver, it was like deja vu, or at least a repeat performance of my first visit. To my dismay, I found Derek's mood swings were still acute; one moment he was fine, then almost in mid-sentence, as it were, his anger would flare up and then he'd go into a cold silence, shutting me out of his world completely. After work, he'd sit hunched up with a book for hours on end without communicating. This went on for two weeks.

I was miserable. Being a stranger in this place, I had no one to talk to, and although I loved the beauty of North Vancouver, I couldn't help thinking I had made a big mistake coming back.

And then, one day when we were actually talking, Derek told me he was feeling particularly sore and stiff across the shoulders and his neck was hurting. He'd been this way for weeks.

I encouraged Derek to think back and see if he could recall the first time he felt this discomfort. He was surprised to recall he remembered feeling the pain and stiffness in his shoulders during our first surrogate session.

Immediately we decided a hypnotherapy session regressing him to that occasion would be in order. As I regressed Derek he concentrated on the pain in his shoulders and I directed him to another time when he was aware of the same sensation. He began describing an agonizing death. It was during the American Civil War. He was viewing the scene as one of the Confederate soldiers lying in wait to ambush a Union wagon train.

The wagon train approached. He knew there must have been a lookout somewhere as he heard the loud crack of a rifle firing. Immediately Derek screamed out in agony as he felt the searing pain of a bullet entering his right eye socket; the impact of the bullet jarred his neck and shoulders like a whiplash. Derek recognized that this was the identical pain he had experienced when the pilot announced the plane's descent into Vancouver.

Through further questioning, I discovered that this past-life experience was not one of Derek's former incarnations as I had at first suspected. Instead, Derek was viewing the lifetime of that Confederate soldier who had remained earthbound after death. I was astounded to learn that this entity had eventually attached himself to the young client for whom we did our first surrogate-session and then had hooked or transferred on to Derek. (A depossession had occurred, but because of the psychic link that was created as Derek communicated with the client during the session, at the moment the entity left the client, it transferred to another host—Derek—without either of us knowing.)

I cringed as I realized that this rough, tough, ornery character had been body-hopping since death, and there was no way he wanted to leave his present host. This most definitely was not one of Derek's own past incarnations. Derek was the victim of an entity attachment! No wonder such a marked difference in Derek's whole behavior and personality became apparent immediately after the surrogate session.

I thanked God for our training. The rest of the session became a clinical depossession, or 'spirit releasement,' as it is nowadays more politely named, and, I'm so very happy to relate, this time the intruder was successfully dispatched to the Light.

The results were instantaneous. Immediately after the session I asked Derek to check his body to see if there was any physical discomfort. The pain and stiffness he'd been carrying around for three months in his shoulders had gone. He hasn't had that searing pain in his eye socket again either. But, the biggest blessing of all was that Derek's whole personality and behavior returned to 'normal' immediately.

Pardon the pun, but there are certain dead giveaways that pinpoint the presence of an entity-attachment. By giveaways, I mean the entity lets the cat out of the bag, so to speak, not intentionally, more by a slip of the tongue or the apparent manifestation of aches or pains for which there is no medical explanation...or even newly noticeable mood-swings.

In my opinion, there must be countless multitudes of people walking around with entity attachments controlling or influencing their lives. I believe we were guided to 'Uncommon Therapy' to assist us in all aspects of our work and lives.

We both already knew about and had accepted the theory of reincarnation, and we certainly understood that certain conditions might be brought with us into this current lifetime. In other words, we set ourselves up for certain experiences that can be triggered by people, events going on around us, or even inanimate objects. And with the assistance of using past-life regressions, we can find out why certain things are happening to us now, physically, mentally, or emotionally, as all memories are stored at cellular level and may be brought forward, then when acknowledged, released.

Many people who know about reincarnation and past lives go for regressions so willingly, seeking to assist themselves, wanting to understand why certain conditions are plaguing them. But now, since our 'Uncommon Therapy' training and Derek's experience, I'm always suspicious when people claim to have been this or that in a past life. In whose past life? Is it his or her own or is it the life of an entity or spirit that's hitching a ride because he or she doesn't know where else to go? Who is actually being regressed? It's not necessarily the person going for the regression, although that person 'sees' and 'hears' and 'feels' all that is going on, just as if he or she is actually going through the past life experience.

If you have an entity on board, you have a usurper using your body and influencing your mind, too. The thoughts in your head are not necessarily yours...someone else can be thinking them for you, while you believe they are your very own. Have you ever been known to say, "Whatever made me say that," or "Why on earth did I think or do that?"

To understand more about this strange phenomenon, I recommend reading the book *The Unquiet Dead* by Dr. Edith Fiore. She explains uncontrollable urges or mood swings, memory lapses, or physical aches and pains for which doctors can't find a medical reason, and—a biggie here—hearing voices inside one's head. These could be symptoms of entity attachments.

We regarded Derek's session as a great success. We certainly did receive valuable lessons, from both client and therapist perspectives, having witnessed this first-hand experience of an entity attachment. Both of us had been aware of the terrible change in personality and the uncontrollable mood swings, then observed the 'releasement' and resulting return to 'normal' disposition and functioning, with an immediate cessation of pain and all physical discomforts.

* * *

This incident serves to illustrate how important it is that we pay attention to what our physical bodies are telling us. Certain pains or discomforts may in fact not be ours, but due to our 'sensitivity,' our bodies perceive and respond to those sensations caused by the presence of unseen influences. I can attest to this.

In the course of normal, married life for me, although sex seemed wonderful at times, it didn't seem all that great at others. And by the time I met and married Derek, I was burdened with arthritic joints that ached and hurt whichever way I moved. You know...the ingredients of old-age pie. Consequently, sex wasn't my number-one favorite pastime because it seemed as if the physical discomfort intensified at that time.

It was uncanny. Every time I began enjoying Derek's amorous endeavors, I developed a major cramp, a violent charley-horse spasm in one of my legs. I can't think of anything else to put such a quick and untimely end to a romantic evening. Fortunately for me, Derek was the epitome of patience and understanding and he'd willingly massage the area until my leg returned to normal.

But one day, when boudoir rejection seemed to have reached epidemic proportions, I suggested to my forlorn spouse that he do some hypnotherapy detective-work. Derek felt maybe the issue stemmed from one of our many past lives together that had set us up for my 'behavior.' Was I ever in for an eye-opener, but not in the way we anticipated.

As Derek began the past life regression he discovered I had two entities with me. One was an elderly arthritic man I'd known when I was a small child. I don't know whether I was more scared of him or the walking cane he used to point at me whenever he was sitting outside and I walked by. The other was an elderly neighbor woman who had also known me years back. Both had attached themselves to me, thinking they were being of help. These old codgers didn't exactly view sexual activities as their 'cup of tea' and quite literally cramped my style, so no wonder my sex life was in such a slump!

Fortunately, the story had a happy ending. The demise of the charley horses occurred as soon as Derek convinced my 'helpers' that they were hindering me. These two old souls agreed to go on to the Light, taking with them the physical discomforts, aches, and pains that were part of the energy of conditions present at the time of their death, thus continuing their own soul journeys. From then on, there were no more muscular cramps to interfere with our amorous pursuits and my experiences with arthritic pain diminished considerably. It was quite amazing. Before then, I'd never have dreamed there was any reason for my cramping other than encroaching old age or lack of calcium.

We couldn't help thinking that we were probably not the only couple to have experienced invisible 'bedroom' interference, right?

Chapter 2

From the time I met and married Derek, things moved with such speed it was hard to comprehend exactly what was going on. If we view life as our classroom, knowing we set lessons for ourselves, then surely it stands to reason that we also test ourselves...and those nearest to us. So I can't help wondering what kind of exams Derek and I set for ourselves. In view of the intensity of our relationship so far, we must have been going in for something equivalent to a university degree, maybe a master's, methinks. Did I just hear someone ask if that would be of the arts, sciences, or masochism?

It's as if a strong current of energy was determined to sweep us along in its path. If we were destined to work together, why then was our path not smoother? Prior to the 'spirit releasement' session for Derek, our marriage had come so close to a very abrupt end. But after seeming to have settled our differences, we began projecting the idea of opening our own business. I missed my kids so much that I made up my mind the new venture would be in Edmonton, although that would mean leaving Derek temporarily.

On the Sunday evening prior to my departure from Vancouver, Derek and I went into the bedroom to meditate; I was armed with note-pad and pencil just in case Derek started channeling his guides. Right on cue, he began describing the scenes and thoughts coming to him, and I began taking a few notes. He spoke of a bird that sings its song and only takes from nature what it needs, then said, "I see young children with smiles and big bright eyes. Already they are all-knowing, but they have to go through life experiences. I am being shown the simplicity of the old ways. Aborigines in the Amazon, Africa, or wherever, took only what they required from nature, giving thanks for what they had taken. White man considered the Aztecs and Incas to be uncivilized because they used sacrificial rituals to honor their gods and goddesses. Some were human sacrifices, but many chose to be sacrificed, thus expressing the full extent of their beliefs while being examples to others."

At this point I chipped in, saying I knew that North American Indians following the old traditional ways make offerings before going hunting. An animal usually walks out of the bush as if offering itself; perhaps that is because those Indians only take what is needed, they don't kill just for the sport.

Derek continued, still in meditative pose: "I feel quiet at the moment. The North American Indians listen when you say something. If you interrupt as they talk, they don't say anything more, as if they sense you think your words are more important than theirs. They allow you to be you, which is a lesson in itself."

I interpreted Derek's words to mean that there wouldn't be anything more coming through that night, so I took a deep breath and detached myself so that I could begin my own meditation. Mentally building positive energy around myself, I created a pyramid of light. Settled securely within it, a picture of a forest with mountains behind began to form, and I heard myself asking Derek, "Were there mountains behind the scene with the Indians?" He had spoken of a forest with light coming out from the trees. I wondered if I had tuned in to the same place, but as I sensed I was getting no response, I mentally expanded the light and the pyramid, going higher. I don't know how long I was there, but I was asking questions in my mind about Derek and me, why our relationship to date had been so tempestuous.

I mentally began sending love to Derek, from my heart to his and then, gradually, my awareness returned to the room and I seemed to be getting 'answers' to my questions. I felt compelled to pick up the note-pad and pencil to write, but the words flowed so fast I didn't have a chance to stop and think about, or compose, what I was scribbling down.

"Is this me or is something going on here?" I asked myself and stopped writing for a split second. Oops! It felt like words were piling up inside my head, wanting to spill out. I began writing again, not knowing where I'd left off, or where the train of thought should be. I carried on, writing as fast as I could scribble down the words. I know I was aware of certain words and phrases, but when I read through afterwards, I knew I had been given a helping hand.

When the words stopped flowing, I tried to read what I had written, but light from the burning candles was too dim for me to read the hastily scribbled words. What did all this mean, writing down words with a pencil that seemed to have a mind of its own? I'd heard about automatic writing. Was this in fact what had just occurred?

As soon as I became aware that I was alone in the room, I snuffed out the candles and went into the living room to join Derek. I asked if he cared to listen to what I had 'received' and then I read the words out loud:

"The lessons that you both are learning are ones of patience and tolerance—of selves and others. Be not hasty in condemning one's self or the other, for that which seemingly deserves to be judged, is of its own being, unjudgeable. All intolerances come from judgments made, by one or the other, when judgment is unwarranted.

"That which provokes harshness and judgment is merely a call for more love and tolerance. Tolerance is the allowing of being, or beingness; hence, the bird spoken of earlier symbolizes its own beingness with that of all spirit and humanity enjoined in the Oneness of All-That-Is.

"The hardest lessons to learn are those of non-judgment, for judgment transgresses the beingness, the totality of Oneness within the Universal Light which is Love.

"Judgment is the lesson to which all are subject in their seeking wholeness of purpose and At-Onement. When in a state of Oneness, which is the total love and harmony of Beingness, the call for judgment has been transcended. Tolerance and patience are the tools to surmount those judgments wherein unconditional love has not yet been attained as the state of grace in which Beingness is manifest.

"Be loving and gentle in demeanor by becoming of the habit to pursue harmony. In pursuing harmony, the habit will manifest as ever-increasing understanding and a brushing away of the strands which are yet present in the veil. Through perseverance, non-judgment, tolerance and unconditional love will be the tools by which the veil is lifted, as the mysteries are unfolded. Strive for peace between yourselves and those whom you are choosing as students and teachers, for to truly give of yourselves requires the love which transcends all faults and entrapments of the ego.

"You are both close to becoming the vessels for teachings of the inner or deeper levels of spiritual unfoldment. Be kind to each other and love each other as one loves a child, for indeed, both of you are children of the Light, and it is befitting that you honor each other as such. Blessings to both of you.'

The words had a strong impact. Derek asked to see what I had written, and re-read certain passages. We both began sharing our thoughts and feelings, and then Derek walked over to where I was standing and put his arms around me. We both felt like a couple of very privileged, silly kids who had been given a tender and loving chastisement and an explanation as to why our lessons had been coming so hard and strong. We had been triggering impatience and intolerance in each other, firing it back and forth, willy-nilly.

Those words I had scrambled to write down certainly became a turning point in the quality of our relationship. A new scenario, a new reality, was created.

As already mentioned, I sincerely believe we all have free will, but when we are to move in a different direction than we have taken, the energy will be created to get us back on track. The energy to get me back to Edmonton had been generated.

This certainly seemed to me to be a confirmation that we have the free will to do what *Spirit* wants. Guided we most definitely are. Though perhaps 'steered' would be a better choice of words, and I say this most respectfully!

* * *

On the flight back to Edmonton, witnessing the majesty of the Rocky Mountains resplendent in white array, looking pristine and peaceful, I was filled with anticipation and high hopes for the future. As the plane began descending towards the crisp blue-whiteness that sparkled from the morning sun's pale caress, the snowscape seemed to be bidding a dazzling welcome, as if confirming I was doing the right thing. Alighting from the plane, expectancy ran through my veins. I felt the way I did as a child, knowing I was on the verge of something very special.

After a wonderful reunion with my children, I lost no time finding out what suitable business premises were available. I wanted my own office and one for Derek, plus a lunchroom, an area for hands-on healing, and a large space where we could hold classes. I had already put that request out to the Universe months before....

The first realtor I called took me to a suite of offices perfectly suited to our needs. It was just what I'd mentally ordered, except it looked like it hadn't seen a coat of paint for several years. But when I finally took possession of the keys and walked around the office again, I realized that, although eight hundred square feet of space didn't sound much, when it's portioned off into five separate rooms, that's an overwhelming amount of painting to be done. There were no funds to pay professionals to do the job and I had a gamy right shoulder.

It seemed I had an almost insurmountable task ahead of me, and I knew I couldn't count on my offspring. One was working and two were attending school. The fourth lived on the far north end of the city; without access to a vehicle, it would be too tedious and time-consuming for her to traipse all the way to the West End, taking into account after-hours bus schedules. Ho hum!

However, I was soon to learn that when you least expect things, they happen! My youngest daughter's boyfriend was the first to volunteer help. Not only did he fill cracks and holes in the drywall and do the sanding, but he began painting, too. On weekends and evenings, my eldest girl brought an army of helpers equipped with paintbrushes, rollers, and trays. It was a wonderful feeling, receiving help from so many people I didn't know previously.

These wonderful workers volunteered their time and energy and made painting a fun time. They wanted to see the office open as soon as possible, as they had heard about and expressed an interest in attending the classes we planned to teach on psychic development. Even though at that time I didn't consider myself as possessing any particular psychic gifts, from my years of rubbing shoulders with Spiritualists I did know that it definitely was possible to develop latent gifts such as clairvoyance and clairaudience. Without any particular planning on my part, it seemed, I actually had students lining up, and eager to learn whatever I could teach them. Someone 'up there' was certainly coordinating and speeding things along so that the place would be ready for business just as soon as all the red tape and paper work were completed.

I was thrilled with how things progressed and tried to overlook the fact that my tiny student desk looked sadly lonely sitting in the reception area with just one kitchen chair for company. Yet it didn't matter. There were some very special people here clamoring to start classes. They'd even bring sleeping bags and pillows and sit on the floor, if only I'd begin, they said. And so, I was more or less talked into setting a date in April for a Sunday meditation and for the first classes to begin. Due to the lack of furniture, sleeping bags and pillows would have to be the order of the day, with some of my house plants thrown in for atmosphere and a splash of extra color.

My greatest hope was that Derek would be there by the time I opened for business. I still didn't know when he would be free to leave Vancouver. But I never doubted the knight gallant. And indeed, he arrived, unannounced, on Good Friday, bringing with him a small trailer-load of our furniture and an abundance of tropical plants. I was so happy to see him.

In addition to a filing cabinet, my computer and cart, Derek brought the large recliner—a must for all good hypnotherapists—that I had purchased just as soon as we'd graduated. What perfect timing for his arrival! Now at least there was something to put in my office.

There's one thing to understand about Derek; he has a very special energy about him and doesn't let the grass grow under his feet. I guess he's what you'd call a 'mover.' Bless his heart, before he'd barely unloaded the trailer, he whisked me out to a newly opened hardware store and bought ten white patio chairs and four tables.

"Suitable for the office," he said, "for now."

Patio furniture? I would never have thought of buying white plastic chairs for an office! But, like a flourish with an artist's brush, the scene was transformed. The reception area now looked like we were in business. Also, depending upon placement of the chairs, it became the classroom we needed. Against the enormous southerly-facing picture window, pale lilac walls and the lush greenery of all the tropical plants, white plastic chairs and tables looked great.

* * *

When the squire himself had breezed back into my life, a whirlwind was chasing his heels. Things moved so swiftly after his arrival in Edmonton there was barely time to pause long enough to take a deep breath.

Although I had experienced automatic writing and what I called inspired writing, I had no control over when it would occur. Now, however, Derek thought I was ready to learn how to 'channel' my guides and do automatic writing at will. I viewed, with a healthy respect, Derek's ability to channel. I must admit it did leave me somewhat in awe. But now he believed I was ready to do the same! Derek's enthusiasm was contagious, yet it wasn't without a generous measure of nervous hesitation that I acknowledged it was, perhaps, time. After all, what exactly does 'ready' mean? How are we to know what jumping into the deep end of the pool means if we've never been there before or can't swim?

And so, one evening at the office whilst trying to conceal my apprehension, Derek gently led me into a deep meditative state and then he coached me through the procedure, which more or less turned my life around. Although I was in an altered state of awareness, a light trance, I was fully conscious of what was happening.

I saw the face of a young Asian girl and remembered that I had seen her at the beginning of the meditation. Now she was smiling at me so I began describing her.

"She is Asian, and she looks like she's about ten years old."

"Does she wish to communicate with you, through you?"

"I think so." At this point I yawned. I could hear the words I was saying, yet they were neither my words nor my thoughts, and I could hear Derek's responses.

"I bring joy."

"Good evening," Derek greeted her.

"Have lightness of heart. If I may be bold, sometimes you need more lightness of heart. Sometimes the vehicle feels you make her sad. It is because you need lightness of heart, inside heart, and I give you a flower. It is very beautiful flower. It symbolizes light. And inside the light is much joy. Sometimes, the joy is so beautiful, one must cry. But I wish you 'be happy.' When feeling sad, look at fat, happy Buddha." Derek keeps a small Buddha standing by the bonsai tree on his desk.

"You like this Buddha?" Derek asked.

"Yes. He gives much joy. Big joy inside heart."

When Derek asked her name she responded, *"Mai Ling."*

I was so absolutely thrilled I had 'channeled' this way for the first time. It's what we call 'conscious-voice channeling,' and differs from 'deep-trance channeling,' in that during the trance state, one can hear what is being said and one is aware that the speaker's thoughts are not one's own. Conversely, deep-trance channeling can be best likened to a catatonic state, in which the psyche 'steps aside' so that the spiritual guide, or entity, may channel through unimpeded. In the latter case, when one returns to full conscious awareness, one has absolutely no recollection of what occurred or was said during the trance state; hence, there is no chance of the channeler's own psyche, or mind, censoring or interfering with the proceedings.

Sure, I had received messages through inspired writing, and conveyed messages to other people from feelings or visions that I had picked up during meditations, but nothing like conscious-voice channeling had happened before. My awareness had been so heightened and my 'senses' intensified as I felt the high, fine energy and actually experienced a different 'knowing' while the conversation took place. I realized how different Mai Ling's loving, respectful thought presentation was from mine.

In my opinion, no other experience comes even remotely close to the incredible elation that occurs when contact is made like this. Looking back, it seems it heralded the most rapid growth in the raising of my awareness.

* * *

Derek and I began communicating regularly with each other's guides, and with their assistance, Derek worked up a format for an intensive Channeling Workshop, so that others, too, could learn a safe and easy technique to communicate in this way.

About half-way through our very first channeling workshop, after Derek had carefully coached everyone to the point where he was communicating with their higher-selves or spiritual guides, he began speaking with Daneus, another guide of mine with whom I had recently become acquainted. It came as quite a surprise when Daneus said he wished to introduce us to yet another guide by the name of Kalindras, who would be helping me write a book. The book, I was told later, would be the first of four works. The news was given in such a matter-of-fact manner, like it was an everyday occurrence. Me? I would be writing a book, would I? And not one, but four? Come on now; let's get real!

When asked what would be a good time for me to do this, the response came, "In the early hours, say around 5:00 AM, before noises of the day cause interference."

I began to have very serious doubts. This couldn't be for real, I told myself. Me? Not only up, but also at the office at that unearthly hour? Surely someone was joking. The suggestion was too ludicrous for words. What about days when we held evening classes and didn't leave the office until 10:00 PM or even later?

With so many misgivings about the projected writing time-slot, there was much need for thought. Everyone who knows me well would probably agree that I'm at my most ornery and least lovable self early in the mornings. As my father would have said had he been alive: "A blue-arsed fly is a blue-arsed fly, whether dressed in pink knickers or addressed with a fly-swatter." Loosely translated to fit the situation, this means I am a confirmed nighthawk, not an early morning person, and nothing was going to change that. Nothing?

It was no joke, as things subsequently turned out, although we were reassured by the statement that if we were to return home at 7:00 AM to 'bathe, nourish the physical, and dress for the office,' we would have energy enough to see us through the remainder of the day.

Months later, Kalindras shared with us that it's best to be 'up and running' while the greater population in this part of the world is sleeping, because, during the 'wee hours,' incoming beneficial planetary energies are less likely to be affected by the multitude of man's conscious negative thoughts and deeds which generate dense clouds of negative energy. In other words, we would likely have better 'reception' of the higher energies if we meditated or tuned in early.

At the workshop, it wasn't stated what type of books I would be writing, but, I must admit, I was intrigued at the prospect of being on first-name terms with a 'writing guide'.

Surprisingly, like clockwork, and beginning almost immediately, Derek and I rose early to greet each new day effortlessly, certainly quite painlessly, in what was to become a daily rendezvous with our guides.

There was another surprise in store for me at that channeling workshop. Students brought their own crystals and rocks to work with during the 'crystal' segment, when Derek instructed them how to make contact with the respective deva—the overseeing spiritual energy of each type of rock or crystal.

When it was my turn, I received the telepathic thought that 'Jasmine' would be an appropriate name for my small and clear quartz crystal. Jasmine? To me, that seemed such an unbefitting flowery name. Like all relative beginners, I felt uncomfortable as I began questioning the telepathic thoughts I was receiving. Was I making this up? Fortunately, Derek sensed my reservations and began asking questions. This not only assisted the extrasensory energy to flow, but it presented an opportunity for me to voice the telepathic responses:

"*I hold the key to understanding the essence and secrets of the Light; much has been entrusted to me. When ready she* [referring to me] *will use me wisely. At first there was much contact, but it is as if I was discarded. Closer contact is requested in order for me to release the information, and I must first be asked to impart the knowledge that I hold.*

"The name Jasmine is that of an exceptional, fragrant flower. If Diana uses the essence or essential oil of the flower, the fragrance will assist to awaken senses provided she makes a request, stating clearly the purpose and intent. Conditions must be right; motives must be pure and she must work with the Light in a mutually beneficial environment.'

To be perfectly honest, I was very skeptical. I doubted everything that had just been said. Sure, I would have liked to believe it. Deep down inside, though, I didn't really believe anyone could have a conversation with, or through, a crystal! I certainly couldn't see myself calling any crystal Jasmine. I was in for another surprise.

The following Sunday, an elderly lady telephoned. She had recently moved into a senior's home nearby and wanted to know if Derek would pick her up so she could attend our evening meditation. No problem. Upon her arrival, this dear soul handed me a gift. It was a bright, fluorescent poster that contained information about each of the human body's seven main charkas—energy centers between the base of the spine and top of the head—and their corresponding colors, musical notes, rocks or crystals, and harmonizing oils or essences. To my surprise and delight, alongside indigo—the third-eye or brow chakra—the list of complementaries included quartz, and the recommended essence was Jasmine!

Wow! It sure gave a swift kick in the pants to any self-doubt and disbelief about information received during my 'channeling' whilst holding the crystal.

Prior to receiving the poster, I had absolutely no inkling that aromas or essences could assist in opening or strengthening certain charkas, or that they were in any way compatible with, or worked well with, certain gemstones, rocks, or crystals. What better confirmation could I possibly receive than this?

Up to this point, I'd thought that anyone who talked to rocks must be one brick short of a load, and right raving bonkers if it was a two-sided conversation! Now, I was more than happy to call my crystal Jasmine.

* * *

Psychic development classes and the workshops were helping pay our rent, but regular business was so slow it almost ground to a halt. The shortage of clients no doubt tied in to the fact that our name wasn't in the phone book yet, and because of limited finances we had been very cagey about advertising. We also sensed that, as the summer season is so short in Alberta, folks prefer to spend evenings and weekends outdoors whenever possible.

By September, no doubt about it, we were worried. I was beginning to wonder how much longer we would be able to keep the office going. But I shouldn't have worried or doubted the powers that be. Obviously, the universe intended us to keep open for a while longer....

As luck would have it, Derek picked up a local newspaper and an advertisement caught his attention; a Psychic Fair was coming to Edmonton's Yellowhead Inn the very next day. It was as if somebody had switched on the light. Our business definitely needed some form of promotion, but anything invested in advertising must guarantee exposure in the right quarters. And exposure at the Psychic Fair would advertise our presence to the type of clientele we wished to attract. There was no doubt about it. We couldn't afford to miss the opportunity to be there, so, on the spur of the moment, we decided to go for it.

Derek began making inquiries immediately. A phone call to the promoters confirmed that Lady Luck was truly on our side. One booth at the Fair was still available for rent. And after a few more telephone calls, we found a company that could make us a display sign and deliver it to our office by ten the following morning.

It was a mad scramble to beat the clock. So that we would have something to distribute to fairgoers, we worked well into the early hours, typing out and printing up flyers and posters announcing what we had to offer at the Alyssian Center.

Next came the realization we needed something colorful to add a little pizzazz to our piles of printed paper. Otherwise, how could we possibly hope to attract and keep folks at our booth?

After frantic brainstorming we came up with a brilliant idea to solve that particular problem. We made a hurried trip to see our friend Azad Jaffer as he opened the doors for business at The Rock and Gem Shop on 111 Avenue. Then we quickly explained our situation. I could have kissed the man! Without hesitation, he agreed to loan us some rocks and crystals to add a splash of color to our display.

We arrived at the Yellowhead Inn with about ten minutes to spare, and by opening time we had everything set up and ready to greet visitors. Deadlines do indeed spur motivation, but I wouldn't like to repeat that scenario too soon!

How things of beauty do attract the eye and draw people. The bright purples and pinks of Azad's colored agate and amethyst, the gemstones, and the clear sparkling quartz crystals were a great drawing tool. We were in our element, just loving the atmosphere and enjoying talking to anyone who would listen.

When traffic was slow, I left Derek manning the booth, using the opportunity to get to know our neighbors at the Fair as I browsed among the nearby books and goodies offered for sale. On the third day, I couldn't resist purchasing a small 'dreamcatcher' that had been attracting my attention from across the room. There was something so special about this creation, fashioned as it was from all natural materials. The web, adorned with bead, shell, feather, and tiny quartz crystals, was woven onto a twig that had been twisted to form a circle and then mounted upon a solid bed of milky quartz crystals. I walked back to our booth proudly admiring my purchase.

A man was giving psychic readings at a neighboring table. Amongst his promotional materials was an album containing newspaper articles and photographs. Derek's curiosity, apparently, had been aroused during my absence by a photo portraying the man levitating, and he had introduced himself. They were joking as I returned to our table. The man eyed my purchase for a moment, and then pointed to our sign, quipping, "Okay, you say you can channel; then see what you can get from that," and he directed Derek's attention to the dreamcatcher.

"Sure," Derek retaliated with a laugh whilst hardly drawing breath, "I'm sure Di would love to channel something if you share your levitation secret."

Di would love to? Oh, thanks! 'That's so generous, Derek,' I thought, instinctively knowing our neighbor's explanation would be up-front and simple. Sure enough, the man willingly shared his secret. He and some friends had lifted a chair and placed the back legs through the 'panic bar' of a gymnasium exit door. Then they had thrown a dark blanket over the chair, and our neighbor was lifted up onto it, where he posed for the photograph with a crystal ball in his lap. Thus, the illusion of the man 'levitating' had been created.

By sharing his secret, the man had called Derek's bluff, as it were. Now, don't I just love being drawn into someone's tomfoolery? I squirmed inwardly. I take my channeling seriously; I don't do it to show off, and I certainly don't do it out in public. However, caught in the middle of these two, I was obliged to do something, though how exactly one would channel a dreamcatcher momentarily eluded me.

Within the span of about twenty minutes—after wasting precious moments worrying—I had 'tuned in' to the dreamcatcher, scribbled down five short verses, painstakingly copied them in my best handwriting, and delivered the finished poem to our neighbor. It was only later I realized that the words had spun their own beauty whilst capturing the meaning of my purchase:

The Catcher of Dreams

The seasons of time are but
a whisper in the night
A day is but eternity
woven from the Light

The melodies of nature
sing songs upon the breeze
And laughter in the heavens
brings harmonies that please

The rocks, the earth, the birds that sing
are herein intertwined
The secrets of the heavens too
in sleep will all remind

And in the dawn of new day
when earth and wind and sky
Greet sun and moon and stars above
the dreams have flown on by

They passed right to the dreamer
in peace, reposed and still
But captured in the branch's web
were those that never will.

Until that day, I had absolutely no idea of a dreamcatcher's delightful symbolism, how only good dreams reach the dreamer and bad ones get caught in the web and perish with the dawn.

I know all my friends in Britain may argue that The Catcher of Dreams is an example of automatic writing, but what is automatic writing other than someone channeling an unseen spirit or presence, or even one's own higher self?

The Psychic Fair was a wonderful experience. Although the twelve-hour days at first seemed long, time passed quickly and we left with a new appreciation and admiration for the psychics, seers, astrologers, and all who travel the circuit. Far from my misconceptions, I found the majority to be very genuine, spiritual, and beautiful people, and I felt privileged to have shared time with them. I also had made new friends into the bargain.

* * *

The day after the Psychic Fair, Derek and I drove over to The Rock and Gem Shop to express our gratitude and thank Azad for his kindness in lending us display materials for our booth. We returned everything to him except one large quartz crystal, which had graced our table at the Fair and attracted lots of attention. A transaction was made so it could accompany us back to the office.

It's a case of once inside Azad's shop, we're in no hurry to leave, probably because we enjoy the invigorating energy generated by the crystals and rocks, and the dusky odor that epitomizes mother earth's interior harvest. We browsed for a while, admiring the polished gemstones and items of jewelry.

I think I like the place because there's an easygoing, unpressured atmosphere that reflects the geniality of the proprietor, and there's unlimited opportunity to handle the wide selection of natural, uncut merchandise in trays and on shelves lining the walls. The store also houses interesting accouterments for the jewelry buff.

We were just on the point of leaving when Derek's attention was drawn to a pale green onyx egg with striations of white and brown. "Here," he said, as he thrust the cool, four-pound object into my hands, "see what you pick up from this."

Within moments, under Derek's guidance, I tuned into the smooth, ovoid rock. The vision of an elderly North American Indian began to form. He seemed rather surly, almost menacing, as if he were guarding something very important and would allow no one near. I began describing to Derek what I was seeing. My heart was pounding with an intensity of feeling I hadn't experienced before. It was a little disconcerting at first.

When Derek asked if this was an indication we were meant to buy the egg, I could see the old man gesturing animatedly; shaking a finger at me; he was warning that taking possession was not something to be done lightly.

He made it quite clear that under no circumstance should the egg or the sacred information it contained be treated with disrespect. Sure, we could buy the rock if we chose to, but we'd better not buy it unless we were prepared to take full responsibility for what could happen. I tuned out.

This was getting just a little out of my comfort zone. Here I was, out in public, in the middle of the day, in a rock and gem store, talking out loud of warnings and an old man telling us of sacred information stored within a rock! Folks nearby would think we had flipped our lids! Even so, they couldn't be any more surprised than I was.

Derek and I looked at each other, and then I looked around the shop to see if anyone was watching. I felt a little silly. Azad must really believe we're nuts! This was crazy. But, so what? I must admit, I felt an irrational sense of excitement that told me something unusual was afoot. What a different experience. Nothing like this had happened to me before.

Was this warning some kind of psychic reverse psychology? If so, it worked like magic. We made a beeline back to the cash register. Surprise! Surprise! Close by, in another cabinet, sat a pale green onyx egg slightly smaller in size, yet it looked as if it could have been cut from the same chunk of rock as the first. Without a word, we both eyed this other egg for a moment and then Derek placed it in my hand. Immediately, I just knew that one egg was going to cost the price of two!

Derek asked me to tune in again. He wanted to find out if this other piece of onyx was a twin, or some other rock equivalent, and if we were meant buy it also. The answer came that it wasn't necessary to buy the second egg, but it would complement the energy of the first. Derek also wanted to know if this egg, too, contained important information. The answer was "Yes, some that is the same, and some that is different." That cinched it.

We didn't need any other coaxing to buy both. But what on earth were we going to do with two onyx eggs? I didn't know it then, but those two eggs would open the door to the biggest adventure of our lives.

Our curiosity aroused by the two mysterious onyx eggs, we hurried back to the office, to the privacy of our own space. We felt compelled to check in again to find out more. Was there in fact some 'sacred information' contained within the eggs, or had my imagination been working overtime? We decided Derek should 'tune in' this time and I would ask the questions.

Holding on to the largest of the onyx eggs, Derek relaxed in his large recliner and settled in for a session. As we'd heard that all species of animals, plants, and minerals have their own high spiritual overseers called devas, I directed Derek to connect with the deva of the onyx. When I felt sure he had made the connection, I summarized our visit to The Rock and Gem Shop, how Derek had placed the onyx egg in my hands and the resulting vision and intensity of feelings as I held it. The deva's comments duplicated what I had been told:

>*"You were told that the bearer takes on a responsibility which must not be taken lightly. Once the information has been accessed, all knowledge gained must be put to use in an appropriate manner. The information contained within is sacred. That information is of the past and is to be brought forward to help mankind in its understanding of what the planet is going through now."*

I asked if the second egg we'd purchased had special information stored within it, too.

>*"All have similar information, it is all from the Source,"* the deva explained. *"The information is within their make-up, and what they give out* [release] *as it is accessed depends upon the motives of those seeking the information. Others* [rocks and stones] *have similar information. As you work with them you will understand."*

In Azad's store I had distinctly received the impression that, due to the intensity of the energy with which the communication began, 'Intensity' would be a good name for the first one. I asked if this would be appropriate.

>*"Yes. Your need to name in order to personalize the relationship is understood."*

I had remarked to Derek on our way home from The Rock and Gem Shop that the second egg had a gentler, more female energy than the first, and I felt the name 'Sanctuary' seemed to fit. The Deva agreed.

>*"Sanctuary is befitting. The information stored within the stone is held there as if in a sanctuary. Trust, and because of the nature of the information, purity of heart, must be apparent before the information will be released. It is required that the knowledge is held in confidence until the appropriate time for its release, and in such manner that it will be regarded with the deepest of respect.*

>*"The names 'Sanctuary' and 'Intensity' are symbolic of their energies. The name 'Intensity' gives an understanding that it is not to be trifled with, not to be taken lightly. 'Sanctuary' has a symbology that denotes a place of reverence. The names are for you to remember them within the context of their dual purposes.*

>*"What will be shared is to assist all. An appropriate time to share the knowledge is when you are unhurried and your focus is not on something else. If you choose to work* [with the onyx] *it will require your undivided attention so that the information is in whole, as a unit, and not in parts and bits that are scattered,"* the deva stressed. *"It is not wished to release some information and then* [the onyx] *be placed on a shelf and discarded for a while, brought back on whim for more information and then put somewhere else. It would be appropriate to keep this information to yourselves, for the moment."*

I said that Derek's attention was drawn to Intensity in the store and asked if the egg had intentionally tried to attract his attention.

"There was no intent to direct or influence in any way. When the stone was picked up, you were told of the responsibility that goes with being custodians. You were given due warning. You could have chosen to put it back upon the shelf, as there are others who could also work with it. It may have been by choice, or you may have been directed there. The main consideration is that it is by mutual agreement that you have this rock; if it had been felt that you were not to be trusted, a different decision would have been made by you."

The next time we visited the Rock and Gem Shop, I asked Azad how long both eggs had been in his store. He said about six months. When I asked if many people had shown an interest in Intensity, he responded that several men had been attracted to the onyx egg and had seemed keen at first to purchase, but had put it back on the shelf and selected something else. I wondered if they had been 'influenced' in their decisions.

I was still quite excited, and very much in awe at what had happened. But, deep inside, I wondered what was really happening to us. Could we believe this stuff? I certainly wanted to believe, but equally, I didn't want to be 'led by the nose' by some sharpie from another dimension who was having a joke at our expense. Information aside, the eggs were beautiful in their own right. I decided to put my excitement on hold.

Chapter 3

Normally, I sleep like a log. Derek, too, except when we're undergoing some form of intensive learning, and that can occur at any time of the day or night. And so, we've finally come to accept that if we're awakened during the night by a dream, a noise, or simply loud thoughts, then we're to pay attention. If we don't take note the first time around, it happens again…like the time we'd been 'awakened' shortly after 3:00 AM for the second morning in a row. On that occasion, there was no turning away, no crawling back under the covers, no hiding under the pillow looking for more sleep.

We were both stirring from slumber at the same time. Again, during the sleep state, Derek was shown some important truths, the secrets of the ages; as time was before time began, when we were all One and time stood still. This was the second consecutive morning that Derek was also being told we were to prepare for the task ahead. The task is to show the way of the journey home and the 'way' is one that is to be found and then told or shown to others, so that they, too, can find their own way.

We had no tape recorder with us in bed, and the option to switch on a light was definitely out, as the disturbance would be sufficient to send the thoughts, the vision, back into the night; the same for getting up to find recorder and microphone. So it was either write down, in the dark, the thoughts and words which come pouring out, or trust to memory. And this stuff is so important to us, who wants to leave it to the memory of an earth-bound vehicle, a mere human being whose reality changes as soon as dawn hits the sky? Are you kidding?

With the assistance of a streetlight shining in through the bedroom window, Derek began writing down the words he uttered upon awakening and also those that poured out of my mouth. It was as if we were in front of some invisible podium taking turns reciting an invisible script.

"We are Whole. Since leaving Source (the Godhead) in the beginning, feeling the sense of rejection—which we now express through denial—we, our soul essence, or spirit, were given the ability and freedom to do and experience whatever we wanted, to create whatever reality we wanted. And we were given the tools to do it, creating our reality through thoughts, emotions, and feelings.

"The crystals and stones assist us. We were directed to them so that we would begin channeling. We are being shown this, but deep down inside, we don't really believe it, we don't want to know; this is the denial of the experience.

"We, meaning all mankind, have everything at our fingertips that we need, but we don't want to take responsibility for our actions. We don't wish to know that everything is our own creation, and we deny it even to our own souls. And so we numb ourselves to avoid looking headlong into the experience.

"From time immemorial, memories have been stored at a deep cellular level within our bodies; at times they are brought to the surface to be remembered and released. These memories were created by experiences during our present and previous lifetimes on occasions of extreme emotional impact.

"Our bodies tell us when issues have to be dealt with. The aches and pains we feel are simply echoes of a distant past. But they keep us stuck until we decide to do something about ourselves, instead of going outside ourselves to seek help elsewhere. Each time we go to others for help we are compounding our own denial, because we don't want to take the responsibility for ourselves and what our bodies are trying to tell us. Deep inside, we know we can heal ourselves, but because we have unconsciously suppressed our abilities and lost faith in ourselves, we rely on others to do it for us.

"We are given the opportunity to find a solution, by 'going within,' to reunite once more with our own soul essence, or God Source. Meditation is one route to go. Another is a relaxing holiday where the setting provokes reflection upon one's life. Yet another is lying flat on one's back in the isolation of a hospital bed; this often forces a body, not by conscious choice, into a position that can't be avoided, making it impossible to run away from the situation with which one is confronted. It's giving the opportunity, but do we ever take it?

"Maybe we have to seek out surgery and let someone else take responsibility for our health because we didn't listen to what our bodies were trying to tell us and we have grown accustomed to allowing others to heal us or numb us with drugs. And this is because we, in life's dance, have learned to pass the buck. Instead, we choose to use the excuses, 'I can't do whatever, because I've got such and such disease' or 'I had to have such and such surgery because...I need to be made whole.' Or 'I want the attention, so, hey, look at poor me, I am walking with a cane,' or 'I'm dying of whatever. I am scared to death, and I'm scared of dying. Please pity me. You must do something for me, because I'm incapable of doing it for myself; I've given away my power to others. I can't do anything any more except complain about my lot...or maybe walk over the heads of others to get what I want out of life. I'm good at doing that. At using other people.'

'Being immobilized is not necessarily the ideal way to reflect upon one's chosen life path, but being unable to do anything else certainly provides the time and opportunity. This is why so many people have 'religious' experiences whilst in hospital, even to the point of dying (the near death experience) to help them change their direction or way of life.

"Can you see what is going on? While everybody is expecting somebody else to be their healer, their counselor, their savior, their employer, their peacekeeper, they are merrily embroiled in avoidance, and in the process are happily giving away all their own power, whilst at the same time becoming more vulnerable, weaker and sicker. After all, it's easier to ask someone else than to do it for one's self.

'Only in the initial stages of reclaiming one's powers is it necessary to seek help from outside. But, like babes beginning to walk, we must strive to do it alone. We are on our own the moment we are born, and we go out alone.

'Every excuse in between is a red herring, a diversion that takes our minds away from the real purpose. You know, whether it's a pain in the back, fear of cancer or AIDS, a crusade to stop abortion, what's happening on the job or at school, what the government and society is doing, what the family is carping about, what Mary is doing to Bill, or what Bill is saying about Grandpa or Aunt Edith, or friends bitching about who did what to whom. It's all a big red herring. Everything is!

"Other people—friends, family, acquaintances, co-workers, everyone with whom we come in contact, even those we see across the room projected at us from a television screen—are here within our experiences. They are here to help us work out a personal salvation which will release us from the continual reincarnation cycle, to help us move out beyond the 'poor me' or 'martyr' syndrome, and take one step closer to Source.

"All of life's bitching and carping and aches and pains, our puny material goals and ambitions, they're just anything and everything to take our attention away from the real truth of our need to return to perfection, to Source, and we've become masters of evasion.

'We're all so busy with our own petty little roles that we evade the real truth, we evade our true purpose in life, and we blame others for what we have chosen to experience in each lifetime!

"All the old prophets, masters, artists, musicians, and sages had a glimpse of the Truth. Some told of it; others were afraid to tell. Some were killed in the name of it. It's all life's dance, isn't it?

"In reality, we are just like the grain of sand around which the oyster creates a pearl, working away with undivided focus. This lifetime is the pearl; it is the end result, the proof positive of all our lifetimes, our whole existence. It's the product of our whole life's work, *lifetime after lifetime, of slowly creating and polishing the jewel, and with each lifetime it became a shade larger and more beautiful, because it IS.*

"But the purpose behind the original grain of sand? What happened to it? That is the real purpose of our life, to seek and find it again. Each lifetime is an opportunity to unload a few of the impurities it picked up while it was in the sea of all-life experiences, the sum total of all our incarnations."

There was a moment's pause, a silence. And then, *"Just look at the symbology we have been given. We've been led to Intensity (the onyx egg). Bringing us back to Source is the egg. What does an egg symbolize? Life, of course! That's where it starts, but where is where?"* There was another pause before the next statement.

"Above all, we're being told, The World Resounds to the Joyful Cry 'I AM.' Those were the words in a book of photography by Henri Cartier Bresson, produced for a World Life Exposition in the 1960s to celebrate The Family of Man, I believe.

"We are also being told, 'I AM my brother's keeper,' which means it is time to stick our necks out once more. This is why we have been led to the egg and past life regressions and all the channeling.

"We brought the information forward centuries ago and were killed for our efforts. What we are being shown and told is letting us know that it's time to write it all out again. And the Universe is saying, 'The Time is Now,' whether it's 3:30 in the morning or not. We are being taken along a set path, and conditions are being created and tools given to us to access the information which has been suppressed, for whatever reason, until now."

There was no going back to sleep, of course, after all that. We backtracked a little to digest what had been said, acknowledging, "Yes, we have been given tools to use." But isn't that perhaps an over simplification?

We chose to become interested in reincarnation and past-life issues. Then came a desire to study how to do past life regressions safely. Hypnotherapy, one of our tools, is the end product that enables us to access the information we seek.

Considerable work was required and sacrifices were made so that we could pursue our goals, and we did it all willingly, though at the time not knowing why. We were certainly given a shove to open our business, which was done on a shoestring 'wing and a prayer.' And we were prompted to share our knowledge with others. So, really, what did all this mean?

* * *

I had often wondered about the significance of my preoccupation with health and weight. Our early morning diatribe certainly gave me much food for thought. There had been several instances in my life when I had been swept off the wellness path and hurled headlong into an abyss of disease and crippling pain, first with multiple sclerosis over twenty years ago, then with a degenerative disk disease and arthritis of the spine. Resulting inactivity had spawned a well-upholstered frame, of which I was all too conscious. Through years of 'hands-on' and spiritual healing, 'self-healing,' an incredible past-life regression and an innate stubbornness and determination, I was able to throw off the yoke that shackled me and regain good health. But many of my questions, such as "Why on earth did I attract and manifest these conditions?" had remained unanswered until that morning.

I now sincerely believe that when a person is ready to receive answers to questions, a response may come when it is least expected, though sometimes the answerer doesn't always seem to know the difference between AM or PM, as Derek and I found on more than this occasion.

Fortunately, we're quick on the uptake. The tape recorder was all set up and ready to go, so we were prepared when the next extra-early morning wake-up call happened and more health and weight-related 'answers' began to flow. As I later transcribed the tape, I knew I would be sharing those words with others.

I have a sneaking suspicion that when words just flow this way when we awaken from sleep, the message comes from either Derek's or my own Higher Self, to bring thoughts and words into our conscious awareness. By Higher Self, I mean the higher aspect of our own soul that communicates with us through dreams. It could make itself known to us in the vague state of consciousness between sleep and wakefulness when we are perhaps 'ready' and more likely to listen to such wisdom, as was 'spoken' on that second occasion:

"You know yourself that all things, all lessons are chosen, and the scenes are set for the learning to take place. Lessons are chosen because the soul seeks ultimately to return to perfection, to the Oneness. The soul is born onto this earth plane and undergoes certain experiences, depending upon whatever choices were made before birth, and certain events occur, certain conditions occur. The outcome, also, is predetermined by choice.

"Let us use weight as an example. There are many people who may be viewed by others as being overweight, yet they are quite happy within themselves, and appear to go happily through life. If the soul has chosen to experience life with this extra weight, who is

viewing it as a problem? Is it society? Is it the people close to the soul? Or is it the soul itself?

"A weight 'problem' means there are lessons being learned through the weight condition, but whose lessons are they? Are they for the 'overweight' person, or are they for others? 'Do I feel it is a problem? Does it affect my health?' one could ask."

Do I feel it is a problem? My health? Was this Higher Self speaking? As I transcribed the tape, I couldn't help suspecting that this was so.

"What is viewed as a problem is in fact just a judgment placed upon an experience which self or another is undergoing. It can be likened to a classroom assignment. The experience has been chosen, like the assignment, as a vehicle through which learning may occur.

"Maybe the choice was to suffer discrimination or reaction within the perpetuation of others' ideas, such as a judgment regarding the ingestion of certain foods, their components, or the quantity that should be consumed. Their only importance is to provide the subject matter or tools for learning.

"Being oversensitive or worried about what others will think or say about one's weight or size is an indication one has not yet learned to love self.

"Unconditional love is the tool with which one can release the condition and let it go. As soon as one has learned to love self, others' judgments or criticisms will have no effect. At that point, the 'problem' will cease to exist and the condition be released."

I devoured this information in the same way that starving Israelites in the desert must have feasted on manna in biblical times. It spurred me on to continue transcribing:

"What is important is to recognize the need to accept and love self and all others unconditionally. If more lessons are to be learned from the experience, then the condition will remain. It will remain until there is a total love of self, until one is no longer distressed by his or her appearance, by what he or she feels are others' perceptions.

"As long as the ego is bruised or hurt or damaged by rejection or criticism from other people, the problem is perpetuated, because by dwelling upon the weight condition, that unique, creative part of self creates more of whatever condition is uppermost in one's mind. If one is joyous, one creates more joy. If one is sad, by dwelling upon the sadness, one creates and projects more sadness.

"The human vehicle is a precious instrument through which a spiritual being is experiencing its chosen lessons whilst in the physical reality. Not only is the physical body a temple which houses the spirit, it is an incredibly complex, versatile mechanism. You can and do actually program your physical bodies to assist you in the life-lessons or experiences through which you have chosen to learn. Size, shape, weight, strength, and health are some of the facades which you utilize to attract or create those conditions through which you may learn."

On a later occasion I had gone to bed feeling a bit down; yet another well-intentioned person had given me an unsolicited copy of a diet designed to accomplish weight loss. I fell asleep, mentally asking, "What am I being told? Is it time to try and get rid of some of my surplus 'padding'?" I wasn't too surprised the next morning when, once again, words began flowing as I awoke:

"*Those who judge others have something within themselves to learn. It may not only be the fat or thin person who has a so-called 'problem,' the ones regarding that person as having a 'weight problem' also have an issue with weight.*

"*In actuality, there is no such condition as 'overweight' or 'underweight.' The shape or size of any individual is correct at that particular time for the lessons which have been chosen.*

"*Understand the physical form takes on its weight and other conditions to assist in that learning. Become aware that when it is truly proffered the acceptance, love and respect due to it through loving self for all that self is, you will release yourself from the bondage of trying to make self into something which will please others.*

"*When this is understood, you will all love your bodies unconditionally, whether fat or thin, tall or short, for providing the opportunities to experience these lessons of choice.*

"*The soul yearns for reunion with the God Essence and undergoes certain experiences through the physical body to bring it closer to the state of perfection it seeks. These experiences provide the soul with an opportunity, whilst in the physical, to express unconditional love, through patience, tolerance, and love of self and others.*

"*In the process of striving to attain a higher level, or the level of perfection it seeks, conditions are sometimes induced that promote dislike of self. You strive to receive recognition and acceptance from others, yet you reject yourselves, your physical bodies, for whatever reason. Although unaware of it, you project that rejection outward to others and in turn, this rejection is projected back, reflected back to you. As you think, so you create; if you think negatively of self, so you create more about which to be negative. Your thoughts are your most powerful creative tools.*

"*To change the cycle which has been created, it is necessary to reverse the negative thought patterns and consciously begin accepting self. Think positive thoughts about yourself, recognize the wonderful being you truly are; see the divinity within yourself and learn to love self again, so that these are the uppermost thoughts in your mind.*

"*As these are projected outwards, they in turn will be reflected back by those who sense and feel the positive thoughts. Thoughts are energy; they are perceived and felt by others telepathically; other people become affected by your thoughts and respond correspondingly. If you think of self positively, others respond positively to those thoughts by recognizing the positive energy being projected.*"

I was deeply moved by the words. Obviously, I needed to change my thinking. Then I recognized that this message was being conveyed in the second person, and therefore, was probably not from Higher Self. That blew my theory about thoughts received upon awakening. Nevertheless, I was determined to find an answer, sooner or later, and continued transcribing that message which Derek, fortunately, had recorded:

"Reinstatement of self-love and self-acceptance will promote a positive sense of self-worth. And as the old behavior is re-programmed or turned around, by the positive energy of positive thought patterns, one unconsciously begins to project outward, to mirror outward a non-judgmental, all-embracing sense of unconditional love. Renewed self-acceptance and love of self at last will become manifest in all thoughts and actions, bringing about a new outlook upon life, and as this is directed to every other human being and condition outside of self, it is reflected back to self.

"If you see yourself as fat, or others as fat, and have a problem with that, you have chosen a weight issue as a learning tool.

"The lesson, to seek, find the divinity within, and then generate unconditional love to self and all others is a primary lesson for all to learn in this lifetime. Once it is learned, all will know inner peace and contentment.

"One way to begin the process is by honoring yourself. Honor yourself for all the choices you make, for whatever way or method you have chosen in order to learn. And honor the choices of others, even if they appear to you to be on the opposite end of the scale. They too have chosen experiences for learning. Honor and accept them for the choices they have made.

"You are all an aspect of each other. As each learns for self, each learns for the other. Honor that learning, too. Avoid getting caught up in criticizing others' choices or making judgments. Whatever they choose to experience is right for them at that time. Allow them to be.

"When people become fully comfortable with themselves, seeing their bodies as the physical shrine which houses the soul, recognizing the beauty in all things, seeing the beauty within the large and the small, the most refined and even the crude, truly seeing the beauty within what others may deem ugly, understanding the delicacy within the coarse, as all these lessons are learned, people will be able to release, to let go of conditions which they utilized as vehicles for learning.

"When people realize the perfection of the divinity within, the beautiful works of art that they are, the miracles of creation, when they can see their own light, truly see the beauty of themselves and others, no one person will judge self or another," the early morning 'messenger' concluded.

Derek hit the nail on the head when he said, "That's what I call a truly enlightening communication. And I can really see how some people find it difficult to love themselves, because with their own negative thinking they've actually created and projected such negative conditions to manifest in their lives."

Ouch! I reminded him that advertisers and television producers who continually parade anorexic females in front of us reinforce such thinking; we fool ourselves into believing 'painfully thin' is perfection personified, so we just can't match up. Then we're bombarded with advertisements and 'infomercials' for this or that weight-loss program or products.

Fortunately, I am now able to recognize that such sales pitches and scenarios actually help folks like me to become more aware of the conditions we choose as a means for learning. I now regard the advertisements as merely a test to see whether or not I've learned to love me in all my glory, whether it's fat, freckles, warts, wrinkles or all other such good stuff!

I couldn't help wondering what happens in cultures where it is considered a sign of importance and affluence to be of a larger stature and indicates one is able to afford the best of foods. In those cultures, do people who are thin suffer from weight issues, particularly if they cannot gain extra pounds to demonstrate their wealth?

At that hour of the morning, although I wasn't sure of the source of those helpful words, it did remind me of an evening at home when Derek was exchanging words with Daneus, one of my guides. Daneus was speaking on a different aspect of the same topic:

"How many souls living on earth are dissatisfied with their physical appearance, the shape and size, or the color of their teeth, the color of the hair, their skin?" Daneus asked. *"There may be freckles or blemishes upon the face. How many are happy with their height, the size of their feet, or the length of their nose or fingers?*

"The underlying discontent is something that is buried, not apparent on the surface. This discontent with self and how one looks and how one feels, in addition to having been chosen by self as a trial, a test or a lesson, if you will, is all tied in with the desire to be perfect again in order to return to Source.

"In the same way, many souls manifest disease as a result of hurt, anger, fear, frustration; it is a cry at soul level for recognition, for love, for help. On another level, the soul remembers perfection and is choosing to return to Source once more," Daneus explained.

"Someone who sees another as being imperfect, for whatever reason—ugly, fat, thin, miserable, cruel, and so on—is merely seeing his or her own self-imposed imperfection

reflected back to self. All other people are a constant reminder of this self-imposed state of imperfection and our soul's yearning to return to the perfection of the God Essence.

"The ultimate desire to be restored to perfection is such a vast subject it cannot be covered in a few sentences or a few words. Suffice it to say the soul strives to return to Source, to the perfection, the state into which it came into being at the moment of creation.

"Life is like a brilliantly composed symphony being played out by a highly skilled orchestra with all its parts harmonizing perfectly. When there is a variation that perhaps causes a discordant note, it is but an expression for the musician and all who hear, and carries a message that he or she needs to fine-tune the instrument. Such a wonderful orchestra should receive the greatest applause possible," Daneus had concluded.

Derek had agreed and thanked Daneus for sharing such words of wisdom.

I found it intriguing, to say the least, as I asked myself a question: were messages of this nature, with their underlying importance of self-acceptance, being given to us for a specific reason? Were we still being too critical of ourselves and other people? Had we still not learned to come from a place of unconditional love? Or were we just being reminded of the need for everyone to release all negative judgments?

Chapter 4

Three days after the Psychic Fair, I felt the need to ask advice on a little matter that had been on my mind for a few days, so Derek invited his guide, John, to speak with me. We hadn't exchanged words for quite some time, and I really appreciated the opportunity to speak with a 'fatherly' soul.

John explained that my spirit guides were working closely with me at this time. He sounded almost apologetic as he said he hoped I hadn't felt that I had been put on the spot, (he was referring to the 'happening' in The Rock and Gem Shop when Derek had placed the large onyx egg in my hands) as this had not been the intention. It was an opportunity, he said, to give me practice, not only to build up my confidence, but so that I would become more comfortable using my psychic abilities. I asked if the dream catcher episode had arisen for the same reason and he said, "Yes."

Then John told me that over the next few days I would be communicating with many of the crystals that were to accompany us to the next Psychic Fair we planned to attend. This would prepare me for future communications and was all part of a plan that would be revealed in due course. And then, as if he was aware of the concerns I'd had when 'sensing' the presence of some unpleasant energy at the last Fair, he suggested a method by which we would feel secure. That is, by mentally generating a light from the center of our own being, expanding it outwards in all directions so that it fills our booth, and taking time to re-generate it periodically throughout the day. Just knowing we are secure and protected by that light creates the very protection we feel we need.

This was neither the first nor the last reference we'd receive about creating and using 'inner' light to strengthen our own energy fields and make a shrine of our environment. If our guides were to suggest I stand on my head and scream three times in order to feel safe and secure, and if the suggestion felt right, then that is what I would willingly do.

During the course of the next few days I continued laboring on my book. Sure, I was sitting at my computer at 5:00 AM sharp, but it was a chore and there certainly wasn't any 'inspired' or 'automatic writing' happening, even though I had performed my preparatory ritual by inviting my guide, Kalindras, to be with me.

One morning, after struggling with words for about twenty minutes, I decided I'd better save the document, but, at that precise moment, the computer pulled a 'software failure' stunt again and the screen went blank, so I lost what little I had written. To say I was miffed would be like saying Mount Everest is just a small hill in the Himalayas! I was following our prescribed formula for success, so what was wrong? I sensed something weird was afoot and didn't like it. I went into Derek's office to whine.

As always, Derek empathized. He suggested I make myself comfortable in 'The Chair' to find out why the software failure had arisen again; he suspected I was having difficulty with the computer for a reason not apparent on the surface, but for which there must be a reasonable or logical explanation. Putting me in The Chair was his 'logical' way of finding out, and within a few moments Derek began guiding me into an altered state of awareness.

I sat there, waiting for something to happen, when the thought struck me that I should be writing a song. I relayed the thought to Derek, adding how silly it was, as I didn't know anything about music. Then it seemed as if I was listening to my voice talking, at the same time being aware that the thoughts behind the words were not mine; they appeared to be coming from a presence standing slightly behind me, to my left. And I 'knew' this presence was a guide:

"Although the night is long and sometimes the path seems dark, it is always lit; we are always guided," the presence began. *"And in the things that we do, though we feel we're guided, sometimes the path still seems long and dark. But, as we look closely, the eyes adjust their focus and we realize there is no darkness. For as the eyes become more accustomed, they see light, like the dawning of a new day. In all shadows there is light, just as in the fullness of the day there is light. Light is within the perception of the beholder.*

"And just as grains of sand appear to be minute, if we place our awareness into the grain of sand, it becomes a universe. No matter how small, in our perception, within each there is a vastness, there is an eternity, and within each, there is light. And it is light that connects all things.

"Even the finest filament of thread is brilliantly lit with the light of creation that is woven throughout the fabric of the entire universe. And each universe is within another universe, each with its own energy, its own light, each with its own filaments. The light

moves in waves, gentle waves of energy, and there is a vibration by which everything is synchronized, like the swelling of the breast when a breath is taken and then exhaled; it is sent in all directions, as are the filaments of light.

"*Life is but a breath. All of creation is the breath of one energy, one voice, one sound, one universe that is all universes; this is where the knowledge begins; this is where it grows, as each breath is given out in the continual cycle of light and energy,*" my guide finished.

Then I began explaining to Derek the intense feelings of which I had become aware before the telepathic flow of thoughts and words abated. "It felt as if I had become swept up inside a giant heartbeat of energy; it's hard to describe, but I was hearing sound-waves, although there was no sound, just a strange type of reverberating energy from within going outwards, similar to the after-tones of a struck gong. There is a reverberation there, like the pause in between the notes; I knew then that the pause is where life is; it is in the pause between the notes, yet every note is a pause.

"At one stage it seemed like I was drifting off; you'd taken me down to a certain point and I was waiting for more instructions, and then something just kicked in. I wasn't sure about what was coming next, so I just began talking. Perhaps this is how the book is supposed to be done from now on. Maybe that's why there was not much writing done over the last couple of days while I've been sitting at the computer struggling; the words weren't flowing the way I felt they should."

After exchanging thoughts about what had just transpired, we were in agreement. The preparatory work had been done to set the scene, as it were, writing about our backgrounds, our yo-yo relationship and training.

Perhaps this now was how we were intended to go with the book. We decided we'd tune in the following morning in the same manner and see what transpired.

Actually, we were right in our assumptions, although the next day we missed our early morning start. I was feeling somewhat discouraged, disappointed at myself for not being able to get up before the birds. I was feeling a little sad, too, that we'd had to sell our car to pay the rent for office and home.

Because of our later-than-usual arrival, it was not appropriate to channel; anyone could walk in to chat or make an appointment. I decided it would be more appropriate to meditate briefly in my office. I followed my instinct and moved to my room. However, when I began to meditate I didn't understand what I was being shown. I just saw three adjacent planets in the sky, nothing else. As it didn't make any sense to me and I couldn't still my mind, I gave up and walked out to the reception area.

Still feeling a little dejected, and without even a shred of enthusiasm, I sat in front of the computer screen and rested my fingers on the keyboard.

But how oddly things unfold. When you don't expect things, they happen. My fingers began running away with themselves, as if driven by an unseen force. I couldn't help smiling at first as I read the message, but it left me with mixed feelings.

Even though the head feels thick and the body is filled with tensions, words will still flow; the inspiration will be given to you. It matters not the time of day that you are given the inspiration, although early hours are the ones when ideas will flow more easily; there are conditions which present themselves better during the hours when there are few distractions.

This new situation you find yourself in is but temporary, and we understand the human condition is affected by prevailing factors. However, it is important that you do try to carry on with the work at certain set times, although, as we say, the inspiration will come, the words may be given, at any time.

You saw three planets in your vision this morning. This will become the focus for a change in understanding. Just as you assist your students to recognize when their cosmic guides are with them, you will become aware also, and desire to communicate. You have been aware of the presence several times. Only upon such indication will it be advisable that you seek communication; signals will be made known to you when the time is appropriate; but, for now, it is preferable that you focus upon the work at hand.

If you apportion times for duties to be dispatched and mental appointments made (for 'tuning' in) if schedules are adhered to, the practice will bring about a natural flow so that things of worldly, spiritual, and cosmic relevance will operate with a more even balance, so that functioning is even.

We do realize that more time must be apportioned for things of a physical or earthly nature such as the running of business. But it is suggested there is a need to draw up and maintain a schedule to follow, so that you do not begin to feel overwhelmed by the tasks you have chosen to undertake.

Three planets aside, what was this electronic message trying to say? I could write any time, but if we regimented ourselves and followed a routine, there would be enough hours in a day to get everything done, writing included? The skeptic in me questioned how following timetables could ensure 'a natural flow.' I printed out the message, intending to show it to Derek, but I guess that particular moment was not quite the right time. I howled hysterically as I looked up at the comical sight of Derek standing in the doorway, all poised to make a grand entrance.

Recently, during a meditation, I was given a vision of a cap, set with crystals. I noted how it should be constructed and I 'knew' the cap was to encourage activity in those parts of the brain not normally used by us human beings. I'd given Derek a quick sketch of the cap. Here finally, after many dedicated hours of work, I could see Derek had completed its construction.

My shrieks of laughter must have been heard ringing through the building as Derek, wearing his masterpiece interpretation of that cap which he had just finished making, came closer. He looked like an elf wearing an overlarge hat covered with bent wheel spokes that sparkled with shiny droplets of dew (tumbled crystals) at their lower ends.

Laughing until our sides almost split, we took turns wearing the prototype to find out if we could detect any different 'brain' activity. What a riot. We guffawed and hooted as tears streamed down our faces and our whole bodies ached from the impromptu 'research.' I'm not too sure about my brain, but my innards certainly got plenty of exercise as my belly shook from the loud squeals of mirth.

Nevertheless, we determined to wear the cap at specific time periods every day. If we subsequently found our psychic abilities had increased dramatically, we would consider manufacturing it and putting it on the market. If we found no perceived difference, say, after a month or two, the worst that could happen is that we would keep it for a wonderful Halloween prop. And it's always good for a chuckle. Derek looks so cute wearing the cap I say he should get a smock and leotards, or a long robe to go with it!

Who knows what could happen? Maybe some day we will teach people how to walk through walls whilst wearing crystal encrusted skullcaps. The practice just could catch on! And if, down the road, it becomes a fashion trend, then remember, you heard it from us first. (With a little prompting from our 'friends'!) In all seriousness, though, we already know that if we feel a little tired before putting on the cap, within seconds we feel a wonderful surge of energy coursing through the body. You certainly won't find a more holistic energizer, and it couldn't have made a better entrance.

* * *

You know, it's great to be told you're going to be writing a book, but there are one or two slight drawbacks when you don't really know what topic you're supposed to write about. For one thing, it certainly makes it extremely difficult to do any planning or even to write an outline. It's sort of like operating on whim and fancy, and 'when the wind blows.' I guess the need to 'apportion times for duties to be dispatched and mental appointments made' had some merit.

The very next day after receiving that message, as I was deciding what to do when, I picked up a small quartz crystal that Azad had given to me during one of my visits to the Rock and Gem Shop. About one and a half inches in length, it had a clump of smaller crystals at each end, and looked as if it had been broken off a cluster. It was nothing spectacular to look at, but it reminded me of a legless miniature French poodle. As I held it in my hand, I mentioned to Derek that I could feel an odd sensation inside my left ear, like a gentle tickling.

Without a word, Derek steered me quickly towards The Chair in his office; his sixth sense was already at work as he recognized a cue. 'Knowing' something important was about to take place, he quickly clipped a lapel microphone onto my jacket. What good insight that Derek had such a presence of mind to ask, "Now you've acknowledged the sensation, what would it like to say?"

I felt compelled to reply, *"I have much to tell you, due to circumstances that have brought us together, and you have much to hear,"* then, without pausing for breath, the following words of poetry just poured out of my mouth:

"The time is now to listen, for I have a tale to tell
And as you hear the words from me, you will recount them well.
The words are just a stepping-stone, to bring the paths to now
The memories of long ago, the promise and the vow.

A time was set for us to meet, and here it's come to pass
'Tis time to work together, the memories to amass.
'Tis time for wealth and fortune, the spiritual kind
The secrets of the Universe at last here to unwind.

And as you listen closely, I'll help you understand
I'll take you to each universe, each foreign and like land
I'll take you further inward, to the depths within the sky
For deep within each being, the universe doth lie.

The nature of the knowing is simple, still indeed
'Tis time to reawaken, to bring out the new seed
For each is sown within them, to nurture true and fast
'Tis time to be reborn again, the pure Iconoclast."

Derek asked what the poem meant, and I heard my response: *"It is to do with religious persecution. I am underground and I see hundreds of skulls stacked one upon another right up to the ceiling. People were being sought out and put to death. They took to living underground. I can see a dim image of a man holding what looks like a parchment document. Someone in authority had a list of names of wanted people.*

"There was a whole underground movement. The only way to survive was to live underground. And as each person died, the skulls were placed on top of those of others who died. I'm not sure if it was a mark of respect or for enumeration. The bodies had to be taken apart. It was a horrible thing that they had to do, but there was no other way the others would have survived. There was a pit underneath the ground where the bodies were disposed of after death, after the heads were removed and stacked.

"Everyone was known to everyone else," I continued. *"It was as if they were a family, an incredibly big family of believers. There was a vow taken that we would all meet again in another time...because we knew we were right in our beliefs...and we knew we would be back together again, to declare our beliefs once more.*

"Now I just see grayness. There was a woman who was taken naked and dragged through the streets. She was pregnant at the time, and she was hung and she was cut open, slashed all the way from the throat to groin...everything fell out...and she was left there as a spectacle, a deterrent for what would happen to anyone who was caught. And those who saw it, they promised each other that they would return again, when they would band together so they could be in a better position to put the world to rights, and all injustices would be removed.

"Word of what happened spread far and wide, and even those who didn't know her, but only heard of her and the promise, they were moved. Each knew that one day the time would be right, and then they would return; they would all meet.... As the news spread, there were several thousand people altogether that made the vow," I went on with the interpretation of my poem.

"It's almost like, from what had happened, a shock wave had gone out and people took to hiding underground, and those who were being sought after that, who had been saved from the same fate, they died in the shadows, as it were.

"But it's alright now to stand up and be counted. It's one of the reasons for our not wishing to do any clairvoyance or anything that would set us apart, to be identified. I am not sure who stacked up the skulls, if it was those who were doing the killing or, if the people themselves did that for the ones who died. I just know that the rest of the remains were in a big pit covered with huge stone slabs.

"The horrors of oppression caused such a great chill to sweep through the hearts of a despairing people that a vow was made to meet again at the dawning of a golden era when

there would be freedom to express their beliefs. Deep within the hearts of many who will read these words, there will be an awakening. Something at the very core of their being will be stimulated into action and the words will serve as a key. And so will a remembering be set into motion," I concluded the poem's interpretation, my voice barely a whisper. *"We will understand at the appropriate time."*

As I handed the small crystal to Derek, I knew the poem was to be called "The Awakening Time." I was stunned. This smacked of pretty strong stuff and 'stunned' was an understatement. Wherever did all that come from? I became aware that I was now sweating profusely and my head was pounding. I could feel the adrenaline flowing and was filled with a nervous excitement.

Instinctively, I knew that something important definitely had transpired and this was no ordinary poem. The impact of the words was just a little too much for me to handle right then, like something was tugging at my gut.

Derek encouraged me to take a few deep, slow breaths to calm myself. After several deep breaths I got up, removed my jacket and walked into the kitchen for a glass of water. However, as I reached for a glass my head seemed to clear and I immediately turned round again. Obviously, I didn't need a break to calm down. I felt compelled to go back into Derek's office. I stood by the door for a few moments, speaking my thoughts aloud. And then Derek reminded me of what his guide, John, had forecast. It dawned on us that I must be on some sort of a 'crystal-channeling roll.' If that were the case, then it would be pretty pointless to stop now. Daringly I picked up a cluster of quartz from Derek's desk and sat in the recliner again. Derek clipped the lapel mike to my blouse and almost on cue I felt a 'sparkle' of light, then a quick boost of energy. I began speaking again, but this time not waxing poetic:

"This is a multi-faceted, multi-directional energy booster. It is to assist where there is slow glandular activity, where the whole metabolism needs a boost. The person must also believe that this will work. It should be placed upon the throat. Don't just hand it to a person you think may need it; he or she must come seeking its help. When used in a healing setting, the energy of the crystal will assist the person to feel bright and light of heart."

I handed the cluster back to Derek. As he placed another in my hand, I immediately sensed its energy and began again: "Laughter.... Lightness of heart. This crystal will impart to the holder the ability to laugh at self with love and understanding. Also, it generates joy and a sense of adventure. Life is a joyful adventure. Listen to the laughter and happiness. See the laughter, feel it, know it is there. Although intangible, laughter is a precious gift that brings healing and a wondrous sense of joy. Look within the symmetry. This will take your spirits high with joy."

What a delightful feeling. That was one quartz crystal cluster I would willingly make room for on my desk, I told myself.

After working with a few more crystals, I returned to my desk, where I felt compelled to remove a favorite crystal from its pouch. Instantly, I could feel my whole body energy changing again and my throat began to feel strange. It felt like I needed to talk a mile a minute again.

I began a telepathic conversation. Why couldn't we converse this way and I'd type the conversation straight onto the computer? The response I got was that if my throat feels enlarged and strange, as it did now from the need to speak, what would happen to my head if we were to use telepathy? All at once, the top of my head began throbbing, and my ears felt like popping. This crystal packed a tidy punch. I got the message loud and clear and I made my way back into Derek's office. The crystal channeling, it seemed, had really begun.

Over the next few days, Derek and I took turns working with the quartz crystals. I guess John was right: some of the information we received was quite incredible, and we easily could perceive the differences between the individual pieces. The energy of some was very strong and had an energizing effect upon us; yet others had such a gentle, soothing energy. It was a wonderful learning experience. If this was what we could expect while 'reading' or channeling information from the crystals, I decided, then book me for lots of overtime!

During our first Psychic Fair we'd had a reunion with someone special. You know the type, so very exceptional that when you're standing close, you sense an ethereal quality. Even if your back were turned to her the first time you met, you would like her instantly, because the 'presence' is there. And with this lady, it was music. I'll swear I hear the music of the spheres when she's around. Maybe it's just a memory of beautiful times gone by, long ago and far away, but she exudes a delicate air like a fine melody. It's not the least bit surprising when one learns that she's a music teacher. I left our booth so she could chat with Derek and catch up on what's been going on these last few years.

A few days after the Fair, this same lady was sitting in Derek's office for a past-life regression. It's always interesting to know why certain people, family included, are in one's life; a regression can be a fun way to find out.

Two nights later, Derek and I went to see a movie that proved to be so boring we left and decided to walk through nearby Kingsway Garden Mall where we bumped into our musical friend of the recent reunion. This time, however, she looked glum. She was feeling tired and rather under the weather. I couldn't help thinking there must be a reason why our paths had crossed again, but what was it?

We all went back to our Center to chat over herbal tea. After a while, Derek brought out a small quartz crystal cluster and placed it in her hands. Her face lit up and she started laughing. Derek asked her what she felt, holding the crystal.

"Laughter," she answered, "I feel bubbly and full of joy. Isn't that interesting?"

Was this Spirit's way of giving me confirmation that what I had 'picked up' from the 'laughter crystal' was correct, thereby increasing my confidence in my own abilities to channel, or was there some deeper meaning to our reunion? I guessed time would tell if this was why we had met again so soon.

* * *

What an intense time. Without doubt, something was in the air! I sat in The Chair again a few days later, all set to go at 5:00 AM, and this was to become the first session of our 'apportioned' time schedule, even though it didn't get off the ground for another half an hour (and it lasted only a few minutes).

Quite suddenly, I experienced the sensation I was going deeper and deeper while falling backwards, and I began feeling extremes in temperature. One moment I was hot, the next, shivering cold. Finally, I relaxed into a calmer, meditative state; I became aware of words I had written a couple of years earlier and I began speaking them aloud:

"In the beginning I was with God and thou knowest this. I come in my nakedness to greet you anew, and this in the awakening time. You heard those words before; it was an indication of what was to come. In the beginning I was with God and the beginning was God.

"There is a new dawn coming, and with the dawn will come upheaval and challenge, and man will be tested to his ultimate limits. Chaos, destruction, man against man, brother against brother, child against child, but the new dawn will come and a new realization will begin. Within each man, woman and child, eternity has but begun.

"Many Light-Workers have come to show the way. Their lights will shine like radiant beacons for the people, who will come in droves, for they will be confused and seek guidance. You are to show the way, to give light, to guide.

"So it is that each will see their own light and their own connectedness. Peace will be restored, and there will be a great rejoicing. As it was in the beginning, it will be always, for time is but a breath, and the awakening time is here; the awakening time is now. And so shall it be dreamt and felt, and those that dream it shall become it, for within them are the hopes and the realization of humankind.

"The brothers and sisters of the universes are here among you to help. They have been among you for a long time. Their influence has been felt and seen by many, and as the understanding grows, harmony is the promise.

"There is much work to be done. Direction will come through sleep. It is wise to record the dreams, and each time I come, I will bring the words. As this work continues, it will become easier. The procedure will become automatic. It will become as automatic as the writing.

"Greetings. It is best always to greet, rather than say good-bye."

I emerged from the brief session a little startled, but with a feeling bordering veneration; inwardly I was strangely peaceful. Afterwards, I told Derek that, while everything was taking place, I felt very humbled and small, and the fine, high energy made me feel like all the hairs on my body were standing at attention.

I never know what to do with this class of message. I usually end up filing it away. But I couldn't wait to check and see if the words given to me two years ago, during a bout of what I now would term 'automatic writing,' were the same as those which started this session. I spent several hours searching through boxes of old documents until I found the paper I was looking for. Bingo, a perfect match! Now I really had goose bumps.

Wow. This was the third mention of the awakening time; the first was made two years previous, the second came with the poem of that name which I'd channeled recently when holding a crystal given to me by Azad, and the third, now.

Finally, the penny dropped; I realized "The Awakening Time" was to be the title for the book. Maybe I didn't have an outline, but at least I had a title. It sure sounded better than "Intensity...An Eggstraordinary Affair," as I could have been tempted to call the book because of the intensity of our whirlwind experiences.

But now what? I asked myself as I read the printed transcript. I guessed that from now on we should always sleep all wired up to the tape recorder!

Chapter 5

We soon realized that my book was to be centered on our efforts to 'access' the information that we had been given to understand was stored within the onyx eggs Intensity and Sanctuary. And so, on a daily basis, with very few exceptions, Derek and I were settled in at the office promptly at 5:00 AM, tuned in and hooked up to microphones, all ready for a 'session.'

Whoever was channeling first would sit in a large recliner now affectionately known as The Chair. We would take turns. When it was Derek's turn to channel, I would facilitate, leading him into an altered state of awareness and then, once contact had been made with whichever guide Derek had asked for, I would begin asking questions. The session would last until the energy wound down or we terminated it. And then we would trade places, reversing the roles to go through the whole process again.

Sometimes we spoke with the Onyx Deva, sometimes the energy of the egg itself. In our constant attempts to access the information, we continually varied the process; we took turns communicating with our spiritual guides, our higher selves, our cosmic guides, oftentimes whilst holding the eggs, sometimes not. Occasionally we felt inspired to call in the Quartz Deva.

Whomever we felt inspired to ask, we asked, and then we asked some more, all the time seeking clues or advice on how best to access the eggs and their information; we even asked for guidance as to whom to ask; you name it, we tried it.

Many times we strayed off topic and asked questions that had absolutely nothing to do with Intensity and Sanctuary. Until the procedure was really established, there were few hits and many misses. Derek and I weren't even sure how we should be 'critiquing' what we received during these sessions. We decided we would simply transcribe each day's channeling, then after typing it up, we could print it out, let it all sit for a while and eventually attempt to put all the documents into some semblance of order, as the book is shaped.

One morning Derek was in The Chair, holding Intensity in his lap, and I began facilitating. When I felt that Derek was connecting with the Onyx Deva, I inquired about the symbology of the egg, and he replied:

"It symbolizes the start of all life, the Oneness, the creation. The beginning of your story starts with the egg, and it is highly symbolic in regards to all forms of life, as you know it. An egg itself has an outer shell of protection; within, there are the inner aspects of life, the beginnings of life.

"Life springs forth from the initial egg, whether that egg is within a human, an animal, bird, fish, reptile, or insect. The egg is the starting point, the origin, as is the seed. Life starts and is nurtured within. As it develops, it matures, and in most cases, only after it matures does the life form emerge. "When the egg, or life, is at a sufficiently mature level, it can allow itself to be open; it doesn't need the outer shell for protection any longer. You may liken maturity to the shell. Once it is broken open, the real life, the real light shines forth. Then it carries on with its next stage of growth, its own purpose."

"Why did the onyx egg attract Derek's attention in the store, prompting him to place it in my hand?" I asked, pleased that the question and answer session was off to a good start.

"There are as many reasons why things happen as there are different paths, different avenues that one can take. What occurred at the time the egg was picked up was that a choice was made; it was of accepting the responsibility for what happens, and to care.

"Without the acceptance, another avenue may have opened up in a different way. You see, there is no great influence being placed upon a person, giving the inclination to do a certain thing, without there being freedom of choice to do it."

"When Derek first placed the onyx egg in my hands, I was told that it held the 'secrets of the ages.' I believed there was some very special, profound message or information that was going to be given to us. If so, how are we to access the information?" I asked.

"Communication will occur in the same way that it is taking place now, but a little at a time. The energies must be compatible. Those being used to channel the information need to refine their energies in order to receive the higher vibrations. As these vibrations or energies match up, a freer flow of communication or telepathic exchange may occur, so a rapport and mutual trust can be built. At the moment, this is the initial start," the Onyx Deva answered through Derek.

"Is it preferable for Derek to do the channeling, or me; or would it be better for us to take turns?"

"It may be done either way. As the energies are built up for the channeling, and the intent is pure, it matters little which one of you does it," the Deva responded.

"Would it be preferable for us to work with the onyx eggs on a daily basis, by setting aside a certain time each day?"

"Yes. The energies will build up a lot sooner than if done on a haphazard basis."

"It seems information also comes through quartz crystals and other stones. Will working with the quartz crystals in the same manner yield the same information as when working with the onyx egg, or will it be different information that we receive?" was my next question.

"Working with both [quartz and onyx] *you will be given information from different sources, to add to what you already know, so that your understanding is increased and your own truths may be compiled. This is so you are not being led only in one particular direction. Using the analogy of a tree, you take from one branch, but there are other branches that hold fruit, also. So, as you sample from each of these other branches, whether it's through the crystals, or whether it's channeling a particular energy, a stone or onyx egg, you receive different information. It is for you to become well versed or rounded with communication through many avenues, as opposed to just doing one thing, which would give you only one perspective.*

"It would be very beneficial to do this on a regular basis. The process is similar to when you carry out healing work; your guides give you assistance at those times. Regular communication allows your channels to become strong, and there will be no doubt in your mind. You will know what to say, and you will know what are truths and what are not. You will have an inner knowing, an inner sense; you will be speaking from a different level, a higher vibration and you will become so accustomed to the vibrations you will be speaking from your true selves."

"Would it be preferable for us to seek to communicate with the Oneness by doing this work outdoors, amongst nature somewhere?" I asked.

"This is not necessary," the Deva answered. *"As you hold the onyx you are holding an aspect of the Oneness. Throughout the ages, man has been urged by the small voice from within to seek out his God, instinctively following the dictates of his own heart for the best location for communication with the Godself and Higher Intelligences.*

"Man went to great physical lengths in his search for Divine communication and in many instances his search took him to the tops of mountains, as he perceived he would be in closer proximity there. The energy of those places was especially conducive for man to receive communion with his God, not because he was at the 'highest' point, but because of the energies that were created for him with the assistance of the mountainous formations of rock. The energies of the mountains' rock structure provided assistance to do that.

"Many sought to communicate at special sites built from stone and other natural materials that combined to assist man on his spiritual journey. When man seeks enlightenment, he must seek within. For the knowledge and understanding, the information that you are seeking, location is unimportant. More important is motive and intent," the Deva continued through Derek.

From my perspective, nothing mind-boggling was being said; this could even be Derek talking.... Yet I could sense a 'different' energy in the room.

I leaned forward, peering through narrowed eyes, almost squinting, as I looked more closely at Derek's face. I'm not sure what I expected to see, but momentarily I was taken aback; his appearance had quite definitely 'changed' and I could see a slightly pasty, almost ghostly looking countenance superimposed over his own features, with no skin tone whatsoever. There was no mistaking it...Derek's eyes were closed yet a pair of black, wider-set eyes was looking straight at me. A little unnerved, I blinked a few times, in an attempt to check out what I was seeing, but Derek's face stayed 'different,' although the image was not constant and seemed to fade in and out. Someone or something was definitely with him and speaking through him. I sat on the edge of my seat and listened intently, as the speaker continued.

"*Everything within life itself, including gems and minerals, is a reflection of the Oneness. Each stone, each gem, is such that it has its own identity, its own energy, just as human individuals have their own personalities, their own energies.*

"*Everyone has to search, find, and become acquainted with their own energy, their own uniqueness, and when comfortable within that uniqueness, each realizes he or she is one tiny part of the entire makeup of matter. It is within man's uniqueness at that point that he assists others to find, to realize, the Oneness of everything.*

"*Information which is within each of the stones will be released on a gradual basis, as in each of your days there are lessons that you learn, progressions you undergo, and each is appropriate for its time. There are other forces besides the energy of the onyx egg or mineral, which affect the transmission, and as each step is taken, different conditions are brought into play.*

"*Knowing there are qualities within the eggs or crystals is a way for you to understand, to realize the Oneness, of how we are all part of It,*" the Deva concluded.

By this time I couldn't think of an appropriate question to ask and closed the session. Derek's face changed back to normal. After that day, I often saw the pasty visage when Derek was working with either one of the onyx eggs, and I became very familiar with the energy that was present on those occasions.

* * *

During another session, as I channeled whilst holding Sanctuary, Derek turned off the music which had been playing. At that exact moment—when the music was cut off—so was the 'transmission.' But as soon as the music was switched on again, I knew that the energy of the music was compatible with the energy of the egg, which, as before, began to feel as if it were pulsating. I only became aware of the pulsating after the fact, when Derek had turned off the music and then switched it on again. Was this pulsating the energy of the egg...or the Onyx Deva?

Derek asked if he was right in assuming that both onyx eggs, Intensity and Sanctuary, were similar in nature but that each had different qualities. The answer was "*Yes.*" Then he asked what are the qualities of Sanctuary.

"It has the energy of peace and tranquility; the name that you gave it. 'Sanctuary' is most befitting as it suggests a safe and secure place where one can retire for contemplation, in which one feels totally safe and secure, the ideal place in which to be with the universal energy, communicating with the Oneness."

As the words had started flowing I sensed an energy coming in waves; I was not 'feeling' it like I usually do, I was sensing the energy in a different way, as a knowing, and I knew that a great distancing had taken place between mankind and the spiritual energies. I also knew that at one time, everyone was able to 'tune in' or communicate like this. If the pulsating was the energy of the Onyx Deva, I asked myself later, then from where did the 'knowing' come? Had I, in fact, tuned into the Deva's consciousness, or had the experience re-awakened a past memory of my own?

"Are the onyx eggs also in communication with the Oneness and all other crystals in the mineral kingdom, the quartz, amethyst, tourmaline and so on?" Derek asked.

"Yes. They are part of the Oneness, and therefore they just are."

As Derek asked that question, I could 'feel' the answer, and I could 'see' an energy traveling in all directions, linking up with everything beside it, like fine veins of light. I knew then that, just as we have an arm, or a toe, or a finger that is connected to the rest of the body, that small toe or whatever isn't the whole body, but it is an important part of everything that is joined together.

No matter which cell in the body, no matter which tiny part, it is playing an important role, as the whole is in communication, and there is a harmony, a life which is going on within the body, the brain, within each fiber. One particular part of a toe, say, doesn't necessarily hear, but it does have a consciousness that is aware of what is going on in the left ear, because there is a knowingness...because there is a connectedness. The same principle applies to the mineral kingdom, there is a connectedness, and indeed not only with other minerals, but also with all of creation.

Derek continued, questioning the Onyx Deva, and asked how the onyx, rocks, crystals, and the different aspects of nature communicate.

"Each gives out its own energy. There are different symbols within each energy. Within the mineral kingdom, as with the animal kingdom, messages are transmitted via

energy. *When natural catastrophes occur and changes take place on the face of the earth, this isn't something which happens on the spur of the moment. There is a gradual building of the energies and this is why animal, plant, and mineral life can be detected responding to these symbols, these energies, and they begin to act in ways that are not normal for them, for they feel the changes that are coming. They know, each blade of grass knows, each tree, each flower, each rock knows.*

"The changes begin almost unnoticeably and gather momentum as in a crescendo, and if man did but once more realign himself with the energies of nature, he would be well prepared. Many changes are on the way," the Deva continued in prophetic vein, *"they have already begun. Like wheels that have been set in motion, the energies build up momentum; the set course is followed. Changes are coming for the evolution of the planet and for humankind. Roles and functions, certain energies, will change as man adapts to a new frequency.*

"The change is necessary to bring new understanding, to bring enlightenment, to restore the balance of the harmonies of nature, all in one accord, and the world once more shall become a sanctuary. It shall be as it was in the beginning, but it will be more meaningful, as humanity will have completed the cycle, and the whole of creation will have completed the cycle for a return to its original state.

"Become aware of the behavior of your feathered friends and any other pets you may have. When they begin to act differently and show signs of agitation, you will know the time is here. Do not be surprised if at some stage you feel the urge to set your captive friends free, but should you wish to do so, it would be best to wait until after the changes have occurred, otherwise they may not survive," the Deva concluded.

* * *

Why was I surprised at the topic when I awoke in the wee hours one morning with a partial verse of a poem, on the same theme, running around in my head? This time I was caught 'with my pants down,' metaphorically speaking, as I ran to the bathroom repeating the words over and over again so I wouldn't forget them. As I made my way back to the bedroom I was still whispering, "There be no light for the sunlit fare to feed the owl with the spotted glare." Repeating the words relentlessly, I rummaged around for pen and notepaper and climbed back into bed. I knew that if I didn't keep repeating the phrases over and over, they'd vanish as quickly as drops of water being drawn into parched earth.

I don't know if it was the whispering or my movements that woke Derek, but sensing something afoot, he reached for his pocket-sized tape-recorder and waited patiently as I climbed back under the covers.

The remaining words came very slowly at first, as there seemed to be a high, fine energy emanating from quite a distance away, and either it or I needed to catch up and 'mesh' again. There were gaps here and there where I lost the odd word or two, but when I typed the poem later, I 'knew' what the missing words were and was able to include them:

The owl with the spotted glare

There be no light for the sunlit fare to feed the owl with the spotted glare
There be no sound from the dead of night to bring the dawn and the hands of light
There be no trees in the darkened moon, the air about will be blackened soon
No space nor time for the eyes that see, for all about will in darkness be

Those eyes will long for the light of day and in deep despair with anguish pray
for those that had seen the lot of dread as eyes beheld that the sun went red
And deep inside of the tiny bore terror will strike at his very core
through the darkened earth in rigid clasp as a hellish mirth exhales its grasp

But sun breaks through with a shaft of gold, shattering darkness, banishing cold
And in the light of the dawning day Earth will arise so to make her way
to begin again as she did before and greet the Lords of a banished lore
adjusting now to a different Light, therein no day, therein no night

In timelessness of a giant span to become at last as all began
The timelessness like the giant eye from the universe within the sky
But the further out it's further in, for the joy of all can now begin
so to lay at rest the bloody past whose deeds therein did remain amassed

Within the silence of bleakest days without the light of the colored rays
shines eternity, a mighty blast, bringing sanctuary to man at last
For through his fears he brought about the turning point to within, from without
and he must know now his greatest needs are created so by his thoughts and deeds

He who looks within will see how bright is purity of the greatest Light
The brightest hopes are the greatest seeds that illuminate and meet all his needs
like sparkling gems of utopic state that ionic fusion initiate
to create anew in the dawn of light that the gold-eyed owl may feed in flight

Immediately after 'receiving' the words (which were accompanied by an incredible vision showing violent earth upheavals, darkness, and then blinding light) I conveyed my thoughts to Derek:

"Although it will seem like panic and chaos during predicted upcoming earth changes, there will be an orderly sequence of events occurring. It is not to be viewed as a cataclysmic occurrence in the darkest sense, not a death but a birth, a new beginning. Those acting from terror will create more terror for themselves, but those who accept the Divine Will and go with the flow will have the easier transition; for them there is no pain, there is no agony, just a change of consciousness. The eyes of the owl (the owl with the spotted glare) is symbolic of man whose vision is obscured; he's being likened to the bird of prey because he's a predator; he's taken from the earth, the sea, the skies."

Sleep, after that, was like the guest who would not tarry. Who on earth could possibly sleep after delivering or receiving such a powerfully profound message? The experience left us both wide-awake, with a sobering sense of awe bordering disbelief; certainly, we had been given much to think about. We were in agreement, though. Taking our druthers into account, we decided that we'd go with the flow of acceptance at the appointed time.

* * *

By the end of November 1994, I felt frustrated. It seemed that, although we definitely had been receiving some 'nice' information whilst trying to access the 'secrets of the ages' or whatever was recorded within the eggs, it wasn't exactly what I had anticipated in the beginning. I was hoping for something that was exceedingly profound, perhaps something that had not been written about before. We'd been coming in week after week, and we still hadn't hit upon any 'Open Sesame' format that would allow the information to flow. Sure we were asking questions and getting what I would term as lukewarm answers. But I wanted more. What we were 'receiving' didn't exactly seem to me to fit the bill, and I felt like we were merrily going around in circles getting nowhere. But worse than that, I knew my exasperation was beginning to show. I began another session a little more aggressively than usual.

"I'd like some direction as to the exact procedure we should be following. This whole scenario stems from the first time Derek placed the egg in my hands; we were told there is information contained within the egg. That was many weeks ago. I would like us to be able to access exactly what was referred to at that point. Is there any way the information can be released to us without us having to ask questions? Or is there a procedure we can engage in so that the information will just flow?"

"As you are proceeding at this time, the vibrations, the energies, are lining up," came the response from Derek's guide, *"and with each question you ask, you can make judgments as to whether the information which is coming through is valid. As these communications develop, even though it may not flow as rapidly as you wish or be as astounding as you feel it should be, there is information given within what has been said. And as your channels improve and become stronger to receiver the higher vibrations, at that time other information will come forth."*

I thanked him for being so patient with me and explained, "I'm really not sure what I should be doing. We realize that when the communication is going to take place there are many things that have to be lined up, and maybe I'm a little over-zealous, wanting something to just fall into my lap without doing any work, expecting wondrous words to run pat."

The guide then continued: *"As you become more accustomed to the energy and trust and allow, this will surely occur. It will occur as naturally as you breathe. At the moment, you are undergoing exercises, which assist you to reach a state of total relaxation, confidence and trust.*

"It takes considerable orchestration on both sides for this to occur, and, as you allow yourselves, when the transmission has begun, to very gently take a back seat, what you are seeking will occur. Do not be concerned if this does not happen as soon as you would wish. When the energies are properly aligned, using the onyx in the manner as is being done now will bring about a speedier transition into a deeper, trance channeling state.

"You have the tools; as you work with them they assist also in lining up energies to bring in the higher vibrations. Using the onyx and quartz together helps to accelerate the process; you are learning more and more, your channels are opening up. As you use the tourmaline, sugalite or amethyst, these also become your tools and you learn how to work with each."

"Can we inadvertently incorporate too many different things at one time? For instance, I always carry an assortment of crystals on my person and I also wear the tourmaline on a chain around my neck, and sometimes I wear an amethyst cross," was my question.

"If the body is not accustomed to these energies it will respond to let you know when it becomes too uncomfortable. You will know."

"Is there any hard and fast rule that we shouldn't put certain types together, or a possibility of any one or more of the minerals or crystals being incompatible with another?"

"As you experiment with different minerals, you will learn which work well together and those which don't. Assistance will be given."

"Did the process of shaping the onyx into an ovoid shape have any detrimental effect upon the onyx?" I asked.

"No. As it was shaped, one energy merged with another; there was much skill used by one who enjoyed his craft, working with a great deal of artistic interpretation. The mechanical means used were in no way detrimental. It was not merely a commercial venture."

"Some say that when a rock or crystal is in its natural form and is stationary, it has more female or yin energy than male, and when its shape is changed or fashioned into something else, the energy changes and becomes more male or yang. Is this true?"

"Sometimes. In this instance the onyx (Sanctuary) *has a more female quality or energy to it. Although it took on the ovoid shape, the fashioning has not changed the characteristics of the rock; it is still onyx, and although it has been given a purpose and different shape, its energy is female. A baby grows into a child attending school; the child experiences a lot of learning, and its progress may be likened to metal being forged and shaped by a blacksmith. However, as the child's personality and other aspects may be molded by the lessons, it does not change sex. He is still a male or she is still a female after having gone through school. If involved in an accident where serious injuries are sustained and maybe limbs are lost, the person does not change sex. Does that assist?"* the guide questioned.

"Yes," I answered, feeling a little silly, and changed the subject by asking: "How often should the onyx eggs be cleansed?"

"Whenever you feel it necessary. When there has been negativity flowing into the area, everything will be receptive to that negativity, including the walls, furniture, books, even the plants and the soil in which they grow. All may be affected to a greater or lesser degree. All are willing receptors that will also willingly accept a cleansing and recharging through positive thoughts of love and light. Do what you feel is appropriate. If you sense at a certain time that something requires a cleansing, that thought is in your mind for a good reason. That is the time to cleanse."

Satisfied with this explanation, I turned my attention again to the onyx egg lying cupped in Derek's hands. I clearly remembered the time the onyx was first placed in my hands in the store.

I now knew everything has information encoded within it, but I wondered if we would ever be given access to the information, so I asked the inevitable: "Are we ready to receive this information yet?"

"Not as yet. There is still trust needed."

That blew my high hopes once again, and I mentally performed my little dance of impatience. Did this mean I was still going through lessons of patience and tolerance? I guess so. I decided not to push the issue further, for now....

Chapter 6

My energy was flagging as we arrived home one evening at around 11:00 PM, so, without more ado, we headed to the bedroom, yawning and ready for sleep. This getting up early to be in the office at 5:00 AM can leave a body weary by the time eleven at night rolls around. Derek undressed quickly, set the alarm clock and then walked towards the window to close the drapes. There was a tone of urgency in his voice as he called me.

"Di, quick! Come look at this...."

There were lights darting around in the sky doing an aerial version of synchronized swimming. I looked out of the window until I realized the 'show' was just a commercial advertising venture projecting beams of light into the sky. Disappointed at not finding a colorful display of the northern lights dancing in the skies at the very least, I expressed my annoyance at being hoodwinked and turned to move away.

"No. You're looking at the wrong thing. Come over here," Derek whispered, pointing, "look right up there in the big clearing past those clouds."

My eyes followed his direction. Way up in the sky was a flotilla of moving 'stars,' but these were not all headed in exactly the same direction. I wasn't sure if I could trust what I was seeing.

Derek wanted to go outside and get a better look. Whoops! Time to get dressed again! I didn't want him to go out alone, just in case.... Perish the thought of little green men coming down and finding us altogether in the buff! And I had no intention of seeing in tomorrow's newspaper headlines: 'UFOs grab hypnotherapist, hysterical widow claims!' My mind was racing ahead, but it felt as if I was wearing lead boots that wouldn't catch up to my brain. It all seemed so unreal.

I tried to dress quickly. Derek made a very brief telephone call to our friend Amos, to check if the same phenomenon could be seen on the north side of the city, then, hand in hand, we made our way outside.

A few large clouds were moving slowly overhead, but between them we could see 'stars' proceeding in the same direction yet at a faster speed. We counted twenty, and then there were more, all moving steadily and quite visibly. We craned our necks as they passed by overhead, disappearing, and then reappearing again. Two of them, in unison, seemed to separate from the others and appeared to be headed in our direction. Just as I was hoping they would come close enough so that we would be able identify some shape or form, they simply disappeared, and at that point the sky was quite clear of clouds. When we looked for the others, they had gone, too. I checked my watch. I couldn't remember the exact time we came outside, but there didn't seem to be any apparent time loss.

After a while, Derek decided he'd better make contact with one of his guides, and sat on an old chair on the patio for the impromptu communication. We were quickly reassured that everything was fine, and that we were simply witnessing a mass sighting of ships from different galaxies, ones that were working with the 'Light.' It was time, the guide said, for the awareness of people on earth to be raised, time that they realized there are different beings waiting to assist the planet during great changes that are to take place and, in fact, have already begun. Many people would witness this mass sighting. During the next few years it would become increasingly difficult to refute the existence of other planetary beings, those already here and those waiting in the wings, so to speak.

With the explanation, we felt comfortable enough to go back into the house, but we went to sleep holding on to each other. If Derek was to be taken for a little 'trip' during the night, I wanted to know about it and be there, too! I guess it was my imagination and the old journalist in me coming to the fore. If there was a scoop to be had, I wanted a place in the front line.

Surprisingly, we both slept well. I don't remember dreaming, but in the morning I felt privileged to have witnessed the night's sighting. Amos, our friend in the north of Edmonton, filled us in with a report which confirmed that what we had seen in the west end also had been visible from the opposite end of the city!

Eagerly, we turned on the radio to listen to news reports broadcast from several different stations and we scanned the local newspapers. Not a mention anywhere of a mass sighting, not a whisper, even of a solitary one.

So, what had happened? Were three of us going bananas at the same time, two on the city's West End and one on the north? There must have been more folks who saw what we saw. Was it a case of others not wanting to share what they may have witnessed, for fear of ridicule, or waiting for someone else to speak up first? Or had other people perhaps seen no further than the advertising light-beams show?

There was a chill in the air that morning and, although the distance from our house to the office was short, I was glad we decided to drive the old beater we'd recently acquired.

My mind was still on the late night sky happening. When Derek invited his guide, John, to be with us, I was very pleased. Talking to John would give me an opportunity to chat with a good friend again. I loved his energy, and could feel such warmth and love emanating when he was talking.

I asked about the sighting. As usual, John shared words of wisdom, including not concerning ourselves with what may have been going on in the skies. Yes, we had seen what we thought we had seen. But he gently reminded us of the task we had chosen to undertake, pointing out that if we concentrate on outside 'distractions,' as it were, it would become our reality, our focus, and steer us away from the job at hand. There was much to be written that will take all our focus, he said, then asked was that not the reality we had chosen to concentrate upon at this time. Of course it was. Our conversation was a good reminder that we do indeed create our own reality by giving energy and attention to whatever is on our mind at any given time.

***

So much was happening so quickly during the autumn of 1994, it really was a wonder that Derek and I retained our sanity. It seemed that some strange unseen force was testing out our sensitivity; our 'alert sensors' were heightened to such a degree that even a flea rubbing its legs together would have sounded like thunder. And nothing we did took place half-measure, whether it was a sneezing fit that carried on for twenty minutes, a bout of loud hiccups that lasted half an hour, pronounced physical discomfort of one sort or another, or even weird problems with the computer. There was no doubt about it. Something was going on. But what?

For a few weeks I had been bugged every now and then by an annoying, loud clicking sound in my left ear. I tried repeatedly to ignore it, but finally the distraction became too intolerable to shrug off any more. It was time to ask for Derek's assistance to see if we could find out what on earth was causing the annoying phenomenon.

We began the session as we always did with a prayer, asking for God's protection and guidance. Next, Derek started to gently lead me into an altered state of awareness, but before I could really access my 'safe place,' I became aware of another distraction, a twitching sensation running up and down my left leg, like something was jumping from muscle to muscle.

Of course, I told Derek what was happening, but when he asked who or what was doing the distracting, I answered, "It's gone now. As soon as you tune into it, it goes."

Then, as Derek started into the procedure again, I became aware of the 'something' really distracting me once more. It seemed whatever it was wanted to stop us from finding out what the clicking in the ear was all about. But Derek continued talking in a soft monotone until he could tell from my skin tone and the way I was answering that I was in an altered state, and he instructed me to follow the distracting energy back to its source.

The following is a transcript of that very strange session:

"It looks like a dark ball of energy. It took off like a bat out of hell!"

"Did you follow the energy and go as fast as it went?"

"No. I couldn't. It's back again." I began receiving a telepathic message and relayed it to Derek. "It says, 'You couldn't follow, you weren't fast enough.'"

"I want you to surround the energy with a whole mass of white light. Send some healing light to that ball."

I did as Derek directed, mentally projecting a ball of white light to completely surround the energy, and then gave Derek a verbal report of what was happening.

"It looks like it [the white light] dissolved the ball. It looks like it's disappeared. I'm being left alone now."

Derek continued with the technique we use to take me to my 'safe place,' and then he led me to a contact with my spiritual guide and began asking questions again:

"We wish to know the source of the interference that's causing clicking in Diana's ears."

"It is felt the purpose, the nature of this clicking sound, is to distract her from what she is doing. It is an outside source."

"Where is it coming from; is it coming from ETs?"

"If that is what you wish to call them, yes."

"And who is doing this?"

"Others who wish to know."

"What is it they wish to know? It's not as if the two of us are highly technical, or have some position in the government with access to vital information. We're just ordinary citizens."

"We understand that theirs is of a different makeup; the spiritual connection differs from yours, due to a different perception or understanding of the mutual evolutionary progress, and for that particular species emotion was overlooked. Emotion was there originally, but through countless generations of non-attention it has become dormant and they are wishing to improve upon that which they are, so as to become more like yourselves."

"We would rather share information than do things underhandedly in a way that could cause others discomfort."

"This is understood. But they are without emotion, and therefore the understanding is different. Your particular use of the word 'underhandedly' implies that there is emotion. It is believed the acquisition of that which you come by naturally would place them in a superior position, from their perspective," the guide continued. *"They wish to incorporate the best from the human makeup. The things that you are teaching help raise the awareness of the people, which assists them to tap into their full potential. En masse, this could create a strength or power that has potential far undreamed of by you. And your observers would wish this for themselves."*

"I've heard that the combined energies of a group of people has ten times the power of a single person."

"The more who are awakened to this, the greater is the significance of your work, and the more impact it could have. These beings fear that the 'backward' human beings, as they perceive you to be, may become very much 'forwards' and be in a position to reclaim much of that which is mankind's inheritance. As man's abilities increase, this could mean that ultimately the creative powers he reclaims could be used inappropriately, such as in an aggressive or military sense. You see, the old saying that the sky is the limit, is very much applicable."

"I can see how some of them could be acting out of fear, just as people on earth right now are acting out of fear about their [ET] presence."

"It is not fear that motivates them to monitor your activities. But, in part, you are correct. It is perhaps good that most people on earth are unaware as to what is going on; many are not quite ready for this, although many are like sleeping children ready to be aroused into wakefulness."

"I can see how our work could do this."

"You may feel that your modest contribution is very small. However, it has the makings for opening not a small gate, but a floodgate of potential."

"Can you advise us on how we could protect ourselves a little more? It doesn't seem that using white light is adequate to protect us from these other influences."

"It would appear that assistance comes to you from another direction. Using the light with intent is the best protection at your disposal for now, and the reason will be clearer to you later. In time you will learn techniques to transport yourself out of range, if you wish, as fast as those that are trying to tap into your source, and you will be able to project yourselves at the speed of thought. But, at the moment, you are like babes beginning to crawl. The next stage is standing, then walking, then running, and then 'flight.' These stages will unfold for you when the time is appropriate. In the meantime, any other assistance will come from those others of your brothers who are also with you, who cherish and have undertaken to protect you."

"You have helped us to understand a little of what's going on. We're just becoming aware of the different energies, realizing how they can transport themselves here within an instant of a thought from what we perceive to be thousands of miles away, and how it appears the walls literally have ears. Is it correct that when we start communicating, and particularly when we are, say, directing a planetary healing, we open up a frequency which can be, and is, picked up by other life-forms anywhere in our immediate vicinity and even as 'far away' as in another galaxy?"

"That is correct."

"How very fortunate we are to have the techniques we've learned that enable us to communicate with such as yourself and those who are assisting us."

"It is wise that you have chosen to continue in your own spiritual endeavors. When you are ready, you will understand more. At the moment, it is appropriate you know only that which has been revealed to you so far. As you begin to stand on your own feet, gain your balance and then walk, your awareness will increase."

It took us a while to settle down after that. How could any other species think that our innocuous teachings could possibly endow people with special powers or abilities? After all, we were merely teaching a method of meditation using guided visualization; showing our students how to 'protect' themselves by using their imagination, and giving instruction in different hands-on healing techniques. Were we, quite by chance, teaching something else, perhaps empowering students in a way we could not see or perceive?

What was going on? I wondered, again. This was all very interesting, and ego-boosting, even, but was it really happening? I wasn't one hundred percent sure I wanted to believe what had 'transpired.' In fact, I would have been happier if the whole business had gone away and I didn't have to look at it again. Was I in denial, or what?

Not knowing what to believe, or what else could happen, I decided I would transcribe the taped session and enter it into the computer. Afterwards, I printed out a hard copy, but, fearing something of which I had no inkling, I made sure not to leave any record of the document on the hard drive. I copied it onto a special disk that I promptly gave to Derek to hide in a safe place. That way, I guess, I felt more secure, although from what, I am not sure. Of course, it goes without saying that the disk mysteriously disappeared. Had Derek put it a place so 'safe' we wouldn't find it again, or was there another factor at play?

Derek and I made a mutual pact; we wouldn't discuss with anyone the 'clicking in the ear' incident. A couple of days later, however, two staunch friends stopped in at the office. These were folks we knew we could trust, so we decided our friends would be the exception, and we broke our pact...temporarily. I'm glad we did. The strange saga took another weird turn.

After one friend read the transcript of that session, he knew there was some pertinent information within the document. He said there were certain key phrases that spoke volumes, but the weirdest thing was, he couldn't for the life of him remember anything he'd read. He looked at the document again and with a puzzled expression on his face said he couldn't find what he was looking for, as the words seemed to have disappeared. Nonplussed, he followed me into the kitchen to take me up on my offer of a cup of coffee. From the kitchen I could hear Derek talking to our friend's wife and I heard him say, "What do you make of this?" He apparently gave her the document to read and within seconds he called me back into the room.

I arrived there in time to see our friend's wife swaying, and then she put a hand up to her forehead, as if to steady herself. "Everything's black," she said. "As soon as I took hold of the paper and began to read, everything went black, like something's stopping me from reading."

Derek guided her to a chair, all the while keeping the conversation going, and, as he gently sat her down, he asked this very clairvoyant lady to describe what was happening. With each response, he bombarded her with more questions, thereby creating and holding an energy link so he could continue to maintain contact. As long as she kept talking, focusing upon the questions and answers, she was locked into whatever the 'something' was.

"Now I'm seeing a giant eye looking at me. It doesn't want me to read the paper. It won't go away."

"What does it want?"
"It's here to observe. It's an observer."
"Why is it here?"
"To observe."
"What else is it here for?"
"There's no response."
"Ask it why it's here."
"It says it isn't allowed to respond. It's just an observer. It has to go."
"But now we've found it out, we've locked into it; so it can't go until it says what it is here for."
"It has to go. It's being summoned. There's a bright light flashing in the distance, calling it back."
"Why did it stop you from reading the document?"
"It didn't want us to know what was written. It has the technology to blank things out, causing loss of memory. But it doesn't have the technology to physically take the document from me."

Her voice took on a tone of agitation. "It's being recalled. It's getting an urgent message. It must go. The light is getting closer and the flashing is becoming more urgent, more rapid. It will get into trouble if we don't let it go."

"It's already in trouble. We found out about it."
"It has to go."
"Come on, Derek," I intervened, "let it go."

Derek finally complied and terminated the conversation that had held 'the observer' locked into our friend's energy link or 'frequency.' She heaved an audible sigh of relief.

"Whew! I don't ever want to go through that again," she said, "it's like I was blacking out, and when you began talking, it felt like I was paralyzed and then I could see this giant eye. I was really sensing the urgency when it couldn't get away."

By this time, her husband had joined us in Derek's office. He'd heard everything from the doorway, and remembered that this was similar to what had happened to him, except he had been able to read the document at first; it certainly answered why he couldn't find any 'key phrases' or remember anything of what had triggered his interest. Things hadn't gone black; he just couldn't see anything. It was only because of his wife's parallel experience that he was prepared to believe what had happened.

Our friends didn't come to our office for quite a while after that....

We certainly realized the benefit of following suggestions given to us recently about directing our attention to matters of a more spiritual kind. We chose not to dwell on things of this nature, lest they become our focus, our reality. In other words, at this point we chose to play ostrich. But just because one can't see something it doesn't mean it's not there. Were we in for a few surprises?

* * *

A couple of days later I was sitting in Derek's recliner in his office again, chatting. It felt as though there was a tight band around my forehead and I knew it had nothing to do with the crystal cap I had been wearing. Several times, lately, I had been aware of a strange sensation in my face; I'd even been awakened by it during the night and I wondered if the two sensations were connected in any way.

In an attempt to find out what was going on, when Derek suggested that I go into (focus upon) the feeling, I followed his instructions. It wasn't long before something seemed to 'click in' and I began receiving some kind of mental, telepathic communication.

"I get the thought they have had me in some type of line of vision for some time. This isn't as clear as it should be, but, I'm getting it's a beginning. I'm only getting fleeting glimpses. It's like there's a room full of 'people' quite pleased that we've made contact. They are saying at this moment the visual impressions will be what I'm wishing to see."

"One that you'll accept?"

"Not just what I'll accept, but something that I'm comfortable with. They are conveying that I am wise not to choose something that cannot be changed. I'm feeling very spacey...a sense of outer space is going around in my head [no pun intended]. They are communicating telepathically. I sense the word 'Greetings.'

"For ones that we assume to be emotionless, there is a lot of love being expressed. I am getting the impression they are saying that the most stubborn, like me, are the most difficult to 'use,' but bring the most rewards when contact is made. It wasn't intended for contact to take place today, at this time, but they are satisfied with the event."

Derek laughed and said, "Well, they've got to make an appointment, as we insist on appointments for contact here."

"I sense amusement. I am relieved they appear to have a sense of humor. They're saying, 'Here's another stubborn one! This is the one who pushed it today.'"

"I didn't push it today. Someone was playing with Diana's face and I wanted to find out who was responsible."

"They say they're just establishing the signals, that's all. I'm sure I got a name, but it's like I can't remember it."

"Well, they are going to have to tell you again."

"The response is, 'This one is very pushy!'"

"Well, if it wasn't for me being pushy, we wouldn't be making contact right now," Derek laughed.

"They're saying, 'That is right. He does think he knows all the answers,' and I'm getting the impression they're quite enjoying this."

"It sounds like we have some comedians there!"

"What beautiful energy. They say there's more fine-tuning needed, but they feel this is enough contact for now."

"Even though I pushed it a little, I'm very glad that I was able to assist," Derek chuckled.

"There is much love being sent. They say we're not strangers, you know, and that we will both recognize some dear friends when the time is right."

Derek brought my awareness back to the room as he said, "So they feel free to call us stubborn."

Needless to say, I was stunned by what happened. Could this really be happening? Could what be happening? I don't know, really. It's like my 'normal' reality had been put into a brown paper sack, given a good shake and then poured out again. I just plain wasn't sure what was happening and mentally reeled, trying to get my bearings. If I had been asked at that point which way was up and which was down, I wouldn't have known.

Which reality is real, anyway; which dimension is real? Or am I just going slowly crazy?

I bet I'm not the first to think I'm off my rocker when this type of thing happens. First a 'spirit ball' that bursts through a wall and nearly sends me flying, then rocks and spirits of rocks talking to me, then 'observers,' and now this. Could anything else possibly happen to top all this? Not likely! And did it have something to do with wearing the crystal cap? Hardly!

I couldn't help thinking, 'Thank God I felt a good rapport with this bunch.' I guess there are good guys and there are different ones.

So, what is this strange, compelling thing that suggests we are going to be working in the mornings at 5:00 AM? And then off we trot, to do its bidding, albeit a little sideways as, still half asleep, we stagger into the office in the wee hours, or what to me are the wee hours? If we create our own reality—and you've heard that from me already—then what did I actually do to create these weird happenings?

"Things will begin leveling out," I kept telling myself. "There's a pattern beginning to emerge. I'm sure when the time is right we'll understand what is really going on. For now, though, we'll just have to take it one day at a time."

* * *

Thanksgiving Day of 1994 was another extraordinary day, the kind that was rapidly becoming the norm. At the office we began, in a leisurely way, to create our protection around us by generating and expanding our own light from within.

After taking care of the preliminaries, we were planning to channel more information about our quartz crystals. However, I soon became aware of a distracting, annoying sensation in my left ear, which became very persistent, despite my attempts to block it out. Something was either stopping me from working with the crystals, or simply trying to get my attention.

It was time for Derek to play doctor detective again. As I tuned in to the annoying sensation in my ear, Derek began asking questions so that he could access the source of the distraction. I was able to report, "It just wants to witness things. It's an observer. I'm not getting where it's from. It says they are from somewhere too far away for your comprehension."

Derek asked if 'it' was working with the Light, and the answer came, "Not in the sense that you mean." When he asked if it was looking out for the well being of us all, I responded, "They are looking out for their own well-being; I sense our well-being is inconsequential. The telepathic thoughts being conveyed are that we are to be observed. I sense they regard us as a different species and we're fair game."

Derek indicated the door and made it clear that the 'observers' could watch, just so long as they observe from a distance; he said they were disturbing me and would only be permitted to observe from the outer perimeter of the room. But they made no attempt to retreat. In fact, the sensation in my ear became more pronounced.

By this time, I was beginning to get just a tad warm, if you know what I mean. So I addressed them out loud, saying firmly, "We give you permission to observe...but from the doorway over there, providing there is no interference and providing you intend no harm. And we say this with respect." I mentally directed a ball of light towards the doorway, indicating where they must go.

With such a disturbance I had opened my eyes, and I watched as Derek brought our 'heavy-duty' crystals into the room and placed them around my chair. Then he psychically brought in the energy of crystals from another location. As I closed my eyes again, I became aware of an increased surge of energy within the room, and I felt the intruders retreating to the doorway.

Derek continued with the process of putting protection around us, and it was back to business again as he invited the Deva of the quartz crystals to join us. After exchanging greetings with the quartz Deva, Derek began asking questions, and I began channeling the responses.

"Do you feel it is appropriate for us to carry on the session with the observers present?"

"There is nothing new they can learn here. They are already aware of what goes on and are merely curious. They have seen this occur before, but they do not understand your emotions, the way that you sense, or the way that you feel the Light and love, or the way that you are aware of the gentleness of the energy that is with you at the moment. I am sure that you also can feel the energy surge. It is being generated to encompass your energy field also."

"Yes, I am aware of the change in energy, and I thank you."

"You are wishing me to communicate. I am not sure what it is that you wish."

"We would like to know more about the crystals that Diana is holding and how best to use them."

"The crystals will work well together. The two energies combining may be used as a key to seek the information you wish."

"To do that, what is the best procedure to use?"

"You know several procedures. All are appropriate. Through the 'trial and error' process you will find what is best for yourself; what is best for one person may be different for another."

"Would it be advisable to call upon yourself, or the energy of the specific crystals we are working with?"

"This is individual preference. I cannot tell you what you must do...either method is valid. If you wish the assistance of the same energy that is present now, then you would adopt the procedure you used this morning. If you are wishing to access a deep-trance state,

the procedure is slightly different. Whatever is your intention, your purpose, then it is for you to choose."

"What can you tell me about the crystal given to Diana recently?"

"A baby enjoys a telepathic communication with guides as he reaches out to grasp that which is still visible to him. The child reaches out to each item in turn; it doesn't capture at once everything that it sees. It focuses attention upon one particular point, one object, and tries to embrace that one. It will bring it up close and examine it through smell, taste and touch, try to consume it, feel it, talk to it, and then, when it has found out everything it can about that one particular object, it will let go and reach for another. The crystal will assist you to reach out and focus upon the one area you wish to receive information on, so you may pursue that."

We continued with several more crystals before calling a halt to the session, which Derek had recorded whilst carefully numbering and labeling the crystals. Then we moved to the reception area, where I sat at the computer to begin transcribing the information we had just received.

To speed up the process, Derek offered to assist by operating the taperecorder for me. But, as I started typing out the information, I felt a series of distinctive, sharp, jabbing pricks in the tip of the middle finger of my left hand.

"Ouch! Ouch! Ouch!" I complained and held my finger out to show Derek my invisible infliction.... Of course, right on cue again, Derek began to ask questions about the jabs to my fingertip, and, as I felt my awareness shifting, I began receiving another telepathic communication.

The unseen observers were back, intruding into my space once more, and one was now suggesting that surely our intelligence warranted a more direct approach to receive information "instead of playing children's games going through minerals!" It was the same observers that we had allowed to watch from the doorway.

Derek asked what was meant by 'a more direct approach,' and I relayed the message that we could be talking directly with them, the observers. Derek asked what that would entail. They suggested that they could 'download' the information to us quicker than us using the procedure we had adopted with the crystals. Then Derek enquired, "Wouldn't that require us giving you permission to use our physical bodies?" This was becoming more than a little ridiculous. Derek was very wary, but inquired a little further to find out if what he was hearing meant these 'observers' were seeking control. There was no immediate response, so Derek repeated his question. After some delay they responded, "Yes."

I heaved a sigh of relief as I then heard Derek's immediate, "Sorry, we can't agree to that." Very calmly he told them he felt it would be like us committing suicide if we agreed to their request, as that would be like giving them an open-ended contract to take control whenever it suited them. Derek then asked if they would do the same if our roles were reversed. After a long hesitation, the response was that they could understand our reluctance.

At this point Derek's tone became almost apologetic as he said he realized there were other people who would no doubt quite willingly accede to their request.

The intruding observer agreed, and said that, although that was so, it would be more of an accomplishment to have our cooperation; however, if we wished to 'introduce' any of our enlightened friends who were seeking 'alternate experiences,' they would consider that.

Why on earth would they need an introduction? We certainly hadn't been introduced. They'd simply made their presence known by a few swift jabs to my finger, and earlier, with several pokes in my ear. Were they really wanting a formal introduction to some unsuspecting soul who may willingly give them what they wanted on account of our 'Here, get a load of these characters and have yourself an experience' say so? Again, no thanks!

The next part of the encounter came as something of a surprise. I relayed the message that, as we had given them a boundary, they were respecting the boundary, but only because we had acknowledged them with respect. I guess they were referring to me mentally sending them Light when telling them they must observe from the doorway.

The 'observer' communicated that it was not in their makeup to be influenced by emotion or the spiritual values we have, and that boundaries are only for those who respect them. In other words, they were politely saying that, if they wished to move in, that's what they could do, as we already had offered a point of contact by setting up a 'boundary.' Then they cautioned us not to offer any 'boundaries' to anyone, as that could be used as 'a foot in the door.' If we did not wish any contact whatsoever, it should be a definite "NO!" and not an "okay, but from a distance."

Derek thanked them for the advice, but I wish he hadn't, as they were quick to add they would still be observing us, and, should the opportunity present itself, should we wish to make the contact on their terms, they would be more than willing to accommodate us. (From my way of thinking, it would be more like us accommodating them.)

I was amazed at how cool Derek had remained, but, on this occasion, I couldn't help feeling that sometimes he doesn't terminate a conversation as soon as he should.

With sublime naiveté, Derek stated we have considerable respect for all life forms, whether animal, plant, or mineral, even species from other planets.

I felt the timbre of the observers' energy change to one that can only be likened to cold impatience. They conveyed that they did not wish to be categorized alongside 'minerals' or other lower life forms. Woops, Derek! I think that was a no-no!

Fortunately, this was one of those occasions where Derek quickly became the epitome of diplomacy and tact; he apologized, saying he had intended no disparaging insult, as he was fully aware of their superior intelligence.

The next moment they were gone and I heaved a large sigh of relief.

Things had been tense there for a short while, but all in all, I was proud of Derek. He'd been faced with a most unusual situation and hadn't blinked an eye. He'd talked to the observers as if it were a normal, everyday occurrence. Thank God he hadn't accepted their offer!

Here we are, seeking to learn about everything, and, voila, we're being offered something on a plate, a veritable opportunity to receive communication at a different level! What a level! What an offer! No thanks, not at this time nor any other. For what was being offered, the price was totally unacceptable.

I was so stunned by the whole scenario it was very difficult to continue with our 'child's play,' although my fingertips were now able to touch the keyboard without any painful sense of being jabbed. I needed a break....

Because of our general makeup, the body needs to assimilate what it has learned or heard, to feel its own truths within what has been said. Our perception of what transpires, through what's been said, felt or understood, whether from a spiritual contact or energies from other sources, makes it hard for us to come to a decision unless we can feel safe within ourselves. We know there could be serious and permanent ramifications if we agree to do what we do not know or understand. And how can one understand fully what one can't see and can only feel or sense? These beings hadn't communicated any visual impressions. I definitely needed a break.

For a brief moment we allowed ourselves to think about the mind-boggling scenario that had just taken place. I decided to shelve my impressions until I had more time to digest what had gone on. But then again, was this too important to put on hold?

On impulse, we decided to tune in again to ask our guides what was going on. We needed some kind of reassurance, even though we still had much work to do before allotting time to digestion of a Thanksgiving nature later that afternoon.

We moved back into Derek's office, where, once again, I sat in The Chair and tuned in. When Derek was sure he was talking to my guide, Daneus, he mentioned the frequent 'interference' that had been occurring, and what had happened as we began to transcribe the channeled information from tape deck to computer.

Once more we were reassured, and it was suggested to not concern ourselves with those energies that had recently become evident to us. As our abilities increase, we were told, so does our awareness, and as our vibratory rate increases these energies will retreat, if that is our wish.

Derek asked how these distracting energies fit into the overall plan, and Daneus explained:

"Everything fits into the overall plan; nothing happens by chance. There are finely orchestrated sequences of events that occur. The distracting energies, as you call them, are here, as are we, and you, and all who have become your friends in this office. Each has its rightful place in the plan of all things.

"There are those among us which exist differently, as their vibration is that of another dimension; of this fact you are aware. Perhaps it is better to focus your attention away from them at this time, for to give energy in that direction takes energy away from completing the tasks you may have chosen to undertake.

"There is a considerable re-awakening occurring as awareness is raised. There are many beings upon this planet like yourselves who chose to incarnate for the same purpose as you; they are just beginning to awaken to the call. It was not planned for everyone to awaken at the same time.

"Individually, and for the group as a whole, the awakening and raising of the vibratory level, of necessity, must be gradual. Otherwise it would be rejected and a wall or barrier would be placed around self, to instinctively escape from that which one fears, because this is as yet an unknown [occurrence]. *Indeed, for the majority, what has been undergone today would not have been handled so well.*

"As awareness is raised, senses are sharpened, so to speak, and this does spark awareness of different species that exist within other dimensions. Your progress may appear to have been slow, but there has been a perceptible awakening.

"Within darkness there is light. Although light casts shadows, it is not the light that is the shadow, but the reflected energy from which the shadow is formed. In the same way, as the wind blows it cannot be seen, although the effects of what the air is moving can be seen and felt; it assists in pollinating and it acts as a cleanser. Its force can also be very destructive, yet everything that occurs in the path of the wind is designed for a specific purpose. Nothing happens by chance."

What was Daneus saying? If nothing happens by chance, then why were we encountering intruding 'observers'?

Either the heat in the room or my own body temperature became too intolerable at that moment, and we had to discontinue the session. There had been a change in energy that I wasn't able to endure for long, and I was left with a feeling that perhaps I would have been a little more comfortable if I had never become aware of beings from other realities or dimensions.

What a day! Talk about grist for the mill. I couldn't help wondering what we were supposed to do about this and other strange encounters we'd experienced recently. I certainly knew we wouldn't be able to talk about it over Thanksgiving dinner. If the kids knew what Mom knows they'd be blown away! Just thinking about having to keep my mouth shut again made me want to scream, but I realized it was best to keep a lid on things. At least until the book is published

Chapter 7

Derek and I continued working with crystals; we were like kids playing with new toys. Previous to our first psychic fair we had no real knowledge of them. I knew my birthstone was amethyst, and I'd heard people claim that quartz crystals were good for work in the healing arts, and certain colors could stimulate the charkas. That was about the sum total of my knowledge.

Up to that point, my interest in crystals was no more than lukewarm, and I honestly disbelieved when others enthused that this or that crystal had special properties. I guess I was too busy with other pursuits at that time, or I simply wasn't ready for the wonderful world of rocks and crystals. But they made such a dramatic entrance into our lives, and all that changed. Now, Derek and I are both confirmed enthusiasts.

I guess to others we must appear to be an odd couple. Not only do we spend 'working hours' together, it seems we spend all of our other time together, as if we can't get enough of each other's company. Either we're gluttons for punishment or we have more to work out than other people.

One evening at home, as I sat meditating while holding two very special quartz crystals, Derek began a conversation and one of my spiritual guides responded.

"*By the time you learn the full extent of the information contained within the crystals, many changes will have occurred within your lives.*

"*Knowledge itself is sacred. Ancient civilizations, light years ahead of you in understanding and technology as you know it now, relied heavily upon the use of crystals, the properties of which, as yet, man has not really tapped into. You have begun to use them and recognize their importance, but there is still a wealth of information that is a mystery to you.*

"*The more you work with crystals, the more you are attuning to other vibrational frequencies. Handling the crystals on a regular basis and wearing them is assisting with rais-*

ing the personal vibratory rate and growth, and as you feel you are becoming more attuned, there is indeed more happening within your bodies than you perceive.

"It is invaluable for you to sit with the crystals, using them as you do in your meditations and keeping them around you at all times," my guide offered.

"Diana is having remarkable success in remembering her dreams as she sleeps holding onto an amethyst crystal. The amazing thing is that the crystal is still in her hand when she wakes. We're really careful what we say to others, as they might think us crazy, seeing we're not only wearing crystals and talking to them, but sleeping with them as well," Derek quipped.

"You are rapidly being prepared for future work as there is a sense of urgency. No longer is there time for lengthy 'apprenticeships.' The pulse of the planet is quickening in preparation for major earth changes that will occur after the turn of the century. But, for now, each transmission is just an exercise, although you may find you receive surprising information at times. Gradually you will learn to trust the information coming through.

"To assist, you have the influence of your crystals. They are your tools. You may surround yourself with them until your work with them on an absentee basis has become more established; the crystals mainly are tools assisting you to build up your awareness and your frequency. There is much that we can teach you, but it can only be done a little at a time.

"We like to call it the 'gentle approach' so that you are never overburdened or alarmed by some of the information you receive. If there is too much done or given at one time it could unhinge the delicate balance within the body. It is almost like inviting into yourselves another being, let us say, light-years ahead in understanding and wisdom, one operating at a highly accelerated vibration. The human body, because of the density and mass, is slower. It isn't as if you can plug the system into an electric outlet, adjust the dial and turn everything on to full power. The body must assimilate the energies slowly, over a period of time.

"If you look back to one year ago, you will recognize that incredible change has occurred in your understanding, attitude, and abilities. You are aware that your reactions to things now are far different from even a few weeks ago. As scenarios are brought into play, they assist you to realize how quickly perception changes; you become aware of how, each time you draw criticism or judgment, it rings a little bell so that you become aware of what you are doing.

"Lessons come in many forms; they frequently serve as a reminder—as do drivers who appear on the road in front of you and cause frustration—that there is still something unresolved," my guide concluded.

* * *

I think the thing that surprised me most about crystals is their individual uniqueness. We expect people to be unique, but rocks, mere minerals? How could they be unique, you may ask, except by shape, size or color? By their energy, of course!

But why was I so surprised to learn that? Probably because I never had any interest in any of the science subjects while at school. You could say I was the 'duffer of the class' in that department. Now I understand that all of us, all of creation, whether human beings, animals, fish, reptiles, insects, trees, plants, minerals, earth, water, the sun, planets, even the air we breathe, all have their own unique energies. We are all comprised of matter, minute cells, molecules or subatomic particles vibrating to a particular energy frequency.

Over the ensuing months, we made contact many times with devas of the different types of crystals, and were surprised how readily our questions were answered. Sometimes, in our conversations with the Quartz Deva, we received more than we bargained for. One day Derek asked how crystals could assist in the healing process. The response was spontaneous:

"When disruptions have occurred and caused the energy flowing throughout the human body and its energy field to become obstructed, the crystals may be used to clear those blockages. This allows the energies to proceed correctly through the meridians of the body. The crystals will also assist in aligning the major and minor chakras. They are also beneficial in realigning the subtle energies of the other bodies [mental, emotional and spiritual] *so that the magnetic flow will be strengthened and healing allowed to occur on all levels, if that is desired.*

"There are many formations or layouts that may be used when placing crystals around the body for healing or to realign the person's energies," the Quartz Deva continued. *"Before beginning, it is suggested that the healing intent be made known and a request made of each individual crystal for assistance, so that its specific energy is given a purpose. It would also be prudent that the intent of the assistant* [the healer or facilitator] *and the receptivity of the recipient be made known, so that a mutual understanding may occur.*

"It is suggested, also, that the assistant aligns his or her energies with those of the crystals before placing them around the recipient's body, and then, after placing them in the desired formation, he or she create a picture within the mind, seeing the energies flow, seeing the energies coursing through the body, and visually sensing them flowing freely and unrestricted throughout the procedure.

"This visualization process is important and necessary, as is a request that healing occur for the highest good of both the participant and the assistant," the Quartz Deva explained. *"It allows the healing channel to work in the best possible manner with the*

assistance of the crystals. You may summon the assistance of others [crystals] *not physically present to help with the healing process, but they too must be made aware of the intention. It is most beneficial to communicate mentally, visualizing what it is that you request, and seeing a positive outcome.*

"Until you are more familiar with using the crystals to assist with the healing, a general procedure you may try is to place several around the body a short distance away, making sure that the points all follow a clockwise direction, and so that a circle is formed, starting at the top of the head," the Deva suggested. *"If you have sufficient crystals, place them adjacent to the shoulders, elbows, wrists, knees, ankles, and one just beyond the great toes.*

"Begin the process by touching the crystal located above the head and directing the energy flow around the circle. You may use another charged crystal to start the process, or you may mentally visualize that you are using another charged crystal to do so. But remember, if the recipient has never been exposed to crystal energy before, it is best to exercise caution, taking no longer than a few minutes the first time. If necessary, the energy circuit may quickly be broken by removing one of the crystals from the circle. Encourage the recipient to sit up slowly afterwards. For some, the experience will be quite memorable, as the energy will have been felt. Others, however, whose awareness may not be so acute, may feel they experienced little, although they too will have benefited from the experience," the Deva concluded.

* * *

On another occasion, as I was taking a break away, I was sitting in Derek's room chatting, unconsciously fingering the tiny facets of the Awakening Time crystal I was holding. At Derek's suggestion, I tuned in, and in a short time the Quartz Deva was communicating again:

"This crystal is a key to unlock many doors. It may be used during meditation where the focus is inward and will assist in awakening memories if it is wished to tune into past journeys of the soul. The crystal is a focus; the holder may focus upon its surface texture or project awareness inside the crystal. This may be done when another person is present, although it is perfectly safe to do so alone; one will always return to the present reality, even if one has fallen asleep during the meditation," the Quartz Deva went on. *"With this crystal you may unlock many doors. One door may lead to another until the desired point of focus is reached."*

"Is it best to specifically request assistance, as opposed to just expecting it?" Derek asked.

"This is appreciated. By holding the crystal and focusing upon it, you are already in contact with the energy. And as you work on a regular basis with your crystals, a rapport is built. After a while, acknowledgment of the crystal can be likened to switching on to that energy in the same manner as when two people smile at each other, there is an unspoken greeting and energy is exchanged. As each crystal becomes familiar to you and energy is exchanged, the communication has already begun. Mental greeting is the beginning of the communication. If at any time you wish assistance from any of the devas, they too share a willingness to communicate."

"We've noticed that crystals in certain stores seem lacking in energy. Why is this?"

"Sometimes crystals project dormancy; this is to detach themselves from the negativity of certain conditions. They appreciate any positive attention that is given to them; however, after communicating with a crystal that belongs to others, it is a courtesy to mentally return it to the state in which it was found," the Deva suggested.

This information was possibly directed towards a large crystal we had psychically invited to our home the previous night.

"Do the different shapes of the crystals, the obelisk, sphere, pyramid or crystal points determine their energies?" Derek asked.

"The crystal in its original form has a specific energy as has an obelisk or wand that is cut to emulate the energy of the single or double terminated crystal form; when cut they retain their individual, intrinsic properties. The shape of the sphere [crystal ball] when it is best suited to being a sphere, does vibrate with a specific energy. You will find it has an extremely pleasing 'feel' or quality to it," the Quartz Deva was quick to explain. "The geometric structure of the rock or crystal shaped to form a pyramid carries with it an energy that is different from the other forms. It has the energy of the crystal or rock which is magnified by the form into which it has been shaped, and you will feel a decided energy peak emanating from the apex."

"There's powerful energy at the pyramid's peak, like a laser beam," Derek agreed. "How should it be used for healing? Should the point be towards the areas needing healing?"

"It may be held over the specific area or directed to it from a distance. When holding the pyramid and directing energy, the apex may be pointed towards the area you wish to receive the energy. The healing energies and your own will then pass through the crystal. As you use your own focus, you direct both energies to the recipient. You may also place the pyramid underneath your healing table."

"Because each crystal and mineral has its own energies and properties, should we check with each one when doing healing work, to find which would be the most appropriate to use?"

"Instinctively you will know. You will be aware in the same way that you are when you channel healing energies and you are directed to work with a specific person in a specific way. You will be inspired to pick up one crystal, perhaps more. Trust each thought that comes, as it is a direction that is being given you telepathically; each inspiration that comes is being specifically given to you.

"As you work with your crystals, you will identify the energy, the specific key of energy that each crystal emanates, so that eventually, instinctively, you will be able to identify each according to its true vibration, rather than the vibration of a name or the vibration of a quality or word that describes the quality. Each has its own unique energy, its own unique vibration," the Deva concluded.

* * *

In another conversation, the Quartz Deva shared that our Awakening Time crystal will assist with viewing things anew, as if symbolically awakening from sleep and seeing things differently, more clearly, as through the eyes of a child. The Deva then said, *"When seeing beauty and light, feeling and sensing it with all the senses, and delighting in just being with all it sees, within that small child the knowingness is alive."*

"Will the use of this crystal enable Diana to go back to when she was a very young child and review from that perspective?" Derek asked.

"That would be possible. However, if she wishes to return to that point, she will also be aware of circumstances which were not as pleasant as others. It would depend upon your purpose for doing this. Belief, too, is required. If you were told a crystal would assist with time travel, but did not believe it could take you back and forth in time, then you would not be able to access that vibration. The crystal has no 'magic' and we say that because you understand what it implies; there is no magic that will transport a person, an individual.

"Each crystal has its own information. Work with one at a time. Work with it thoroughly, and consistently. The crystals will assist as you are using them as a point of focus, and within the crystals themselves is recorded much information. However it is sensed there is a slight confusion. This is because you yourselves are not sure what you are experiencing or wishing to experience. Unless you are quite clear of exactly what it is that you wish before you attempt to communicate, the answers that you receive will be rather vague."

Before beginning the session, I had been vaguely hoping to tap into the 'Big Bang' theory.

"It is sensed there is hope that by holding one of these crystals it will release information that you have other ways of accessing," the Deva stated. *"We will attempt to generate a picture of the beginning of creation. However, there are no words that are adequate to*

describe this. For within each picture there is a vast communication and each person would view it from a different perspective. The holder will be able to describe what she sees and the feelings she experiences.

"For what it is sensed that you are both seeking, it is suggested you access the moment of your own conception in space and time and the light that you are; to chart its course and follow it through to where you are now. But to do this will only give you a record of your own unique journey. Although each soul is from the same source and is of the One, it has chosen its own unique path of evolution on its journey to the point where it will be reunited again with the Oneness. To record and communicate about one's own journey would give an indication to another soul of what transpires; however, it would take almost a lifetime of reading.

"This is why it is important to be specific and ask for exactly what you seek," the Deva stressed, *"because out of the vast universe of information, you must pinpoint one fragment for that to be brought to you in your understanding. To ask for the whole history at once would be similar to bringing down an avalanche of information that would be heaped upon you, metaphorically speaking.*

"I feel as if I have been but of little help. I sense disappointment within the holder. I trust the disappointment doesn't last long. Also, you may find in your searches sometimes there are conditions that surround you or prevail; this can create a difference in the information that you do receive, as though a censorship is occurring.

"You will find that with all information you receive, as you are going through the process of recording it for your own purposes, more information will come. Often, although much information may be shown or given at one time, there is more.

"For instance, with the vision shown at this time, words could not convey all that was being conveyed. However, as the holder begins to write or record in the chosen way, memories will be triggered by what was seen and the memories will flow, and she will indeed be quite surprised. She will know the meaning. Go with the inner knowing.

"Before beginning, each time, ask that the inner knowing be allowed to come through, so that the space in the head is not taking control. Each time you are recording your thoughts and observations, ask first that the inner knowing be allowed full reign, so that the truth will flow. And I wish you much joy in your endeavors."

The session was concluded with the Deva asking me to take hold of Derek's hand while s/he generated a blessing energy to both of us. What a beautiful way to be told to be more specific when asking for information.

* * *

The next time Derek spoke with the Quartz Deva, it was to ask for a few pointers in the care and cleansing of crystals.

"Some people we know leave their quartz crystals in the window to be cleansed by the sun. Is this good or bad for the crystals?" Derek asked.

"Placing them in front of glass or a window through which the sun shines causes the intensity of the sun's heat to be magnified. If this is done for too long a period it may cause discoloration of the crystal and even cracking. The best time to expose crystals to the sun is during the late afternoon."

"Some people claim crystals should be cleansed by placing them in the sun, while others say they use the moon's energy, or the earth, or the wind, or place their crystals in sea salt, or water to which sea-salt has been added. Others we know cleanse their crystals using prayer or light, breathing upon the crystals, or holding them above the smoke of burning sacred grasses or leaves. Which method is best?"

"Each method has its own validity. It is best for individuals to arrive at their own method of cleansing. Thought and intent, combined with whatever procedure is chosen, are the greatest cleansers. However, as you become familiar with each crystal, as that bond of trust forms, and it will, in the same manner that any bond of friendship is formed, you will instinctively know which is the better procedure to adopt. Whatever you feel inspired to do will be conveyed to you by your crystalline friends," the Deva assured.

* * *

One afternoon, on impulse, Derek made a quick visit to see Azad at The Rock and Gem Shop. Whilst there, his attention was caught by some small pieces of sugalite and he was inspired to pick up a handful. He was particularly intrigued by the texture and different shades of this lovely purple rock, also known as royal lavulite.

Quite pleased with his find, he returned to the office, and placed the rocks on my desk, like a caring cat placing a mouse at his master's feet. Derek had no idea why he had been inspired to buy the sugalite. Neither of us had even heard of it before. But, as Derek scooped up the sugalite and took it into his office, I should have known this was another mineral that would rapidly take us into a crash course of expanded awareness.

The next morning I awoke remembering having dreamt about sugalite and realized it would be a good topic for our early morning channeling session. My guides, a trinity known to me as 'The Three,' answered my call. (As

I'm not sure which one communicates, to simplify things, I normally refer to them as 'my guide' or 'my guides.')

They suggested we might find it beneficial to invite the deva energy to join us. And then they gave us a configuration to try when using the sugalite: placing a piece over the third eye, another over the heart chakra, and one on each shoulder where the collar bone meets the shoulder bone, so that the shape of a cross is formed. (It also forms a double pyramid, the bottom one inverted.)

Derek left the room. He had gone into that sanctuary of delights called his office, where, after carefully inching past the ever outstretched arms of hanging plants, trees and shrubs, he opened a desk drawer and from within his compartmentalized treasure chest of mother earth's bounty, he drew out the pieces of sugalite. Returning with them, he placed four pieces upon me in the prescribed formation and then directed me to connect with the Sugalite Deva.

As we connected, I felt a strong, almost hard, fine energy, one that was quite different from the onyx or quartz devas with whom we'd communicated before. After exchanging greetings, Derek began asking questions.

"Is there another purpose for the sugalite in addition to using it for channeling?"

"Yes. You will find our energies to be of assistance. This is not to say that one energy is better than another. Each individual should try to find the one that is most compatible with self, with one's own energies. Every portion has its own unique energy and when using it you will find telepathic communication becomes clear. For some, it may function as a catalyst; those with the ability to 'see' may find that sense enhanced. For those wishing to 'sense', the properties assist," the Sugalite Deva was quick to share.

"What can you tell us about the configuration that we are using now?"

"This is useful for many purposes, including balance of the upper chakras. Portions may be placed upon the chakras also; but working with them requires that each person seek for self to find what is appropriate. Physical discomfort may be felt when placed over the lower chakras."

"Should the sugalite be used specifically with the upper chakras?" Derek asked.

"It will be most beneficial when used with the upper charkas, but whatever feels comfortable will be appropriate."

"Will the sugalite work well with another stone or crystal?"

"If this is desired, you may find certain energies are compatible for the work you have in mind. Trust inner judgment."

"Should sugalite be used for extended periods of time, perhaps wearing it around the neck?" was Derek's next question.

"Each must decide. It would be too presumptuous to say it should be worn at all times. It may be worn for decoration; it may also be consciously used for assistance in other ways. If used upon the throat chakra, for instance, it may assist with communication, with toning, balancing that area."

"And for practical use, would it be appropriate to invite the energy of each individual piece to be with us?"

"This would be for the individual person to choose. When wearing, or using, the benefits are not solely determined by whether you invite us to be with you at a conscious level or not, although a greater rapport may be attained on all levels when this courtesy is extended. However, our energy is with you as the piece is held, or when it is placed upon you, or when it is being worn.

"If the holder or wearer is attuned in this way, and receptive, we may assist in directing attention to certain areas within the body. Attention may be drawn to where one has imposed restrictions within self, and if the time is appropriate to remove those restrictions, it may be done by mentally visualizing their removal; seeing this removal as being completed will assist.

"This [referring to the sugalite] *will assist you when checking the body for these* [self imposed restrictions]. *If you sense discomfiture, then it may be an indication of where a restriction is located. When the person is ready to release certain conditions, these* [discomforts] *will be felt. It would be beneficial to do this from time to time as these self-imposed restrictions are only revealed when it is time for them to be removed, when they no longer serve a useful purpose and become a hindrance to earthly progress.*

"If you wish to adapt this procedure as part of a cleansing routine, we will assist in the 'detection' process while you work. Use [a piece of sugalite] *as a scanning tool, holding it between thumb and first two fingers; you yourselves will be drawn to where those restrictions are, and may proceed to remove them. If nothing is revealed to you, there is either nothing to be removed, or it is not appropriate at that time."*

"To my understanding, we ourselves place these restrictions to keep our reality 'in the physical,'" Derek stated. "And this is so that we will continue with the earth experience and not try to escape from the frequently harsh conditions we have chosen to undergo, until we have learned whatever lessons from those experiences were necessary for our progressive advance. At that time we may let them go."

At this point I became aware of an irritation or probing sensation under my right shoulder blade, and began to remove the 'invisible restriction' by imagining I was taking hold of it, picturing myself pulling it out. At the same time I performed exaggerated physical movements to accompany my thoughts. I recalled having felt inspired to do this to my left shoulder blade recently on being bothered by a pain there. I wasn't quite sure what I was doing at that time, but the pain did disappear. I had been wearing a sugalite pendant that day.

Derek began asking questions again: "Will the sugalite assist with the removal of unwanted energies?"

"Ones placed by self."

I became aware of another unpleasant sensation, this time in my right foot, and asked Derek if he could assist me in removing it. As he went through the pulling-out motions, it definitely felt like a thread was being drawn out of my foot. The unpleasant sensation subsided.

Afterwards, I told Derek that I noticed quite a difference using the sugalite; the energy felt purely 'businesslike,' and all emotion seemed to have been put on hold. This had made the transmission clear and to the point, although initially I felt I had more difficulty connecting.

We traded places. Derek taped a small piece of purple sugalite over his third eye to try out its effect. He experienced no difficulty at all and went straight into an altered state. It was my cue to begin asking questions.

After the session, I asked Derek how he liked using the sugalite. He said it felt like he was immediately sitting in a large, empty void; his mind wasn't wandering and he was not distracted by other thoughts. There was no emotion; it was strictly down to the business at hand and he liked that.

CHAPTER 8

Some time after channeling information about sugalite, I read about 'implants' or 'devices' we place within ourselves that affect our health in order to hinder us from 'seeing the light' or remembering from whence we came before birth. I was intrigued, to say the least, and wondered if these devices were the same as 'self-imposed restrictions.' I decided to ask Derek's guide during our next session.

"I've read we symbolically 'implant' devices such as armor, breastplates or such things before birth so we're not quite so sensitive, and that when it is appropriate we can remove these ourselves, as we will become aware of what and where they are on our bodies. Is this true?"

"There are choices, decisions you make for situations from which you wish to learn; these are the so-called 'devices' people choose," the guide responded. *"These 'devices' are issues that require attention. And, as you learn and come to an understanding about these issues which you may have considered were holding you back, you realize that in effect they had been assisting you, at that particular stage of your progress, so you yourself may then release them, allowing you to move on."*

"If we can't see them, how do we release them?"

"In your experiences, you may alter your decisions or choices. It is similar to what occurs in some of the hypnotherapy sessions you do; you go back to a time when you made a certain decision about an issue, and you release yourself from, or change, the decision at that point or perspective. You may come to a different understanding as you are reviewing these experiences, by forgiving self and others for what you may have considered inappropriate action. Viewing the experience as if through the eyes of an outsider may bring new understanding. Some issues may be released by visually sending healing energy to a specific area within the body where discomfort is felt."

From the response, I felt Derek's guide had not quite understood my question. That was unusual. Perhaps my question had not been specific enough. I decided to try again.

"The situations you refer to would be like conditions we have placed on ourselves during this lifetime to assist us to progress. I am asking about restrictions we may place upon ourselves before birth so that we may learn our lessons, and then at a certain point, when we no longer need them to assist us, they actually become a hindrance to our progress and we need to be rid of them. If my understanding now is correct, in fact, we have at least two different sets of restrictions, those we placed on ourselves before birth and ones after birth, or even during a previous lifetime."

"Those that have been placed after birth have been through imprinting; those placed before (birth) through the learning that was selected to be experienced whilst growing up in this lifetime," the guide responded patiently.

"The 'imprinting' you speak of, is that how we view things from our perspective, how we see or perceive what happens to us?" I asked.

"In a way. Imprinting is the effect or result of one's own life experiences colored by others' belief systems that are imposed during infancy, childhood, and various adult stages. In your life experiences, a lot of blame is placed upon others for what occurs. In actuality, what is being reflected to you, or attracted by you, is for your learning and understanding and is in fact something of your own creation, which you choose as a vehicle for that learning. The pre-birth self-imposed 'devices' to which you refer are selected restrictions or predetermined conditions, and they are someone else's symbolism, words that have been used as a means to explain why their author and many other people fail in this lifetime to remember their origin or Source."

If we become aware of any self-imposed restrictions and if we have finished our learning in that area, through whatever manner they were affecting us, we may consciously release them, and thereby free ourselves from their effect. The same thing applies to cellular memories that are often brought to the surface for acknowledgment and release. Derek confirmed this during an early morning discourse with Nehiemir ("Nee-hi" as we affectionately call him), a guide who had made his presence known during a hands-on healing session. I always liked Nehiemir's advice because it was blessed with clear-cut, down to earth, easy to understand language.

"If something should be stirred up, a memory with much emotion, and it is not obvious why that memory is being brought forth, go into the issue," Nehiemer had suggested. *"When such a memory does occur, it would be advisable at that time to consciously acknowledge and release the old emotion which was stored within the body because of the incident being recalled. This allows the body's cellular memory of that incident to actually be dislodged and released."*

"Sometimes, when these recollections occur, the memory is acknowledged, but the condition is not released, because of oversight or the person not being aware why the memory has surfaced. However, this does not mean that every single memory is an indicator of something stored within the body at a cellular level. If one has been talking about certain topics, playing certain music, memories may be triggered," Nehiemir continued.

"It is always best to reflect for a moment to check whether what has surfaced was in fact of a traumatic or stressful nature at the time, and then check out the body for physical sensations, to see if there is a correlation there with the memory and what one is experiencing within the body, perhaps a discomfort. Then, consciously, the cellular memory may be released.

"Whichever method you prefer for release will be effective. You may use a visualization process to see or sense that physical discomfort or sensation flowing out of the body and into the ground below or, using your imagination, you may 'see' yourself physically taking hold of and removing the sensation, similar to the manner in which you release pain during a visualization.

"It is preferable when attempting to release cellular memories," Nehiemir stressed, "that the physical discomfort first be conveyed in terms of pictures or 'visualized' as an object, such as, 'It feels like a piece of cold metal,' or 'I sense a knife,' or 'It looks like a ball of fire,' however the pictorial metaphor of the physical condition is presented. Then that pictured image representing the discomfort or pain may be plucked out or removed."

"This gives the person a definite feeling that something is physically being taken out," Derek agreed.

"Yes. If the picture image that best describes the *pain or discomfort* [i.e. ball of fire] is created in one's imagination first, before reaching down, or forward or behind, to take hold and remove the pain or discomfort, this 'removal' can occur as the physical gesture is made.

"And in a similar manner," Nehiemir added, "this may be applied when you are doing 'hands-on healing' work with people. If they have physical pain within their bodies, ask them to convey that physical pain in picture form so that it can be easily identified as to the shape, size, even the color if necessary. And then, get them to mentally take hold of and remove the pictured item whilst at the same time, you also 'physically' and psychically go through the motions to do the same at the pinpointed area. For example, if described as, say, 'It feels like a knife in my knee,' both of you in unison, use your hands and also use your visualization or imagination to 'see' and 'feel ' or 'sense' it [the knife] being removed."

"So the added energy of both parties using a visualization for the process would be recommended?" Derek asked.

"Yes. Visualization is very important. It is bringing into play the use of your own creativity for healing, and, as you know, you can create whatever it is you desire, if you desire it sufficiently and believe you can do so. But always, when seeking to create anything which you are designing to bring into your own sphere—your own square, as you call it— if you visualize it well, seeing yourself within the scene with whatever it is that you are requesting or seeking, it will materialize sooner. And of course, as you have already learned, when it is something that you are requesting for yourself, add emotion to it, so that all senses come into play. If you are healing yourself, at the conclusion of the visualization, see and feel yourself looking healthy, put a smile on your face whilst you happily and effortlessly mentally engage in a physical activity you enjoy. Put the emotion of joy into the scene."

(At the time this information was shared with us, neither Derek nor I were aware that this procedure is very similar to one taught to advanced Reiki adepts. We were quite surprised and thrilled when we became Reiki Masters/Teachers and found we already had been utilizing this technique for some time.)

"We do wonderful things to ourselves, don't we? All in the name of learning! Unresolved issues are sometimes brought to our attention by an ache or pain or other bodily sensation," Derek commented. "Your suggestions are noted for their release."

"There are other ways that these issues may be released, once attention has been drawn to them. Aches or pains let us know where they have been stored at a cellular level. Some are released in the dream state, some are released through different manipulations of the body, by massage or reflexology, etcetera; that is something you may wish to look into at a later date," Nehiemir suggested.

"It is great to know that some conditions are released during the dream state; we might not be sufficiently in tune to release them otherwise," Derek shared with me after the conversation with Nehiemir.

I agreed. We hadn't gone into the topic of dreams before. "I'd sure like to know what John has to say on the subject; maybe we can ask him tonight," I suggested.

And so, later that evening, dreams did become the focus during a chat with Derek's guide, John, who responded to my questions.

"As you become aware of your dreams and learn how to consciously participate within them," John began, *"you know that you are aware and awake in that dimension or reality, that you are within the dream itself. When you do reach that stage, you will be more conscious of what you are doing during that state, and you will become more aware of how you actually take part."*

"Then it's important we learn to participate in our dreams?" I asked.

"Yes, your dreams are very important."

"Are there any tips or any advice you can give us about participating in dreams, how we can bring that about?" was my next question.

"The dream state is very similar to the wakeful state in that it is another reality," John explained. *"If you believe there is nothing there, or that it is simply a dream or movie to entertain while you are sleeping, that's all it may seem to be for you. But, if you understand that everything stems from your thoughts, that realities are created from your thoughts, as are your belief system, if you believe that you can awaken, control, and participate actively within your dream, then that is one of the major steps in being able to do this. It starts with your belief about what you can do."*

"And the desire to do it?"

"And the desire."

"Should we make a conscious decision about it before going to sleep at night?"

"Mentally make your intentions known to higher aspects of self about what you wish to do within the dream. Then repeat to yourself that you are going to remember your dreams and record them. Be prepared. Keep pen and paper and such, to write them down, or have a tape recorder and microphone handy beside the bed," John suggested.

"Can we actually state ahead of time what type of dream we want, what we want to do in it?" I inquired.

"You may ask for what is most appropriate for you at the time for your learning and understanding, what it is that you need to be shown at this time. In the dream state you are very receptive; you are channels, whether you are dreaming or awake. In the dream state, conscious awareness does not become involved with the ego in what is being relayed. As you begin to understand some of your symbology, what it represents, it will be easier to manipulate your way through that realm."

"So, when in a dream, is the object to consciously control the outcome of it?"

"Yes. It is similar in practice to when there is a situation you wish to transpire within the physical realm, something you wish to create within your reality. You use your imagination, your expectation and desire, and see within your mind's eye exactly what you wish to occur from the outcome back to where you are now, viewing it as if it has already happened. In other words, you may consciously control your life by projecting and creating what you want in it. Similarly, this creative exercise may be used during the dream state to bring about the desired outcome."

"In the same way that one would look back over one's life to the present time, except doing it in reverse, from the future back to now?"

"If, say, you wish to spend your winter in Bermuda, but have no funds to go there, and if, within your imagination, you create a picture and see yourself there, visually see yourself as being there, you are creating this image. You are sending this energy forth, and events will eventually occur that will allow you to be in Bermuda just the way you envisioned; you will have created that reality to occur."

"I have read that when you dream you are killing somebody, say, it's just acting out what is not acceptable to do when you're awake; you can't go around killing people in real life. Sometimes when we are angry with an individual our anger is expressed in dreams, and we experience the emotion that way, to get rid of whatever emotion we are consciously suppressing; we get to release it at that time."

"Yes. When what you are dealing with is very difficult, or unacceptable to do in the physical, it may be dealt with through the dream state," John confirmed.

"And those of us who are not so active in the physical, for one reason or another, we can be absolutely anything we choose to be in a dream, a gymnast or super-hero or whatever?"

"Most definitely. In a dream you may see yourself, express yourself, and experience events in many different forms which may be unavailable to you when awake."

"Are there any taboos or any things that we must not ask for in the dream state?"

"Be careful in what you ask to experience," John cautioned. *"It would be wise to ask only for those dreams which are for your highest good."*

"Should we ask for something in an area that we're working on now in this lifetime?"

"Yes. There are many realities. You have a difficult one that you are living in at the moment. Attempt to deal with that first. The dream reality assists people to realize there are realities other than just the one they are in at the moment. There are other dimensions."

"Is it true that when we dream, the people we see in our dreams, whether friends or family or even strangers, they are all actually just aspects of ourselves?"

"Mostly. It depends upon the dream and the dreamer; in other cultures, the representation may be different. But for yourselves, those people portrayed in the dream are playing out the issue being worked upon, to let you know the path to take; they are a representation of yourself, they symbolize an aspect of yourself, to help with the interpretation of the dream."

"We know ourselves, from accessing dreams with the help of hypnosis, that when there has been a troubling dream we'd normally term a 'nightmare,' it's really not what it appears to be. And if, instead of pulling ourselves out of it, we continue on with the dream, it takes on a different form or context."

"*What you refer to as a nightmare is a message which is being conveyed to you by your Higher Self,*" John explained "*It may be directed towards a past issue which needs resolving, something which is keeping you 'stuck' in a particular mind-set and is hindering your progress. It may be an answer to a question you have been asking yourself repeatedly; it may even be bringing you guidance to take certain immediate action. The message is presented to you in such a dramatic way that you will awaken or 'sit up and take note' so that you will seek out the dream's interpretation.*"

John's explanation confirmed our own beliefs. Only a few weeks previously I had dreamt one such dream with a dramatic message. It shocked me awake. In the dream, Derek and I had gone to his brother's place in the country to housesit for a couple of weeks. We arrived just as the brother was leaving for his vacation. On his way out, he warned us not to use the toilet, as the septic tank needed fixing. After his departure, I realized I needed to use the upstairs bathroom urgently. I asked Derek what I should do. Derek said not to worry, he'd go and fix the septic tank, and with that, he bounded downstairs and went outside. I stayed upstairs in the bathroom, waiting for Derek's signal that it was okay to use the toilet.

Things were getting tense; I desperately needed to 'go'. After an uncomfortable wait, I walked out of the bathroom and looked through the window over the stairs to see if I could catch a glimpse of Derek in the back yard. He wasn't outside. Then I glanced down over the banister. There at the bottom of the stairs I saw a large brown seething mass that was gradually moving upwards. I yelled out to Derek to stop whatever he was doing, as this stuff was coming up the stairs!

There was no response from Derek, so I yelled for him again. Almost immediately he came hurrying up the stairs, but he had no head or neck and there was a brown mess all down the front of him. I yelled, "Oh my God, what happened, where's your head?" And from somewhere close by I heard Derek answer, "Over here." I reached over, grabbed onto his hair and lifted up his head.

I could see exposed bone and clotted blood at the base of the neck. My mind was searching frantically for what to do, and I quickly began a hands-on healing, using Reiki symbols to try and reattach Derek's head to his body. I knew that if we rushed to a hospital it would be no good; I'd never heard of a head being sewed back on. I drew several symbols rapidly in the air, but stopped when Derek said that under certain conditions the symbols were rendered ineffective. Ineffective? I'd never heard that before. I continued frantically directing energy, praying that I would be able to get his head back onto the body, which was standing there on the stairs waiting patiently.

With no other living soul around for miles, I was dreadfully scared I wouldn't be able to save Derek and we had so much work to do together. But nothing was working. At that point I awoke and shook Derek to see if he was okay.

I told Derek of my dream and asked what it meant. But there was no way he wanted to give any off-the-cuff interpretation, as all symbology within a dream is unique and special to the dreamer. He suggested we do a session at the office later to tune into the dream and see what it meant.

Back at the office, Derek began a hypnotherapy session with me, taking me through the dream a couple of times and then asking to speak directly to my subconscious mind for an interpretation. It said the dream was telling me that my system needed an immediate cleansing.

When Derek asked for the meaning of the severed head and the healing symbols not being effective, the response was that the head could not be reattached in the dream and the symbols were ineffective because 'separation' had occurred. When he asked why he was the one who had lost his head in the dream, it was said that, as the dream was mine, the body and head were mine, not his. His body was symbolic of mine and was used as a dramatic way of getting my attention to let me know to begin a toxin cleansing diet immediately.

I'd had thoughts about doing a cleanse, but I never got around to it. My body was letting me know, through minor discomforts, that something needed attention, but I hate going to doctors and only go if something is extreme (the last time was about two years before). The dream was telling me that if I waited until something drastic or extreme occurred, like my system backing up, it would be too late to remedy the matter. My body had tried to get my attention before and I hadn't listened to it, and so the graphic dream was given to me, knowing that I would seek an interpretation of what was being conveyed.

Derek, bless his heart, left the office shortly after that and returned with all the necessary ingredients for my toxin cleansing diet. I heeded the message, needless to say, and began a cleanse immediately. Soon afterwards, I noticed a marked improvement in my health.

After that dramatic dream, it's not surprising that health-related questions dominated our next early morning session.

"I believe people suffering from debilitating diseases have, in fact, chosen them on another level, as an opportunity to begin the journey inwards to find their true life purpose or review their lives," I began. "If that's so, then why is it so many folks seek help from professionals who don't accept alternative medicine as a way of healing?"

This time, it was Robert, another of Derek's guides, who responded.

"Many recognize there is something they can do to help self in the healing process; some recognize there are external influences and there are internal influences which can be called upon," Robert began what was to be a long and definitive explanation.

"And in the experience, which has been attracted to them, what they experience is not necessarily solely for themselves; it may be a joint experience involving yet another set of circumstances around it. If, say, one becomes sick with an infectious disease, there may be an effect upon other members of the family, sometimes upon a community, as in a group-soul experience, depending upon which conditions are being attracted."

"There are many, as you say, who have given away all their power to others within the medical profession; they have bought into the belief system which has been fed to them from infancy, that to seek health, good health, is to seek it through an external source. And so they place their trust in others. And this is all right, because this is their choice. But if they wish to be rid of the health conditions that surround them and free themselves from the cause and not just the symptoms, they must be prepared to look within also. That, my friend, may be a long and sometimes slow journey, one for the determined and strong of heart.

"Most people fail to understand and indeed are quite shocked when it is first suggested that on some level they chose to experience and attracted or created the most horrific of conditions. They deny or reject that concept instantly. However, at some point in their existence—maybe before they came to earth, or after they were born—they attracted those conditions to them. On another level of awareness, they made the choice to experience sickness and disease.

"There are many reasons these decisions are made. One may be seeking forgiveness or wishing to punish self, or to punish others by making them feel guilty for something that has been said or done. Some seek merely to place the responsibility for their own lives into the hands of others, wishing others to take care of them or provide for them financially. Some may feel they will be shown more love or more kindness if they appear to be sick, disabled, or physically challenged. Some have chosen the experience to be an example to others to show how certain debilitating conditions may be overcome. Others choose to experience conditions in which they themselves and others learn lessons of patience, tolerance, and

understanding, lessons in unconditional love, learning to accept self or another, whether disfigured or reduced to a shadow of his or her former self.

"*The list of reasons is inexhaustible,*" Robert continued. "*And all, at some time or another, allow the individual the opportunity to seek, to go within for answers, the opportunity to connect with the true spiritual self.*

"*Whatever the reason for the condition, whether chosen consciously or unconsciously, all experiences are created by self for the learning the soul has chosen. Through having undergone certain experiences themselves, some learn compassion towards others, and they can relate to what others are experiencing.*

"*Denial is a common reaction when an individual manifests a disease,*" Robert explained, "*particularly one he has never heard of before, and then is told he has chosen that condition; disbelief precedes such comments as 'I wouldn't do that to myself' or 'How could I choose that? I've never even heard of it.' The suggestion that the condition is of his own choice may be received as a direct criticism or judgment, even though there is no judgment or criticism intended.*

"*After it is accepted and understood by the individual why he is experiencing the condition, and that he has choices, and has had a choice all along—choices other than whether to stay with traditional medicine or seek alternatives or utilize both—with a lot of determination and willpower, he may regain improved health by taking responsibility for his own life, his own decisions. An improvement in health may occur once the 'poor me' or 'why is this happening to me?' stage has been gone through, unless, of course, the decision has already been made to return 'home.'*

"*Many, however, are too frail to take responsibility for self, because they have convinced themselves that it is somebody else's fault. They lay blame with the cigarettes they have smoked and the tobacco companies which supplied them, or claim the air was polluted and chemical companies were responsible; they whine that the job was too stressful, or the spouse walked out, or the parents were abusive. They are consumed with blame and denial.*

"*It is nobody else's fault why certain diseases manifest. It is because of a choice or decision self has made, often during childhood or later stressful conditions. But as soon as the chosen lessons are learned, a decision to make a full recovery may be made. In some instances, a return to good health may be brought about by the conscious choice to honor the body by making a complete change in lifestyle,*" Robert concluded on that line.

"Often we have difficulty regaining our health because we see and feel the problem on a regular basis; while we feel the ache or pain we acknowledge we have the disorder. Doesn't that confirm with us, 'Yes, I'm sick' and 'Yes, I do have this,' which in turn perpetuates the belief that we are sick, thereby creating more of the condition?" I questioned.

"*Yes,*" Robert answered with conviction. "*Repeatedly telling self, 'I am sick,' most definitely perpetuates the fact that 'I am sick.' It can become ingrained in the belief system. But conversely, repetition of positive phrases such as 'I am well, I am whole, I am healthy, my health is improving every day,' can convince the subconscious mind of a new belief system about health which may cause improvement to occur. Once it is believed and one's mind is convinced that this is the request being made, it will then put healing into motion by sending appropriate messages to the brain and to the creative intelligence within each cell requesting and causing healing to occur—if that is the new choice.*"

"We often have negative influences of others around us that affect the situation. Don't disembodied spirits that have attached themselves to us, or get caught up in our energy fields, bring their 'ailments' with them and also add to the situation?" I asked.

"*Human beings are sometimes plagued with certain symptoms that are not their own. They are sensitive to, and thus affected by, the energy of those who are with them. Very often, physical aches and pains can be the conditions present at the death of an entity or disembodied spirit that has chosen to 'come along for the ride'; those conditions are sometimes the result of the manner in which the death occurred. Or they may be symptoms of a disease or diseases present in the entity's body at the time of death; they are vibrational memories brought forward and replayed through a different body. These are sometimes the symptoms that your medical doctors call 'psychosomatic.'*

"*While medical conditions exist, people do need the assistance of the medical profession, the majority of whom are very caring individuals working within that profession because of decisions to be of service to others.*"

"Aren't certain situations re-created many times in one lifetime to make sure we learn our lessons, until we get rid of the old ideas and beliefs? Say it's low self-esteem, then issues on self-worth will continually be re-created until it has been dealt with."

"*This observation is correct,*" Robert answered succinctly.

"Couldn't that be extended further to include mass consciousness and how it also has an effect upon life? All over Canada, businesses are closing and we see health facilities being cut back. If folks believe there is no work 'out there,' and have fears of cutbacks and being laid off, doesn't that help to generate that situation even further?"

"*Yes. Thoughts are very powerful. But, the occurrence of health facilities being cut back is perhaps a move that has been created by a mass consciousness. The situation, however, does have a positive side to it, as it may provide the impetus for each individual to begin to seek alternatives which direct them to draw closer to the true purpose and intent for which they are in this experience,*" Robert responded.

"As far as cutbacks and the other conditions you mentioned, people certainly create their own reality, whether through mass thinking, or thinking on a smaller scale. You see, a child born into this world who appears to be sickly, if he continually hears family and friends saying, 'Oh, he is such a frail little thing, he may always be sick,' it becomes extremely difficult under these projected circumstances for improvement to occur.

"Although it is not a large population saying these things, it has the same effect; however, if the mass thinking in this case is positive and is of encouragement, assistance and total unconditional love, as each learns their own lessons from the situation, there can be an improvement in the child's health.

"Thoughts affect or create a situation; it is the thinking that sets the process in motion, whether for good, or otherwise. If we were all to begin immediately thinking peace, there would be peace everywhere. If we all begin thinking that each person is but a mirror reflection of self, that each person, whether of a different skin color or size or shape, is a mirror image or a facet of self, a reflection of a lifetime one has lived in exactly the same or very similar circumstances, then each human being would become aware of the sameness, or Oneness, rather than focusing upon the differences. Then they would begin to generate more love to those they perhaps may have looked down upon or to whom they felt superior.

"Each and every soul, regardless of occupation, amount of income, whether there is any income or not, whether they belong to the most humble of castes or class, or are from the highest society, all are exactly the same. They all come into this world in exactly the same way and they all leave in exactly the same way. The locations and the circumstances into which they arrive or depart will be different, as will the experiences, but those are the only differences," Robert concluded on a clear and simple note of brilliance.

Chapter 9

Sometimes I cringe as I read some of the dumb things we asked our guides during those early days of channeling. If we had been better organized I'm sure we could have worked up better questions, rather than snatching something out of thin air at the last moment. Yet there were never any criticisms and our guides ever patiently responded with answers. Occasionally, a sense of humor crept into the proceedings, like the morning Derek began talking about man's consciousness.

"I've read that man's consciousness has evolved, that the consciousness first took on a state of existence as a mineral, then plant, then animal, before evolving into the human being."

"It is suggested you do not tell that to some of your ancestors!" the responding guide answered with a touch of levity.

"Is there any validity to what I've read?" Derek asked, in a serious tone.

*"Evolution certainly has occurred, but humankind has not evolved from a rock, plant, or animal. The planet was first created, as were different life forms, and when the 'souls' or beings came to inhabit the earth, certainly they played around a lot, exploring, testing their own powers of creativity. They were aware of the consciousness of the other life forms and, at will, could go into that consciousness of the others. You say man's consciousness evolved. Man's consciousness is. It was and always has been man's consciousness. However, man's conscious **awareness** became confined, more limited, to assist him in coping with situations that occurred at certain times.*

"Everything about you is energy; everything has its own energy field. The soul energy can pass through all the other energies. If you so wished, if you trained yourself, you would be able to walk through solid walls or objects that appear to you at this moment to be solid. This does not mean that you would become part of the wall, unless it was your particular choice to experience becoming one with the wall for a fragment of time. You would feel the density of it and you would become aware of the energy of it also."

"We would probably need to have a good reason to be doing that."

"It is surprising what curiosity can lead to," the guide suggested.

"Man was once very in tune with his spirituality. When did he begin to drift away from it?"

"Initially, after separation from the God Source, the soul tried out for itself a multitude of forms, sometimes a combination of forms," my guide responded. *"Decisions were made as to what it would like to experience. After each of the experiences, the accumulative thought patterns or consciousness created other realities, causing man to lose track or sight of the God Source. Although still believing that he was invincible, he was already losing touch. And eventually, as he began to lose his sense of connectedness, man lost the concepts, the reality, of who he was, or what he could do or could have become. These experiences took a long time.*

"And because of those wishing to dominate, to be in control of and manipulate other human beings, it became as it is now. Different influences helped to create some of the situations that many souls may not have willingly entered into. There were also influences other than physical ones that had an effect, influences from planetary systems that wished to exercise a decisive role for their own purposes."

"How long has man been influenced by these other beings?" Derek asked, his curiosity aroused.

"From the beginning. But the gradual decline of man's innate abilities was not just because of influences of other beings, it was also self-imposed, as was the decision to become human, to experience a physical body, to experience the emotions, those particular lessons involved with being human, learning and experiencing.

"When one chooses to play a particular game, there are rules to be followed so that each player has an equal opportunity to win or to proceed throughout the game. As the ground rules are set, the game proceeds. The rules stay the same, but as each player follows the rules or guidelines, he has a better understanding of the game he is playing. He finds there are different choices that may be made during the playing of the game, such as drawing certain cards and playing them, from which he learns, as in the golden rule of 'doing unto others' or one reaps what one sows. He learns that every action taken has an effect.

"Within what one chooses to experience, there is the balance and progression as the finer lessons are learned. And the soul not only learns for itself, but also learns in order to assist others in their progress," the guide went on. *"But the step away from the true spirituality has been by choice, and therein lessons are being learned. As time goes by, the void in which man has set himself apart from the rest of creation will gradually disappear and all will be reunited. You see, spiritually, all are still united, but mankind cannot see this. It is not within man's reality, man's comprehension, and yet, every child is born with this knowledge of the affinity and the love still radiating from All-self, The God Source, The Creator, whomever or whatever you perceive God to be.*

"There are still cultures among you that are aware of the connectedness of all things, but, for the others...you are just partaking in a different facet of the learning experience of humankind.

"Within various cultures more people would still be in touch with their true inner-connectedness, but, because of indoctrination by certain religious groups, at the instigation of governing bodies of the times, a belief in the inappropriateness of psychic abilities contributed to the disconnection.

"Early churches established certain doctrines initially out of concern for the many. Because the church fathers could see the dangers of people becoming 'possessed' by those they saw and termed 'demons,' as all beings from other realms were regarded, and because of their own narrowed or restricted beliefs and a desire to control the populace, a very strict set of rules was compiled for individuals to live by," the guide explained choicely.

"Although in those times many people could see the discarnate, as well as beings from other realms, they chose not to see what was about them, as religious decree dissuaded the people from communicating with 'demons.' Through fear of punishment, and because they were often frightened by what they saw, the majority of the populace 'turned a blind eye' and so closed down their psychic vision or third-eye, the brow chakra or energy center, in order to shut out that which they 'saw.'

"Denial became the chosen way, and with it many doors were closed; it became easier to shut out rather than to disclose what they saw, as that would have brought accusation of possessing supernatural powers and punishment by death. Children then were strongly discouraged from communicating with those they 'saw,' and it is little different today.

"So that which was originally intended to protect the people was the very tool by which they closed off not only their psychic vision but their sense of connectedness. Only now are people beginning to re-awaken and consciously seeking to reclaim it.

"Nevertheless, when the masses begin to communicate, a certain energy is formed, as is occurring now. 'New thinking' is being voiced; this gradually filters outwards, and new actions and reactions begin to speak louder than words. People see, they witness for themselves what is occurring elsewhere. They see the written word, they consider it, they absorb for themselves, and then there is word of mouth. It is a very slow process, but a whole country's thinking can be changed in time, and a new belief system evolves." This guide seemed to be very astute and candid.

Derek hadn't asked for the guide's name, yet he felt there was something so familiar about the energy. "And to get back in touch with the Oneness, it's necessary to search within?" he asked.

"Yes. Very often in the process a person becomes more humble, as he recognizes his place in the Oneness of all things. However, some people become humbled in a negative sense, so they believe themselves to be unworthy, and being unable to see their own worth, view themselves as being separate from the Oneness, or not being part of God. They perceive God to be a detached, separate Being or personality 'up there' or 'out there.'

"One does not necessarily need to be aware of the other realities and dimensions before one is willing to connect or identify with the Oneness. But first, one has to remove the shackles of negative judgment. Feeling superior to other people, placing others below self because their beliefs differ from self, judging others by their appearance or the color of the skin, judging others for what they do or their level of education, these are the negative judgments that shackle man and hinder his progress," the guide enumerated.

"Even if mankind is not aware of the other realities and is unaware of the energies within the plants and other aspects of nature which are all a part of himself, if man would at least begin to recognize all of humanity as being part of the Oneness, all being joined together as brothers and sisters within the one family of God, all being the same, each being part of the other, each other being part of self, then the awareness of other realities would grow from that point.

"If man would focus upon developing not only the religious but also the truly spiritual side of his nature, he would rapidly become more aware of the existence of those who at the moment he cannot see. However, the thinking would need to be of a sufficiently mature level to handle this, and the stage of positive judgment reached.

"One may delight in the thought of seeing guides, angels, and those perceived to be higher spiritual beings, but even yourselves, if you were to 'see' all the time, say, bodies plagued by discarnate entities, you may find it quite a shocking sight. With people of a quick-firing mentality, there could be ideas of killing off, or destroying the 'plague' and many more may 'die' as a result, perhaps adding to the number of those entities. Through lack of understanding, or negative judgment, the unwanted sights may be thought of, or appear, to be too grotesque. This is one of the reasons for reality being the way it is in man's perception now. It really is an illusion, how he chooses to perceive what he sees.

"Many of you wish to have clairvoyant abilities, to be able to 'see,' to predict, and hear those of other realities and dimensions. However, the greater majority of you are just not yet ready for this. There is even fear of the disembodied you classify as spooks, ghosts, and others. And if one of these were to manifest during your classes, guaranteed there would be people running for cover."

"That's right," Derek was quick to agree. "During a session not long ago, a friend caught a glimpse of another reality as a cosmic being came into focus. Our friend began trying to hide and avoid its presence by crouching in the chair. Even though knowledgeable of this other reality, the person was still affected by fear," Derek related with a touch of curiosity.

"It is termed fear of the unknown. Often, in order to progress, it becomes necessary for one to confront one's fear headlong. However, that does not mean jumping into experiences *in the name of confronting the unknown. If you were afraid of fire, you would not jump into a blazing inferno in order to determine how hot it is,"* the guide advised with candor.

* * *

Derek had been given a book to read, but it lay around for quite a while before he put his nose between the pages. Then, much of its information not only intrigued him but confirmed the validity of our own experiences and parallel information we had been receiving from our own guides. However, for some reason, I wasn't too keen on taking time to read the book. From the little Derek had read aloud to me as I took a break from my own writing, there was something about it that made me feel uneasy, yet I recognized many of the things that had become 'truths' for me. Perhaps it was because I felt the readers were being told that there is no need to 'protect' themselves when entering into a meditative state, or all that is necessary is to draw a column of light down into themselves, thus bringing down their own 'light body' with the implied guaranteed entrance into a wonderful world of self-awareness and true enlightenment.

My inner prompting told me, 'If it's that easy, there's a catch to it.' There are no such dramatic shortcuts on the road to enlightenment; things are not that simple. Metaphorically speaking, to my thinking, a sprat was being offered in order to catch a mackerel. Because of all the strange happenings in our lives recently, I felt the book's readers were being hoodwinked.

By opening themselves up to a 'column of light' (perhaps a group of wily extraterrestrials with an ulterior motive proclaiming one thing to gullible knowledge-seekers while leaving out the hidden agenda) the unsuspecting, eager seekers of enlightenment could be preparing to open themselves up and thus provide a perfect opportunity or invitation for that species (or whatever energy is hanging around at the time) to enter in at will.

Seriously, there's bees in them thar honey-trees! All of us are bodies of energy, bodies of light, and this 'drawing down of a column of light' is, in effect, giving permission to another 'light' to use or come into our body or energy field.

I know I've said this many times before, but I can't stress it too emphatically, until you know what you are doing and what energies or 'light' you are entertaining, you do need to 'protect' yourselves. For starters, aim to strengthen your own energy field, practicing this for several weeks or months until you become quite proficient at this; next, learn how to connect with your own higher self. Only after that is well and truly accomplished should enlightenment seekers attempt to entertain other 'lights' or columns of light.

From our own experiences, we know there are those who will offer wonderful knowledge, information, stuff that would blow the average person away. You hear it or you read it and think, 'Wow, man, I'm on to something here; nobody has said this stuff before; it's incredible and it tells me I'm perfectly safe and I don't need to be on my guard anymore.'

This is the hook that draws a body into a false sense of security whilst at the same time offering a palatable way to quench the insatiable thirst that we all have to find the one true answer. We think we've found the key, the code...and we trust implicitly. Sadly, for some, the door has been opened, but it wasn't the door to instant enlightenment—it was the lid of Pandora's Box.

One morning, Derek wanted to double-check on certain information within the book to see if it tallied with what we ourselves had touched upon once before, and so he began asking questions:

"I've been reading that the DNA of human beings was altered thousands of years ago by beings from other planets, so that humans could be controlled and their negative emotional energy used as a food source. Is that true?"

"*As with all historians, information will be recorded from the perspective of the ones writing, and from theirs, this is correct. However, viewed from a different perspective, this could be called an oversimplification of what transpired. Indeed, there was not merely one group that interfered,*" my guide began yet another lengthy explanation.

"Then this was done by several groups at different time periods?"

"*Yes. Several different groups have been upon the earth. Tampering with DNA was done so that control could be gained over the human population, and indeed there are those species that do feed upon energy emitted during fear, stress, anger and all of the more negative human emotions,*" the guide answered, with concise clarity.

"*Earth was intended originally to be a center of communication, one of neutrality, where all could come, as to a garden oasis, a flower, a jewel in the universe, where peace and harmony would reign in the presence of unconditional love, the unconditional love of The God Source, The God Essence. As love is the primary vibration, the primary emotion, this is a planet of emotions.*

"Emotions come in many shades and degrees. They can be triggered quite easily; a thought or a desire creates an emotion. When people are in one accord, whether good or otherwise, the emotion or vibration among them is heightened, magnified.

"There are those that thrive upon love. When love is shown to the animals, to plants, to all of creation, that love vibration affects everything. Plants grow vibrantly strong and flowering varieties will produce blooms. Of course they will also grow or bloom because of other conditions: adequate sunlight for those requiring direct sunlight, adequate moisture, adequate nutrients from the earth, but when given love, in addition, they grow larger, stronger, and their rate of growth increases. It could be said they thrive upon love.

"At the opposite end of the scale, as stated already, there are those who thrive upon hatred, anger or strife; there are those who thrive upon stress. These are all emotions, emotional energy or vibrations. Some people whom you know seem happiest when they have something about which to complain—it gets them the attention they seek; they seem to thrive upon the very conditions that they have created and complain about.

"Does it surprise you," my guide asked, *"that there are other life forms that would 'feed' or thrive upon the energies emitted by the stress, the worry, the anxiety, the hatred, in a similar way to those others that thrive on the love vibration?*

"There have been times on this planet, upon the earth, of very little strife, periods in the history of the world where there was little warring. But, as influences change and others come within earth's boundaries, sometimes adverse influences manifest to create strife. As you have already been told, when conditions become settled and harmony is restored above the earth plane, so will it be settled below, upon the earth plane.

"The human DNA being 'altered' by species from other planets may be viewed as the enemy having committed a terrible act eons ago, but there has been a slow, gradual evolution ever since. Perhaps you may understand this if it were likened to an amputation, say of one of your fingers or a limb. The removal of that digit or limb would perhaps cause great concern and handicap at first, but eventually, the body would adapt to its new circumstances, albeit perhaps unwillingly, and life would continue on. And subsequent offspring would not necessarily be born minus that one limb, because memory of the 'DNA' is within every cell like the echo of a distant cry or phantom limb, as it was in your ancestors—not only within those strands of the helix purported to have been removed.

"And, as you are well aware, the newcomers to your planet being born at this time are arriving better equipped than you were. Many newborns are showing signs of being more advanced, more intelligent than the average child born in previous generations. This is because at this period in your time it is necessary for the planet to undergo great changes. Those of superior intellect will be among the survivors and leaders of the future. Planetary changes have taken place before in dramatic ways and the time is approaching for this to occur once more.

"Although there may still be those among you who have ulterior motives, there is little they can do to stop the progress that will be made. Similarly, regarding concerns about those who feed upon or are nourished by negative vibrations, have you not wondered, if these beings have such incredible powers and technology, why is it that they have not yet already taken over the planet? Perhaps it is not necessary at this present time for you to concern yourself, or understand. But know this, you are all being guided," the guide revealed emphatically.

"From everything that's happened lately, sometimes I feel we're being pushed rather than guided," Derek threw in.

"It is understood that sometimes you feel you are being pushed along more than guided. Your lessons appear to be coming fast and strong as the pulse of the planet quickens. However, as your mind comprehends what you are learning at the moment, your path does become easier, you become stronger, and your light will shine, whether it be the light of love, or the light of knowledge."

"There is still much denial about the existence of other life forms," Derek suggested.

"A lot of the denial stems from the fact you have all been raised to listen to the words of others. When a teacher or a parent makes certain statements and the child does not pay attention to the words or give the expected response, it may be reprimanded; perhaps affection or approval is withheld one way or another as a form of control, until the child does listen. The child then grows up believing that those in authority, in control—the governing bodies—have the right knowledge and the right information. It is the way your society is governed.

"Therefore, if governments suppress information about those among you, if there is constant denial of the existence, then, for the human being who is comfortable within his or her own reality and does not wish that comfort zone to be disturbed, why should she or he believe otherwise, unless actually confronted with situations that would cause them to check into their own beliefs and their own belief systems?" the guide reasoned.

"Then what hope is there for the majority of people to change their beliefs?" Derek asked, somewhat sadly.

"Be optimistic," the guide encouraged. "Remember, the human species has an incredible curiosity, and, when under pressure to seek change, the inner prompting comes into play, assisted by a deed here, a word from somebody else there. Under these circumstances, eventually, either many of you will seek further by going into your own belief systems to find answers, or, finding them redundant or unsatisfactory, you will seek elsewhere.

"When that first seed of doubt is sown about the belief systems which are keeping people stuck, then they are fortunate indeed, for that one word or deed opens the door slightly, *very slightly, the door which will lead them towards a new path of self-discovery and enlightenment."*

"We've been told that this will be known as the awakening time in earth's history, the time of self-discovery and enlightenment. Is this the reason for the present overpopulation of the world?" Derek asked.

"The world is not over-populated. Certain areas have a high density of population, but if those populations were spread to the unpopulated areas on the planet there could be space and food for many more. Look at your own country, see how much space there is, how few people occupy it."

"I agree with what you are saying in regards to space and population," Derek responded, "but taking into account the fact that a few hundred years ago the population was much less than it is today, what is the reason for the increase?"

"Many have chosen to incarnate at this time to experience or assist during the changes which are to take place upon the planet."

"Is this the first time around for many that have chosen to incarnate at this time?"

"For some it is the first and last incarnation upon this planet."

"Must they go through the whole cycle this lifetime, or are they just here for the change?"

"This lifetime, as you call it, is not necessarily as you perceive it. The span of time that you are upon the earth plane is but a speck in infinity. There are many universes where time, as you know it, does not exist, and there are many souls or beings or entities, as you call them, billions more than there are living upon this earth plane. And they, like each one of you, have chosen experiences in different places or dimensions as part of the soul's complete experience."

At this point, Derek decided he wanted to know to whom he was speaking, and asked the inevitable. He was, understandably, somewhat taken aback when his inquiry was answered with another question, even though it was delivered in a kindly tone: *"Which do you feel is more important, a gift...or its wrapping?"*

The thought-provoking interchange came to a speedy close, possibly because Derek was somewhat at a loss for what to say or ask after that. But even though it did leave us wanting to know more, we had certainly been given plenty to contemplate as to our existence and possible reasons for being here.

Chapter 10

One day as I began asking questions, I assumed the energy I was speaking to was familiar. I sensed 'something' that suggested we had spoken before; whatever it was, it bordered on a kind of open friendliness.

"Do you perceive any difference, being in this room instead of the other?" (I was referring to our new set-up, using my office instead of Derek's for our early morning session.)

"The energy throughout these offices, shall we say, is very unique; what is being offered here is picked up and perceived by those who enter as an expression of welcome. Those who come do understand and realize they are not judged; they can say whatever their concerns are, they know they will be helped."

"I was just wondering if you notice any difference in the physical comfort at all, if it's perceptible to you. Does it make for easier communication if the physical body is more comfortable?" (My recliner is so much softer and more generously upholstered than Derek's.) What I was really looking for was an acknowledgment that the 'location' for the session had changed.

"When the physical body is comfortable, attention and focus is upon that of communication. If there is irritation or discomfort, then some attention is taken away from the communicating."

By this time I was very curious. It couldn't be 'someone' we'd spoken to before, or the different office would have drawn a comment...wouldn't it? So I asked, "To whom am I speaking?" After a moment, the voice changed in tone slightly and Derek answered. He said he was tossing a name back and forth, wondering if he was 'making it up' or if there really was a name being given. He didn't quite trust his perception. There was another pause, and then the 'energy' took over again.

"The name has been given to him. He is allowing it to take form in his mind. It is Oran."

I couldn't believe I'd asked for a name and finally been given one. So far, during sessions like this, our guides had been reluctant to say who they were—unless it was Robert or John, Daneus, Kalindras, or my healing guide Nehiemir, whom we knew by name before we started formal 'channeling.' They say it's preferable we learn to recognize them by their energy rather than by name. The reason usually given is that anyone can say they are Jim, Henry or Mary or whatever 'handle' is given, but if we can't see them, they may not be who they claim to be. And as each spiritual being has its own unique energy vibration or signature, if we become familiar with that, then there's no mistaking it. It can't be duplicated, just as we can't duplicate someone else's fingerprints.

"Oran? Is that close?" I asked cautiously.

"Yes."

"We have spoken before, haven't we?"

"Yes."

"When Derek asked for you this morning, what title or designation did he use?"

"He asked for a guide who would be able to assist with the communication and the questions which would be asked this morning."

"Will you be working with Derek on a regular basis from now on?"

"This depends upon Derek himself; if he wishes. Another guide may handle the questions differently."

"Did you realize when Derek asked for you this morning that we hadn't prepared questions, and if so, does that make a lot of difference?"

"Yes. It makes a difference. You have been learning about being vague. A degree of aggressiveness, by knowing what you want, is required for what you have chosen to do. To cook a dish following a familiar recipe you would gather all the ingredients together, your intent being upon what you are doing. You add one ingredient, then the next, and so on. You do it without hesitation because you know how it has to be done. There may be a moment's hesitation as to whether the temperature should be 350 or 400 degrees for cooking, but you know the end result that is going to occur whether or not the temperature is set right, because of the knowingness. But if you try a new recipe, you don't know what to expect because you have not tried it before. That is when difficulties can arise."

I'd asked a fairly straightforward question, and was just a little put off by the wordy response. Immediately, I knew this session would test my patience. But I'd give it a fair shake.

"I understand why our hesitancy has arisen," I stated. "We had this scenario of going into a store. You are familiar with how we acquired the onyx eggs, right? It was incredible. Derek picked up this onyx egg, this main ingredient, and handed it to me; then all sorts of strange and wonderful things began to happen; we were told things, like the egg contains special information. And then we begin to ask questions. We're not sure whether we should be asking for the energy of the egg itself, or the Onyx Deva, or specific guides, and we've more or less muddled our way along. We ask all sorts of questions. But at the back of my mind I think, 'Are we supposed to hit upon some magic formula of asking certain questions so that the floodgates will be opened for us? Or are we just being prepared, as it were, as different guides attempt to work with us to see which is best suited to whom?'"

"If, at the initial start, you were to be given this wealth of information that you are seeking, it would be very difficult for you yourselves to decipher or understand whether the information is true or if it is indeed coming from a reputable source. Within your learning and understanding of what has been transpiring, your systems have become accustomed to sensing whether you trust the information, whether you trust the energy that is with you. This learning process is assisting you to determine whether you are being led merrily down the garden path, or whether you need to be on guard, to mistrust everything that comes your way," Oran explained.

"This learning and understanding has served to hone your perceptions whether to discharge or dismiss energies or start over, so that you feel comfortable and safe. It has also been to build up your own vibrations, your own energies, to build up your trust. You already know that it is very easy for an impersonator to slip in; of this you are very well aware. It is easy for another energy to attach itself, even momentarily. So, in what you are learning, whether you ask for the energy of the onyx eggs or the Deva or your Higher Self, a particular guide or energies, this is all preparing you to complete what you intend."

"Would you be able to answer all the questions that we may come up with?"

"Not all."

"If we were to come up with something beyond your ability to answer, would you let us know at that point?"

"You would be advised as to a more appropriate guide."

"Presumably, at your end, everybody knows when we are clear in our minds about what questions we are going to ask and it's not by chance in the mornings we get who we get."

"It was suggested that you ask your Higher Self, before retiring to bed at night; this is so that your Higher Self will make arrangements for the appropriate guide to be present the next day to answer whichever questions you wish to ask. In much the same way, you sometimes invite guidance for inspiration before writing poetry. An 'appointment' is made.

It is not exactly an appointment. You may call it etiquette if you wish, or a way of asking for assistance so that an appropriate advisor may be on hand. If there is a particular subject you wish to address, the appropriate advisor would be made available to answer questions on that topic."

"It sounds like a good plan to follow. The different guides that come through give us all this information, and we dutifully record it all, transcribe the tapes, enter it into the computer and print it out. But then we don't always read it afterwards. It's almost like we need to be trained like animals to respond until finally we catch on."

"You are not being trained like animals. The offer is extended, it is given to you that way, to allow you to learn and accept it at the appropriate speed. If you find that you did not save a document on the computer and you lost all record of it because you did not save it, after losing documents several times, you begin to save them. So, if the procedure of losing the documents helped you to learn the importance of saving, that procedure was a valuable lesson for you.

"If you run short of questions and don't know what to ask next, it is not because you haven't been given direction. When you do feel it is appropriate to do the preparation before-hand so that you are prepared, then you will do it."

"Then Derek and I should sit down together the night before and agree on what to ask."

"Most definitely, because then you are mutually attuned to what you wish to discuss."

On the surface, all of this appeared to ring true. But I had a gut feeling that I should be on my guard, that maybe things were just perhaps not what they seemed to be. It could just be that, after all these weeks of trying to access the 'sacred' information contained within Intensity and Sanctuary, and say, our learned necessity of 'testing the spirits from whence they came,' perhaps I was being a little paranoid. But I couldn't help feeling that, these answers I was receiving today were rolling off a well-oiled tongue rather than 'coming from the heart.' Was it my imagination or not? I decided I would continue, but with caution.

"Since beginning our other work we have built up a particular format to follow and because of that we are more confident when we go into a session. It follows that we would become even more confident in asking questions if we refine or change our format," I stated, searching for words as I wondered if my suspicions were correct.

"This would give you the little extra push of aggressiveness that comes with confidence."

"It certainly would remove our vagueness. One day Derek wanted to know what type of restraint or 'container' we should use to dispose of unwanted energies during the 'surrogate' work we do; his question drew the answer that if we are vague in our description, we will get a vague, or weak, container," I volunteered. Was I taking a risk bringing up such a topic?

"What you may be unaware of, for that particular work, is that the intent behind whatever you are doing must be as strong, if not stronger, than the intent of those you do not see and with whom you are dealing, because they can manipulate from the vantage point of being unseen."

Boy oh boy, there certainly was truth in that statement. Nevertheless, I couldn't shake the feeling that at this particular time perhaps I was being 'manipulated,' so I threw in the comment: "When in an altered state, we sometimes do see them, in addition to perceiving or sensing them. Is there a simple formula we can follow that will enable us to see them clairvoyantly at any time?"

"There is no formula. When you are ready, when it is appropriate, that will occur. You are learning first how fine the fine subtleties are. To be able to walk into a room and just feel the energy, knowing exactly the type of energy it is or what it is about is an incredible achievement and that is what you have learned to do. You are now able to identify several different types of energy. You are learning the capacity that these different energies have, and how not to entertain certain ones. You have made incredible progress in only a short time."

I found this assessment to be true, though a little extravagant. Most definitely I could identify with what was being said, and yes, both Derek and I could smell a rat from time to time. But, at that particular moment, I couldn't help wondering, was I, in fact, participating somehow in a bizarre cat-and-mouse game? Was 'someone' flattering and buttering me up in order to lead me by the nose? And if not, why was I feeling so uneasy? Immediately, I felt guilty at my suspicions, and tried to shake them off as I continued.

"That brings me to a comment I heard yesterday regarding a friend we are concerned about because he has invited in so many of these 'undesirable' elements; we heard he is reporting back to one of the energies we call 'watchers.' Is that correct, or is our informant just making a judgment which is out of line?"

"It is quite possible that this has happened. There is little difference observing what is going on, whether through him or through one of their own vehicles."

"It occurs to me that 'watchers' wouldn't need to use him to be able to observe. We have known them to be here of their own accord. Am I correct in that assumption?"

"Little games may be going on, just to create confusion."

'You bet!' I thought. But Oran's statement did spark my interest. "Is it best to not concern ourselves with him?" I asked. "We enjoyed a very good friendship before. I don't know whether he is isolating himself or whether it is just time for the friendship to drift."

"You will find that he distances himself from you because they [discarnate entities] know of your concerns and they have created a parting; they are very well aware of what you are doing. Your intentions, even the subtle messages, have been observed, and he is being steered aside so that he is kept even further in the dark. The friendship is only being held together at this moment because of his partner."

"We continually send him light and love; does it do any good, or are we fighting a lost cause?"

"There is free will involved. One can take on the grand task of saving the world, trying to clear it of all these entities, or there is another purpose; one can assist others to become aware of the realities they have created."

"Would we be naive in thinking that we could help him?"

"The question raises a judgment for you to make. Nothing is futile. Sending light and love as you do is one way of giving assistance. If a person chooses to continue with the experience he has selected, such as incarnating into a handicapped or totally disabled body, the soul has chosen that experience; you cannot just take away the experience and say, 'Get up and walk.' Some make it so debilitating for themselves they cannot maneuver, and muscles deteriorate to the extent of being virtually non-existent. But it is an existence they placed themselves into. As with your friend entertaining these others, it is an existence he has placed himself into in order to learn.

"Consider whether you should go to endless time and effort for someone who may not want or appreciate what is being done, and may even become vengeful if the experience is taken away from him. How do you feel inside; what is your intuition telling you? If his situation is bothering you to the degree that you cannot sleep, or eat, then possibly you are being told something should be done. If there is a loving intention behind it, a 'something' that is looking towards the best for the person, yet knowing that person made a choice, then sending loving kindness is helping in a way that is neither interfering nor taking something away," my unseen communicant responded.

"Then assisting without interfering would be the best way to go. Should we assume that if our friend returns to our Center he is looking for some sort of assistance?" I asked.

"Yes. If there is no more communication between you, they have totally severed the bonds. What goes on is but another lesson for everyone involved within the scenario. What your friend has chosen to go through is an experience which you are experiencing by observing, without having to go through it, so, you become aware to not give the energies [entities] *consideration or an area in which to play."*

Although there appeared to be much truth and plausibility in what was said, the somewhat slow delivery was so slick and so very smooth that, again, I suspected there was a double meaning in every response; it was as if a forked tongue carefully coached each one. Scratch the cat-and-mouse theory. My communicator was more likely a snake-in-the-grass!

From that point on in the session I became very uncomfortable with some of Oran's answers to my questions; I felt they were beginning to take on a rather judgmental tone, so I stopped the session and Derek and I walked home for a bite of breakfast.

When we returned to the office I was tempted to erase the whole tape, but something urged me to begin typing. It could always be deleted later, if necessary, I reasoned with myself; however, when I reached the judgmental part, I made a judgment myself and omitted it from the document. Then I erased the tape.

When I told Derek what I'd done he agreed I'd done the right thing. He had begun doubting things too towards the end of the session when it appeared judgments were being made, and he said he was pleased I terminated it.

The person I'd been discussing with Oran was Jay, a friend who allowed umpteen different entities to hang around him because he welcomed all experiences. His philosophy was, 'If everything is part of the whole, there can be no good as we know it, and therefore no bad, just different degrees of the same thing.' So he chose to experience everything that came his way, entity or whatever. We don't disagree entirely with his philosophy, but neither do we believe in sticking our necks out in the way that he does.

Jay's saving grace, I sincerely believe, is the fact that he is a very spiritual being; he just doesn't realize he is 'playing with fire' and he's certainly unaware of how little of the time he is consciously 'here' now, and how much of the time the 'others' take over. On more than one occasion, though, he has indicated he is aware of their presence.

I became very suspicious during that session when Oran said that our friend receives more help when he comes to us and that the energy at our offices is 'better' than at the other place which Jay attends for spiritual uplifting, where folks are more 'singular' and 'regimented' by a strict code of beliefs that are very 'restricting.'

It was easy to see the judgments that were being made. I know that among the highest and truest spiritual beings with which we are seeking to communicate, there is no ego, no judgment, and all is unconditional love. Sure, things are explained to us, but in a loving way. So, whenever there is any hint of ego at all, or if things are being said in a critical way, we know immediately that something is suspect and we should either disconnect or dismiss the energy. If we suspect an imposter or trickster has wormed its way into the proceedings, we generally cut things off right there and that's the end of channeling for the day; occasionally we restart again, trusting we will make a proper connection with the 'right' energies.

It should have been no surprise to me when, during our evening meditation, Derek spoke to my guide, Daneus, and began asking questions once again about Jay. I believe he will continue asking until he finds the answer he wants to hear; he desperately wants to help his friend, but we know we can't unless and until we are asked.

"I'm still concerned that my friend Jay has let others take over his vessel, that he will flounder in the harbor, as he hasn't even put any anchors down to protect himself from drifting," Derek confided. "He seems to be in a row boat about twenty feet away from his vessel. What I'm finding difficult is, yes, we know how to assist and get rid of these hijackers, but do we just say, 'Well, that's his reality,' and step aside, knowing he's twenty feet away from his ship [body] and might not make it back?"

"He is still attached to the ship by a rope, even though he is out in his little boat. He still comes to see you periodically and as long as he is keeping that contact with you, don't worry about him being adrift. You see, for every captain, when conditions become difficult and the fog is thick, the light will shine through. And even if he is in his rowboat in dangerous waters, that light will reach him. For now, just be content to be the lighthouse. So long as your friend knows that the light is there, it will reach him," Daneus reassured.

"I guess we can help him most by understanding that and leaving the rest up to him."

"Yes. Send him your light with no preconditions. Send him your unconditional love and that will be his beacon. It is indeed a conundrum sometimes for the wise father to know when to allow his children to continue playing and when to step in."

We began sending out more unconditional love. A few days later, during a little personal conflict between Derek and myself, Jay turned up at the office and became our beacon. I think Derek found the answer he was seeking.

Of course, it goes without saying that Oran became the topic of conversation and basis for my questions the following day as we settled in for our pre-dawn session.

Derek relaxed in 'The Chair,' and after going through the preliminaries, I began the communication. "Yesterday we received a name, Oran. I was concerned by some of the responses and terminated the session." I immediately received confirmation that my fears were grounded.

"That is not the right name for the one with whom you were speaking, but it could be something quite similar. It is best not to concern yourself with names at the present time. If the energy feels appropriate and you feel comfortable with the information you are receiving, then accept it, by all means, but if it does not seem 'right,' then you may reject it."

What had just been said did register, and 'sit right,' but I wanted to test the energy Derek was channeling.

"Do you have a name we could address you by?"

"As has been mentioned, it is not necessary at this time to be concerned with names. As you learn to trust your own inner guidance, as you listen for the quality of the messages, the tones in the voice, the feeling of the energy, you will learn to recognize these. There are many names and many may use similar names, but if you learn to be able to identify these forms in other ways, you will surely know the energies with whom you are communicating. You are learning the subtlety of using ESP, as you sometimes call it, or your intuition. As you pass into a room, unaware of what is in that room, you enter into it carefully."

"I'm concerned about what happened yesterday. I thought I recognized having spoken to the energy before, and I was told that indeed I had, and we were given a name. Everything sounded fine at first, very authentic, very believable, but I felt uncomfortable and towards the end there seemed to be a judgmental tone; I became very suspicious. Is it possible we were speaking to one energy at first, and then another took over? And does it mean that the whole of the transmission is suspect if there is any part of it we don't trust?"

"If you are communicating with a 'con-artist,' a deceiver, some of the things being said may in fact be quite plausible; this is to lure the listener into believing 'yes, this is credible information.' Not all the information received would be unworthy of retaining; the first part may have been a means of getting your attention by giving you some credible information initially, to draw you further and further in," the guide revealed.

"As you finally hone your art of inquiry, you may formulate a particular line of questioning to check out the source. If you don't like a program on television, you change the channel or turn the set off. Any time you feel dissatisfied with responses to your questions,

or are uncomfortable with where you feel a signal is coming from, you may stop the session."

"I don't expect any high spiritual being to criticize another entity or being or group."

"The ones you are seeking to communicate with generate unconditional love; there are no conditions placed, no judgments made, and anything said is always for the highest good of all concerned. What is said about another person, if ever, would be to bring his or her energy or spirit up, and not lower it."

"If, say, I'm in a trance and I'm picking up intolerance with questions being asked or because Derek is perhaps joking, then that would be suspect, too?"

"Yes. And after you go through the scenario of a morning's channeling, as you term it, and you then spend a few hours entering it into the computer, you perhaps do a little editing, maybe erasing passages completely, or adding notes in parentheses to expand upon the point that is made, may we suggest whenever you have received statements that cause you concern, you use them to illustrate what is suspect or not credible, so that the reader may understand how to discern for self if attempting the process."

"You mean, instead of deleting the 'suspect' passages like I did yesterday, you're suggesting we include them, but add that we feel they were suspect and state our reasons why?" I asked.

"Yes, to illustrate, as examples of things that can occur."

"What baffles me is that yesterday, when we started off, I felt a type of rapport with the energy that came through, as if I knew it like an old friend."

"Perhaps the element of doubt was created in order to assist you in different ways. If a father allows his child to do whatever it wishes, the child may display inappropriate conduct whenever it wishes to get the attention of the parent. And if there is no difference in the father's response to the inappropriate conduct, it is very difficult for the child to understand whether or not it is receiving the father's love. Sometimes, there is learning by different means and we do not understand why it is happening. It may be for entirely different reasons than the ones we think," the guide offered.

"What are you saying? Is it that in fact what we received yesterday could have been valid, but towards the end when the information became judgmental it was a cue for me to make a judgment call and query it, thereby not just accepting everything that comes? Was it a test to see if we would sit up and take note or swallow everything at face value, criticism as well, like a pair of gullible children?"

"If the transmission was on an even keel, and had no inflection of, say, judgment or ego, then there may have been no query whatsoever."

"Now I'm even more confused. Just when we think things are going so wonderfully, a spanner is really thrown into the works to cause doubt and deflate the ego," I said dejectedly.

"*That may not have been the intention. You could say the symbolic spanner may have been thrown into the machine to assist in your understanding of the entire workings within the machine itself, just as other influences have been brought to your attention to help you realize that within your reality there are other realities that do become involved, and to a much finer degree than just a 'spanner.' Sometimes, in order for the awareness to be expanded, one's entire system requires a 'tune-up.'"*

After transcribing the tape and printing out a hard copy of the session I decided that, although frustrating, this had been a truly enlightening interchange for us. In essence, the whole Oran situation had assisted us to delve into and learn a bit more about the process of channeling, while alerting us to the fact that, indeed, there is a difference between roses and cabbages, and if we can't see before touching them, we'd better have a good sense of smell...or risk a good prick here and there.

Chapter 11

It's always obvious when the stage is being set for major learning to occur; it usually happens whenever there is a hive of activity around our house. Two daughters and my granddaughter had gravitated home for a few months; numbers increased as a live-in boyfriend entered the scene, followed a week or so later by my youngest son and his cat. Every spare inch of space was being utilized, including the basement.

The arrangement had just sort of happened. If we could all remain amicable and happy and courteous and not too noisy, any nether region revels shouldn't upset the delicate balance of my wedded bliss. In all sincerity, I just love it when all my kids are around, particularly during the festive season—providing they clean up after themselves and I get to use the telephone when I want. I'm not too sure what Derek really thought. After all, the move back home initially had been fathered by his suggestion aimed to assist a young single parent experiencing financial difficulties...then another of my offspring gravitated back to the nest, and so on.... And Derek didn't seem to mind, at first.

One morning, however, the early morning session took place much later than usual. But it felt good to be at the office, particularly when we were settled in for a chat with our guides and teachers and Derek began the conversation:

"It must be the time of year that makes us want to sleep in a little more."

"You are feeling the effects of the break in routine."

"If this was a break, we were very busy; we now have a house full of guests."

"It is good they feel they can come home when the need is there. Each has much to contribute."

"They have unique ways to do that. But I find the old parental control thing slips into the picture; it really likes to take a handle on the situation."

"This is perhaps due to certain souls incarnating sooner than other family members; because of their more senior role they continue to treat the offspring as children, as youngsters, when in fact the youngsters may be as old as the parent. In most human understanding this is not recognized and is sometimes why clashes occur. You may call it a control issue when parents exercise certain rights and privileges the ego claims are theirs because of perceived seniority.

"But if you ask the two daughters with children which one has the control, neither adult will claim it. Very often it is the child who has the control. In many households the parents jump, or dance, to the tune the child sings, because, on another level, the child knows it is equal and has equal free-will, and very often this is why clashes occur. Wills sometimes clash as the child tries to take control because of being the parent or controller in other incarnations," my guide explained.

"Are there species elsewhere that have progressed beyond the parental control aspect?"

"There are those that have overcome the ego."

"Isn't ego intended to help us survive?"

"And to protect you."

"So it's a case of learning balance?"

"Yes, and to learn to not become unsettled by the will of others. When you talk about someone being willful, will-full, each having free will, that will is born of and is part of the One Divine Will. If parents and their offspring alike were mindful of this, there could be some changes in attitude on both sides.

"With children, because the soul has only recently incarnated and is so open, so trusting, so receptive to what is being said and done, the belief systems are quickly established. If children see spirits and tell of seeing someone or something that the parent can't see, they are often chastised for telling lies, or are told it was their imagination, and they soon learn to mistrust.

"Often, at the point at which trust is broken, a feeling of despair sets in, because the child knows what it has seen and experienced. The child was expecting to receive assistance, consolation, or reassurance. It is quite a shock to the young child in all its innocence when it is accused of making a false statement, or it finds that it is not understood or maybe ridiculed for being afraid of something that may indeed have been frightening.

"If a child explains the beauty of a creature it has seen, say, a nature spirit, and is told, 'It is just your imagination,' he may be quite wounded that he is not believed. Should the child be told sufficient times that what he sees is not real, that may cause him to disbelieve what he sees and shut out the clairvoyance that was there. Fear of what was seen can also cause this to occur."

"I can see how a wall could be built up to protect self. Not only would the child not trust the parents any more, it would not trust its own judgment. Can broken trust ever really be re-established?" Derek asked.

"Trust issues between child and parent may never be resolved in this incarnation unless there is the preparedness of at least one of them to let go of past bitterness, past anger, regrets."

"We often feel threatened and become defensive if we are being criticized; is this because of upbringing, when we were perhaps controlled in this way, or does it go back even further to previous imprinting from incarnations where our roles were reversed?"

"It all does have a bearing, but don't forget that your perception of what occurs is what sets the scene for learning. Examine your thoughts and feelings, your perceptions now, of why you feel you were being criticized; then place yourself in the other person's shoes and view from that perspective what has occurred; determine how you feel as the role is reversed.

"Try to truly understand others' feelings and what it is that makes them react to you in the way they do; you may come to a different understanding which allows you to release any hard feelings being held towards others; if this occurs, then the lesson has been learned. This is not necessarily condoning something another, or others, may have done to you, but if you understand the motives or feelings behind the action or criticism, then your own perspective or perception can indeed change so that you are more forgiving and no longer upset by the other's actions.

"Where a parent appears to be continually scolding a child, correcting it, there may be many reasons behind the parental behavior which the child doesn't understand," the guide continued. *"The parent may be going through much stress at the time, unhappiness or grief, and is unable to cope. Maybe the parent wants the very best for the child and wishes total acceptance of it by other people, so tries to form or mold a perfect little character that everyone sees as likeable, intelligent, and well behaved. As the child cannot understand the motives of the parent, and senses only criticism or rejection, it feels frustration; it feels cut off, and because of those perceptions and feelings, withdraws and creates certain other conditions to occur.*

"It is often only later in life, when one has grown in wisdom, that one may begin to understand why certain conditions occurred. That does not mean to say it was wrong to perceive things in the way they were perceived during childhood. But when it is understood that the scene had to be set in order for certain lessons to be learned, it makes it easier to understand self and one's own reactions. This paves the way to understanding others' motives.

"Very often, this new understanding sets the scene for allowing unconditional love to flow to heal the old wounds, the old misunderstandings, judgments, and misconceptions. And as love for self and others is allowed to flow, and forgiveness of self and others is

allowed to flow, a releasing can occur so that the body may be freed of whatever conditions were placed upon self as a result of the early perceptions," the guide concluded.

Well, well! So that's why my kids had gravitated home. It wasn't because of financial hardship, or even the festive season, although that's what it appeared to have been on the surface. It was to recreate scenarios so that old perceptions could be reviewed and perhaps new understandings occur.

* * *

Only four days into the New Year of 1995, I came into the office on my own, feeling somewhat vexed. We were definitely still in the middle of some major learning. The scene certainly had been set. Derek and I had been engaged in verbal 'saber rattling' for a couple of days, triggered by some trivial remark, which I'd let simmer on the back burner. I guess I had been waiting for the heat to be turned up so it could come to a full rolling boil before making a meal out of the issue. I'm amazed at how brilliant we can be in the way we create scenarios for our lessons and to get our own way.

The previous night my man had gone to bed angry, just like me, although I had politely waited and read a book for a half-hour before creeping into the bedroom. In my way, I was so very generously allotting him a 'period of grace' which would allow him to gain his composure, settle down and pretend to be asleep, so that I could do the same.

We'd independently adopted this type of routine for this type of scenario. Derek skulks off to bed without saying 'goodnight,' just to let me know he's mad. I pretend I don't know what's going on. I give him time to 'get to sleep,' knowing full well that he will be unable to, and then I quietly sneak in, climb in and jump on the pretend-sleep bandwagon, too.

The routine usually works, although this time, judging by Derek's coughing, I knew this was no 'usually.' He couldn't feign sleep that night. Between coughing, tossing, and turning, he was trying to pretend. In between one of his turns and coughs I had challenged, "Do you want to talk?" The grizzled response flew back at me so fast it almost took my nose off.

"Talk? There's nothing to discuss!"

"Well, pardon me, sir!"

Of course I wasn't going to take this lying down (pun intended) so I half sat up. You can't actually sit up in a waterbed; it's more like doing an elbow-lean-up; so, from this uncomfortable position and with gritted teeth, we mutually snarled back and forth for a few minutes.

I'm sure many people have been privy to this type of sophisticated and mature boudoir behavior. And so...our late night 'endearments' completed, we each turned our separate ways to get a good night's pretend sleep, which, needless to say, set the scene for the next morning's continuing saga.

I finally dozed off, but was rudely awakened at three o'clock on this particular morning by a large gray and white pussycat houseguest happily caterwauling its little heart out. I heard the cat's master trundle quietly to the bathroom and back to his room. I guess the cat, too was doing its bit to add atmosphere to the brewing pot.

For quite a while I lay there in bed; I was well and truly awake, pretending not to be, until Mother Nature called me to visit the littlest-room-in-the-house. I returned to bed, knowing full well that Derek was awake, too, though silent and motionless.

Finally, I broke the stiff silence and said: "Are you going into the office with me?" Why on earth would I ask such a dumb question, at such an hour, after such a night? I must be crazy.

I can't quite remember Derek's exact response, but I think it was in the negative! At least it triggered a negative response from me, sufficient to propel me out of bed with great alacrity and agility. I was really on form, and within record time I was up, dressed and out the door before anyone could whistle "Dixie" from first to second bar. And so I made my way to the office.

At first, I was almost at a loss for what to do. Why on earth had I created such a scenario? Here I was, all alone, no one with me for an earlier than usual morning session. There was nothing to nibble on, and I felt miserable. I decided I would surely find comfort by meditating for a short while.

Gradually, I felt myself becoming peaceful within. And then I had a wonderful idea. Why not try to channel solo? I could do it; sure I could, if only to prove it to myself. So, quite pleased with my brilliant idea, I set up the tape recorder and pre-recorded a few words.

"It's almost 5:00 AM and this is Diana channeling solo to see what's going to transpire. I will begin by tuning in as usual, and then asking my highest spiritual guide a question about what is the lesson that I am going through as an individual, and that Derek and I are going through as a couple, as a unit, as a relationship, and what is it that we have to learn?"

It was a mouthful, but it was a start. At this point, I set the recorder onto pause so that I could perform the preliminaries. And after tuning in in the normal manner, I mentally asked my question again and then released the pause button to record everything that would possibly be said.

I could sense the familiar presence and said aloud, "I give you permission to use my voice to answer the questions that I have asked."

There was a pause as I began to physically relax, and I could feel the energy intensify as I coaxed my conscious awareness to take a back seat. Then it was as if I heard myself talking from a distance. I knew the voice was mine, but thoughts were being conveyed which didn't seem to be mine.

"*Greetings. As you are experiencing, this is another routine, another method you may utilize for accessing information, or for receiving answers to questions.*

"*When one is asking what one is learning, or what is it that one is supposed to be learning from a given situation, very often one cannot see the picture clearly because too much is obscuring the vision.*

"*Let us go into the first portion of the question. What is Diana learning for Diana? Diana is learning lessons for self while being part of lessons of the family or group as a whole. This is not a unique situation. This is the process by which all souls learn their lessons.*

"*The lessons one learns are for a broader picture, over a much larger spectrum than can be perceived on the physical level. Each soul chooses to incarnate many times, on many different levels, and you are just beginning to understand the existence of these realities, some of them, as of yet, still within your remembrance but unknown to you at this time.*

"*Each journey on the earth plane, as part of those lessons which form the greater whole of all your lives' lessons, begins not at birth, or at conception, but before the soul chooses to incarnate,*" my guide went on. "*And what is being acted out at the moment is a fulfillment of decisions which were made at that time.*

"*Within relationships, many lessons may be set for one particular lifetime. This does not mean that there are karmic debts to be repaid. Karma is not involved; choice is involved. Some of the strongest lessons occur within a large family, learning to coexist with a number of others.*

"*If one has chosen, say, to become a parent as Diana has done, bringing in a number of souls, as was agreed—having in mind this is a decision of many and not just one—the purpose was already predetermined, the conditions were predetermined and selected.*

"*As a young child Diana set goals for herself which she was able to accomplish. She had a dream, she had a vision; she followed it, she succeeded, and this has been a repetitive cycle throughout her life. She chose to raise a family alone. There is another goal; there is another dream at the moment. The current goal embraces the relationship, the husband, and that which they have jointly agreed to accomplish together,"* the guide continued.

"Family relationships differ and change within any relationship in order for certain things to occur, adjustments to be made, so that the true purpose of the relationship can come to fruition.

"Major lessons may be learned by people under one roof. Now under the one roof at the current time there have been gathered together other parts of the relationship so that combined lessons may be learned. The eldest has something to learn from the youngest and all the others, as does the second eldest and so on down the line, even to the feline. Each child has a contribution to make, and each is there so that all may learn. Their position within the unit may be viewed by the prime players to be subordinate, that is, because they are children, but whether children, house-guests, or occasional visitors, each makes a valid contribution, each is there for the others to learn from during the period they are together. Even children of either party who are absent, and children of children living elsewhere, are part of the relationship.

"Now, if one within the unit or family has a problem, it becomes a problem of all, as it affects the combined energy under that one roof. If the energy is to be brought back in line, which means in harmony, in balance with the others, it is a joint effort, a joint choice, and a joint contribution.

"However, at any time, any member may choose to exit the relationship if that part of the group learning is complete, but there remains a bond or tie there, and the relationship is in fact never severed. That only occurs when all the lessons have been completed which creates the true freedom to leave," the guide continued apace.

I know I asked a pretty long-winded question, but it came as sort of a surprise to receive such detailed response. I willingly paid attention to the words I was both hearing and speaking.

"Part of the learning is allowing others to act out their role. If one wishes to wear red slippers every day and another has a fierce loathing for red slippers, the person who loves wearing them could be asked to take them off and put them out of sight. When one realizes she/he has an issue with red slippers, there is the option open to find out why. However, the choice may be made to ignore the whole situation, hoping it will go away, which will never occur. It will manifest again in another scenario, in the same location or elsewhere, although possibly next time it could be green slippers, or blue, or purple.

"The person who loves wearing red slippers could remove them, hoping to remove the aggravation. But is the other person being honest with self if he/she expects them to be removed? What is it about red slippers? Is there an inbred fear of them? Do they annoy because they trigger a buried memory from the past? Are they perceived as a direct threat, or are they perceived as being worn to antagonize?

"Both parties may each point accusing fingers; they may agree to disagree, or strike a compromise. But remember, only by finding out why they are annoying may the lesson be learned; otherwise, red slippers will keep on cropping up, whether in this lifetime or another, whether within this relationship or another.

"Both of you must realize that you have both chosen these lessons. It is something for you both to work on. You may both wish to sit down and ask for a solution how this could best be solved. However, it must be done with an open mind. You may be surprised at what you find out about yourselves," the guide suggested.

"All this is given with much love. It is not telling you what you should be doing; that is also part of the lessons—to find out for oneself... for ONE'S SELF... finding out not for the other, for the older, for the younger, for those in between; it is finding out for one's self, while realizing that all have chosen to be within the relationship for mutual learning.

"The more intense the lessons, the more central they are within each family or unit. Each and every individual on the planet, both seen and unseen, all are learning their own lessons in the greater relationship. And I thank you for being given this opportunity to speak," the guide concluded.

At that moment I could feel the energy disconnecting and I took myself out of the self-induced trance. I stopped the tape-recorder and made my way to my desk where I sat very still for about twenty minutes before leaving the office to walk home.

During the brisk walk home through the crisp snow I couldn't help marveling how situations are created and thinking to myself how incredible all this is. I realized Derek and I are both equal partners in all our squabbles. But was my anger towards Derek created for him to become angry with me, so that energy would be generated to propel me to the office alone? And was it created so that I would channel solo, to show me it could be done that way?

If Derek and I hadn't been squabbling, I wouldn't have been mad enough to walk out of the house and be tuning in at least thirty minutes earlier than normal. And I wouldn't have been alone. And I wouldn't have been so darned determined that I wasn't going to let another early-morning opportunity for channeling get missed, as had been the pattern the last couple of weeks, due to the Christmas and New Year season.

I also remembered that, whilst walking to the office, a thought had briefly crossed my mind as I wondered if the channeling procedure we normally use could be done alone; yes, and what a blast! It's amazing how we create situations to occur; I realized what a large dose of emotion could do to propel us in the direction needed!

But, on a sobering note, had I, in fact, deliberately caused our matrimonial discord, thereby creating the opportunity to find out? I guess so. I wasn't too proud of that thought. And does that mean we create our own reality...by manipulating others to make sure we get our own way? The implications were mind-boggling.

I tried to find a positive motive; maybe we had brought the whole thing about so that we could share how to do this solo, too. Truly though, it's not really solo, is it? Nothing is, because through it all, our guides are always with us.

* * *

I had an absolute ball that day. I was so pleased with myself and thrilled by my fledgling 'solo act.' Above all, I recognized that anger directed positively was perhaps a good emotion. Had it spurred me on to reach for and do something that I wouldn't normally have had sufficient desire or confidence to try, or was it just time to prove something to myself?

I interpreted it as a blessing that Derek had chosen to give the office and me a wide berth that day. We both needed our own space occasionally. The office was mine alone for the whole day, and I felt wonderfully free and adventurous.

I was so ecstatic about what had happened that I began to see the funny side of things; I laughed at our ridiculous antics, the silly little games we play as we go through our life-lessons together. Bless you, Derek, this one was a real gift and I thank you from the bottom of my heart. I realized it would give me a wonderful opportunity to inject a little humor into my writing, too, and I eagerly started another chapter for the book. Before I knew it, the afternoon was done.

I closed my document, printed it out and turned off the computer. Still on a high from writing in a witty vein, I made one or two calls, yakking on the phone for a while, and then I closed up shop and walked home briskly, enjoying the crisp air and the sounds of snow crunching underneath my feet.

I barely noticed the sub zero temperature; I guess my own inner glow from the flush of personal success kept me warm. Shades of mauve swept into apricot-lined clouds as a low-lying sun saluted the arrival of evening. I noticed how prettily the sky was tinged with delicate pastel shades of purples and pinks like fields of Scottish heather.

Back at the house, the scene also was set. Derek, I learned later, had been out all day and arrived home about fifteen minutes ahead of me. I strode into the bedroom to get a comfortable sweater, as I would be walking back to the office in just over an hour's time for one of our Psychic Development classes.

To my surprise, I found Derek was already in bed. It was 5:15 PM. He must be feeling really tired, I chuckled to myself, as I saw Derek lying there, eyes closed, unwilling to communicate, as if pretending to sleep once more. These little sidestepping ego dances are so cute, each of us merrily moving to our own tune. I wanted to go over, there and then, and give him a big hug and a sloppy kiss, but inwardly I wasn't too sure of the reception I'd get; I decided to play it safe and wait until later.

I knew that my little solo event was only important to me. I'd asked questions about what I was going through, and although I wasn't given a solution, I did receive some wonderful insights—applicable to me! Nothing super-fantastic to jump up and down about and shout out to the world, but I had done all by myself something that I wouldn't have dreamt of under normal circumstances; the idea wouldn't have entered into my head to try and channel alone. And I am so pleased I did.

Pleasure at my solo adventure and my effervescent delight spilled through and lit the evening. Our students all appeared to have a wonderful, guided meditation; the full complement of ladies was present, and a delightfully all-girlish energy made the evening a pleasure.

By the time I arrived home, things had improved on the domestic scene. Derek was up, though not quite back to his normal, teasingly happy self. After hanging my coat in the closet and putting away mittens, toque, and scarf, I reached into my briefcase, pulled out the printed transcript of my solo excursion and handed it to Himself. He read it through, making appropriate noises of acknowledgment here and there.

I assumed the worst of the storm clouds had passed. But, just in case my timing was off, I held back on my humorous observations about what had been going on between us. That just might be like throwing a match into a gunpowder keg. If there were any possibilities that my written attempts at humor could maybe cause an explosion, it would be best to wait for another time to show off my other manuscript.

The following morning began as one of those days, you know, the kind where you wished you'd stayed in bed and gone back to sleep. That way, everything would be a dream and could be swept back under the pillow if need be, like, 'Nope, I don't want to look at that right now.'

Both of us had slept in, so there would be no channeling that day. I felt a little guilty, though I knew there was no reason. "Neither of us are supposed to, today," I told myself as we arrived at the office.

When we stepped inside the door, it seemed as if we were in a time warp. It was still the day before yesterday and there was a bitter meanness in the air. For no particular reason, we both behaved like two bears with sore heads. In no time flat, we were at loggerheads and at a decibel higher than I considered professionally acceptable. Had Derek no respect for the other office tenants? And what about me? I was behaving no better!

Falling for the bait once again and right on cue, I felt sick and tired of Derek having to prove himself and his little-boy tantrums if ever he felt he was being criticized. Whichever way you cut it, he was on the defensive; no matter what was being said, no matter what suggestions I made, everything I expressed he didn't like; as usual, he saw everything as a direct criticism.

This was it! NO MORE! "Derek, shape up or get out!" I wanted to say. I'd had more than I could take. I was fed up and worn out by continually having to tiptoe around so as not to break any proverbial eggshells. The time of impasse was NOW. "DO SOMETHING ABOUT THESE ISSUES or get out of my life!" was what I wanted to scream out loud.

Even though I knew what a wonderful, loving, kind, gentle, giving, wise and noble person Derek was, I didn't want him in my life any more at that time. I wanted OUT of the relationship. But what about the book? I couldn't give a hoot!

Things had happened with such a blast of energy and I was hopping mad. I got on the phone to Amos. Derek and I both needed independent hypnotherapy sessions immediately. We were both acting like kids. I made up my mind. He could go first and get straightened out, and then when he arrived back I would go. At least that's what I thought. We both know that if there is a problem between two people, both parties have an issue to deal with; otherwise, each would not be triggering the other; the ammunition would miss its target.

But, while I was on the phone to Amos arranging things, adding more fuel to the fire, Derek became even more irritable because he objected to the fact that I had decided he must go get help first. I guess he had a problem because he felt I was trying to control the situation. It was tit for tat, and vice versa.

I interpreted his responses to mean that he was squirming out of getting help. And so, with grandiose style like a prima donna, I stormed out of the office. Let him stew on his own! If he didn't want to go for help, I would, just to prove I really wasn't the one with the problem. Tsk, tsk! What a joke! It was 11:00 AM.

I arrived back at the office six hours later feeling great. My hypnotherapy session with Amos had been quite surprising. But that wasn't unusual. They always are. I wasn't actually in session for the whole six hours. Because I was still so hopping mad when I got there, to defuse the situation, Amos took me out to lunch.

When our buttons are pushed, as mine had been, the underlying cause is rarely what we perceive it to be; frequently it's an unresolved childhood issue. As Amos regressed me back to another time I had felt this way, boom, I was right there at ten years old, face to face with my brother. He was bossing me around, telling me what to do, and I could do nothing about it because he was a boy, older and little stronger than me, and he had been left in charge.

I was shocked to realize that my anger actually stemmed from a sense of injustice and an unexpressed resentment towards my parents, because my brother was simply doing exactly what my parents had told him to do. He really had no choice in the matter, although he was enjoying playing the role of authoritarian. Boy, had I done my brother an injustice—I'd always blamed him for bossing me around when my parents were absent.... He really had been the innocent turkey in all this...just like Derek! Derek had merely been playing the role of catalyst and the tone of his voice had triggered my response...it was all so that I could get down to brass tacks because it was time to release the old, buried anger and emotion I'd unconsciously stored at a cellular level as a child.

The test for me now would be to see if I was able to tolerate a certain tone in Derek's voice. And, of course, I expected him to go for a session. After all, we both had been triggered.

Chapter 12

It was a good five days after my 'solo.' Much soul searching had been done on both sides and we had sorted through what had been triggering our behavior towards each other. Happily, Derek and I were back on an even keel and eventually things felt right for us to recommence our regular channeling. We had reminded our students over and over again that they should never attempt to channel if they felt 'under the weather' or upset at all. Today we decided Derek would get in 'The Chair' first.

After going through the preliminaries and making contact with the appropriate guide, I got down to business and asked if we had communicated before. The answer was 'No.' I asked if the energy would be communicating on a regular basis and the answer again was 'No.'

This miffed me no end, though I tried to keep a rein on my feelings. What on earth were we shilly-shallying around for? I asked what was the point of repeatedly asking for the proper guide if we weren't going to get one with whom we could become familiar and build up trust.

The process, I was told, helps the guides working with us to find the right energy that will match ours. Now that answer seemed to make a tad of sense. I just might be on to something, I thought, so I continued.

"Are you suggesting that not only does it give us, the 'vehicles,' an opportunity to work with a new energy to see if we are compatible, it also gives the energy that wishes to come through an opportunity to try us out?"

"Yes."

"So, if today we find that the energies are compatible, the next time we wish to communicate, how can we be sure that it is the same energy that we get? Do we just say, 'The same energy as yesterday, please'?"

"No. There is a finer knowing than knowledge. You are not understanding the workings of telepathy. Guides who are with you regularly know through your feelings,

through your thoughts, what you wish. And as you tune in to these energies, you will recognize them."

"So with each different energy 'trying us out,' are they different bodies of energy, or are they the energies from the same soul or energy group?"

"In truth, we are all the same energy; we are all from the Oneness. But, to answer your question, yes, there is a group of energies, several energies—you may call it a collective. If you were wishing to receive information regarding literary works, mathematics, science, you would ask for the appropriate energy to answer questions in those areas or any other area about which you wish to communicate.

"Let us use the analogy of a recording unit, one half of which is horizontally suspended in space, the other half resting on a solid base. In this analogy the receiver represents you. One half of you is in the spiritual plane and the other half is in the physical body on the earth plane. You are functioning at less than half of your capacity, as part of you is suspended outside your physical bodies and this suspended part is the one with which spirit works closely, as it houses the higher aspects of self through which spirit must work to reach you.

"Symbolically, you would liken attunement or raising of the vibrations to moving sliding bars on the mixing board that spans both sides of the recording equipment, and upon which there are many different levels and settings, representing the different aspects of the group or collective energies. These all have to be properly adjusted to achieve the right 'sound' or vibration. When searching out a station on a radio receiver, between stations you may get nothing or you may get static or distortion. Occasionally, as signals cross, you may tune into two different channels at the same time and receive distorted impressions.

"It takes practice on all levels before the higher energies may align perfectly with those of the physical. At the moment, perfect transmission is distanced by just a hair's breadth. The patience and tolerance are noted, as is your dedication. With continued persistence, both of you will receive the rewards in the form that you are anticipating," this guide finished succinctly.

I felt a niggling doubt. I know we all originally came from the one source, and I have heard of 'collective' or group soul energies. Was my question answered or not? I'm not interested in math or science or the like; nevertheless, I made a quick decision to continue on. "I understand everything contains the 'secrets' of the Universe, from the time it was first created. Is it appropriate yet for us to begin receiving the information that would, say, be stored within the onyx egg?"

"The onyx egg is but a vehicle for this information. It is not as you view a library where everything is written down within the books and each book contains specific informa-

tion. *The eggs themselves are a tool similar to the other tools, the crystals, the sugalite you use to assist with the channeling."*

"So, in effect, you're saying there is nothing stored within the egg, that it is just a chunk of rock?"

"You may classify it that way if you wish. But it isn't quite appropriate."

Was this energy detecting the annoyance in my voice? First we are told there is information within the egg, then no, it's just a tool, then we are told a similar set of contradictory information. Hm.... What's going on here? I decided to let whoever was talking continue.

"The stone itself, even though it is part of the Oneness, it does retain information, but not as you are viewing it."

Was this an about-turn? Some kind of back-pedaling or changing tune? I wasn't going to let this one get away with it, but I didn't want to be too impolite, just in case I was wrong in my thinking.

"Maybe I misunderstand. Derek read something from a book recently that confirmed what we learned a long time ago; it stated that everything contains DNA, or information, including rocks and minerals, even the trees and plants. Is that not so, or am I just understanding things wrongly?"

"Information is encoded within, but one must first become familiar with the entities, become familiar with the vibration to be able to access this information, as this information is part of that which is the Oneness," the responding guide added.

"That sounds like a contradiction to what you said before. First you say it's just a tool and then you say there is information there. It's very confusing to get what seems like conflicting information. I'm not sure what we can trust. Now you say we must become compatible with the energies of the egg; how do we do this, how does this occur?"

[Actually, according to the taped record of the conversation, he had said to become "familiar with the entities," not "compatible with the energies."]

"You are doing this at the moment."

"So, if we are doing this at the moment, why is it that we can't access the information?"

"It's not that you cannot access the information. If you were to tune in and ask the appropriate questions, if the appropriate questions are coming through, or you are being guided with this in regards to the information, this is how it will be given."

I didn't detect any hostility in the response, but it didn't make much sense, as we've been asking for guidance all this time. 'Talk about conditioned responses and making us work for our living,' I huffed to myself. But I decided to continue a while longer. "So it all comes back to knowing what questions to ask. Is there some sort of key that we are supposed to hit on by using certain phrases, or formulating the questions? We have already asked Higher Self, and it seems, as yet, we're still not asking the right questions. Is there anything that you can suggest?"

"Ask for assistance of a guide who will ask these questions, or ask for inspiration to ask the appropriate questions."

In my mind, that's exactly what we had been doing. Well, maybe not quite. We'd asked for a guide to answer the questions, and also requested inspiration for the questions we should ask. Was I being too critical? I'd give whoever it was the benefit of the doubt—for now. "We will try that avenue. If it's just one more day, that's nothing."

"You see, within your response, beneath the words, there is a belief of not receiving," the guide spoke quickly.

Now that's not true. I really expect things will take off, just like in the Rock and Gem Store when Derek first put Intensity into my hands. But I'm only speaking for myself. Granted, at that point in my last statement there was the feeling of 'Well, I guess that's all for today, folks,' however, there was certainly no underlying belief that we will never receive. And, after all, what is one more day, anyway? I know eventually we'll hit the jackpot, and the information is going to flow.

"So you say to ask for the appropriate guide or ask for the inspiration to ask the correct questions?"

"Yes."

On that note I ended the transmission. Was that confusing or what? I wasn't terribly happy with any of the answers and I let my feelings be known. Although some notes rang true, I was highly skeptical about the whole thing. 'Ask for a guide to ask the questions or ask for inspiration to ask the appropriate question?' That sounded so screwball. 'I ask for inspiration every day we do this,' I complained to myself.

I was glad we had been told before not to worry if we tuned into an energy we were unsure of, as our guides would take care of us. I even questioned whether Derek's 'guide' was a guide.

Were we receiving contradictory instructions about how to access the eggs, the 'information,' and the Oneness, or was that merely foggy perception on my part? I decided we were definitely not asking the right questions, or simply not asking the questions right.

Before trading places, Derek and I had quite a discussion about the session. I strongly objected to the 'guide' telling me 'there is a belief of not receiving.' Stuff and nonsense! That's never been part of my belief system! I really smelled a rat.

Now it was Derek's turn to ask questions as I sat in the chair. We followed the usual procedure, and finally Derek began a conversation with my guide. "Diana felt uneasy about the answers she was getting earlier."

"It is necessary that you both ascertain the source supplying you with information or answers to questions. You yourselves become familiar with the energies coming through you, but, for the person sitting opposite asking the questions, it is not always easy to recognize or identify those specific energies or personalities."

"I sensed the energy didn't feel quite right," Derek admitted, "But I wanted to see if the answers would seem credible, or were being made up."

"As some of the answers seemed questionable to you, it would perhaps have been better to have terminated the session sooner, but Diana, too, wished to see where the responses would lead. It is advisable to be specific about whom you request. Ask for a specific guide. Do not be vague. Asking for 'the most appropriate' is not specific enough for the information that you seek."

"Sometimes we've asked for a certain guide by name and haven't received a response."

"You do not need to have a specific name until you are able to identify the energy 'signature'; for now, a specific designation or title would be appropriate. It is all part of your learning. When you are reading through the transcripts you will find certain keys, certain small pieces of information that will be valuable to you."

"When working with the onyx eggs, are we to direct questions to the eggs themselves strictly through the guides whom we have invited to join us?" Derek asked.

"It is your choice whether you do this or not. You may wish to channel information from the higher spiritual realms; using the onyx as a focal point, or focusing upon it to begin the process, is one method you may try. However, it is for you to choose what you are wishing to access, whether it is words of spiritual advice or information.

"Before sleep at night, it would be appropriate to ask your Higher Selves to inspire you with questions that would elicit the answers that you are seeking; the inspiration may be in those first thoughts that are on your mind as you awaken. Be guided by what intuitively feels appropriate."

"Books on the market at the moment, are they to pave the way for other information which is coming through?"

"Yes. It adds to the collection of information which helps to break peoples' patterns, ones that have been set up for centuries. Many are ready to let go of certain beliefs, and this information will help serve in that way."

"Some appear to take a few shots at certain religious organizations or sects for the control that has been exercised over people."

"*This is only if they wish to see it as control. Others may not view it as such, even though it may appear to be written down in that form for control. Many feel they are receiving help from those organizations; or they are part of organizations that consider they are doing what is right, and they may believe others are here to destroy, or are jealous of what they have. Each believes according to their choice of experience.*"

"Are we going to be able to access the information we are seeking?"

"*You are accessing some of the information at this moment, even though, on the surface, it does not appear that you are.*"

"In our future attempts to access the information, is it best to tune in to the questions that are to be asked, while at the same time tuning into the energies we're channeling, in order to find out for ourselves what is appropriate?"

"*Yes. Each attempt brings you closer to that which you are seeking. At the present time you have not found the true basis whereby you can trust what is coming through. What you are experiencing is a perfectly normal response and it is associated with the perceived necessity of having a name to relate to.*

"*In your desire to relate with one particular energy, you are, in a way, restricting yourselves from receiving the best or highest energy that may come through. Nevertheless, it is advisable for you to continue with your present procedure until the conditions are right and you are confident within yourselves that the manner in which you are asking and the words or key phrases you are using are correct.*

"*Once you are familiar with your key phrases for the appropriate energy, like gears meshing together, the correct chord will be struck and the information will flow. Each attempt to find this key brings you closer to your goal.*

"*Many changes have been occurring for you, many adjustments are being made on either side with you and your partner and with the energies. You are finding that, as your own vibrational rate changes and adjustments are made, a little disharmony may occur within your normal routine, in your actions and reactions with each other. Nevertheless, as you become more patient with each other, you will realize that this is all part of the process,*" this very informative guide revealed.

"*As fine-tuning is occurring on the spiritual level, it is needed on physical, mental, and emotional levels also. Before perfect harmony can be achieved, it is like this little energy here needs a push in this direction, and this one over here needs a certain adjustment, too.*

"*It will all assist you for the final process when you acquire your key phrase or phrases. There is no magical set of words that you must pronounce to invoke a certain* energy or entity to appear or be present, it is just a group of words that will bring the comfort and the knowing that indeed this is the right energy that you are communicating with."

"We're searching for the right procedure so we may be sure of who or what we're dealing with," Derek explained. "Earlier, Diana asked again about the onyx eggs and accessing information on the Oneness. Are the eggs themselves a focus to use whilst seeking to channel information from the Oneness, or do they contain information?"

"Yes to both questions. There is connectedness with the Oneness and because of this there is information within the onyx, as there is information within all things. It is also true that, by holding the onyx eggs, they are being used as the focus to assist in tuning in to higher vibrational frequencies, in the same way that you use crystals, in the same way that you use the energy of a piece of music to put self into a receptive state.

"By taking hold of something, you are in effect combining your energies with those of the object that you are holding, and a communion of energies or spirits takes place at a certain level.

"Now, whether you wish to access the information that is inherent within all forms of onyx, indeed all things, then that is information which is available to you. And this is not implying that which is within the onyx is inferior or superior in any way to the information which is within all things; it is but a different part, a different facet, a different aspect or expression of the Oneness, yet unique in its own energy.

"But whichever way you perceive it, the answers that you were receiving were in fact correct," the guide assured us.

"While we've been asking questions all these weeks, we haven't been quite getting the responses we were looking for. As I was channeling a few moments ago, being in an altered state, I was aware of the questions and answers, and in the tone of Diana's words I sensed her disbelief in what we are receiving and the feeling of 'Oh, it's just another day gone by'. Is the reason we haven't received anything because within ourselves we don't believe we'll receive it?"

"Maybe your perception of what you were picking up from Diana was not her disbelief, but the concern that you share for making sure you have the correct bearer of information rather than one that can be spinning a fine web of deceit for you.

"But, you see, each time that you sit to channel, and every attempt you make is, in fact, bringing you closer to the goal you are seeking. It is very true that practice makes perfect. It is very true that you already have sufficient information to put into book form at the moment, even though it may not appear to be the information you are seeking to include within the book. This is your judgment.

"The whole process is serving the purpose of building up confidence in your abilities and mutual trust in yourselves and those with whom you are working. It is understandable that you wish only the truth. This is very commendable. Many would be delighted with whatever came through and would write it and sell it as being the truth, and many unsuspecting souls would accept at face value what was written—because everyone is searching for answers. You have the onyx, but you are leaving no stone unturned to find the right answers, and this is good; it hones your skills. It also proves that you are determined in your search," the guide again reassured us.

"We have talked previously about how we acquired the onyx eggs. Is there a specific purpose for these eggs?" Derek asked.

"Yes. Both have a purpose. The one that is being held now, and the other to which your attention was guided, the same information is contained within each. They were fashioned in the ovoid shape purely as a symbolic expression. The egg contains the information of all life, as you know it, the secrets of life itself—if this ancient knowledge, available to all, is to be called 'secret.' Really, there are no secrets; there is just a record of that which was created in the beginning by the Oneness."

"Would it be appropriate at this time for the egg to share some of its information with us?" Derek asked.

"You see, it is not just the egg that will share the information, it is the egg and its energy. That is the energy of the Oneness, and when accessed, will reveal information. It is not specifically the egg that is relaying information, it is the Infinite Creative Intelligence of the God Essence, the Consciousness of All-That-Is, which is within all things," the guide replied with great enlightenment.

"Then, am I correct in assuming that the egg is just a focal point for accessing the information?"

"For you, it is the focus, that is correct, and whatever questions come into your mind when contact is made with the egg, this opens the channel for the communication.

"Your attention was drawn to the egg so that you could be told that the time is now and that you are ready to continue with your work in this way. There has been a purpose set aside for you, something that you must do and which you have chosen to do, in order to assist others on their path to the Oneness.

"Unfortunately, in this age in which you are living, many things have to be brought to the attention of others in a way that is a little, shall we say, flamboyant. It has to be done in a way that will catch the attention of other people, whether it is an event about which you speak, or whether it is information that hasn't been transmitted via the normal means; it must be presented differently so that it will attract attention.

"Many seek information from the written word; there are many who are ready to partake of it; they will read it.

"The egg is a different focus. It is a different way of distinguishing yourselves from others, from other works that have been written. It has been carefully designed. And if the onyx you are holding had not caught your eye when it did, then your attention would have been caught in another way so that the information is allowed to flow. Each time either of you are tuning in to the energy of the onyx egg, you are tuning in to the energy of the Infinite Creator, to the Oneness."

"When tuning into the Oneness, sometimes we sense there are other influences that want to interfere and either misguide or stop the transmission with interruptions of physical discomfort."

"Do not be put off by other influences. You will know as the information comes through whether it is correct information or whether it is from one of these influences of which you speak. If you are fearful that you are allowing one to communicate that is not of the Light, then, by all means, refrain from the transmission. But, if this energy is already with you, be reassured we are taking care of you as we have done from the beginning. We do not say this lightly, as we know the importance to you is great. However, you will know when there are intruders, and if it is an intruder speaking, then you may dismiss it, and the information.

"But do not deprive yourself of the opportunity to communicate because of your fear. As you align yourselves, you are aligning with the energies which are of a very high vibration, although initially you might get interferences from those you don't wish to communicate with, or who don't wish you to communicate. As your own vibrations are raised, you will recognize that communication coming from the source you are seeking. It will assist you, shall we say, in being able to unload any intruders. Just trust. Allow yourself to attune with the highest," the guide advised.

"We want to be sure the information is coming from the proper source."

"And it is appreciated that you wouldn't just press on and deceive. We know that is not the intent and therefore every assistance will be given to you. You have been brought together to complete a work. Other experiences are coming into play merely as a part of strengthening your own beliefs and your own abilities. The interferences, even though unwanted or undesirable, were beneficial because they caused you to become more alert, more aware. You were shown ways to deal with those situations and ways to protect yourselves. They have served a useful purpose."

"I understand. By establishing regular contact we find ourselves becoming more confident," Derek related.

"It is important to pursue what is being given to you. In your determination to continue, the determination to follow the right path, the determination to project your light throughout each day, you have been shown in some small measure how you are to pursue the work. *The more you become involved with it, the more the energy is directed into it, the more it will fashion and function for you.*

"There will be a time when your own light is projected at all times, as you remember and consciously become that which you seek, and then 'protection' will no longer be necessary. But it begins with what you have come to regard as the ritual of creating your own 'protection,' becoming aware of and expanding the light within, the light that you truly are. The ritual is to assist you in your recognition and remembering of that which you are.

"The time will come when information will flow simply as you take hold of the egg, without consciously performing any preliminaries. By that time, you will have become so accustomed to working from within your own light at all times the energy will be with you and you will be aligned, because, by then, you will be living according to the Law of One."

As we reflected upon what had just been said, Derek and I were in agreement: this appeared to be information of the highest order; it reassured us that we were on the right track and could now endeavor to refine our channeling techniques. Had we finally opened the right door? And if so, were we prepared for the next grade of this exacting 'High' School?

Chapter 13

It goes without saying that both Derek and I check and double-check again to see if the information we are receiving jives. If we doubt something, or if we think we are on to something wonderful, we will each take turns asking the same question over again until we feel satisfied that the information tallies. You have to give us an 'E' for effort, or at least a 'P' for persistence.

After weeks of groping in the dark, after being told I was going to write a book and finding things didn't flow exactly the way I expected, and asking for names as we channeled and not getting any or ones we suspected, I was disappointed and dissatisfied. I wanted to get to the bottom of things...or to the top, whichever way you look at it.

One morning as I began 'interrogating' the unseen guest, I felt I was communicating with a sort of 'businesslike' or 'emotionless' type of energy. Emotionless is probably the wrong word I'm searching for; it was just more detached.

I asked if we had spoken before, and received a 'no' response. Then I asked if the guide worked specifically with Derek. Again I got a 'no.' Intrigued, I continued questioning. "If you work with others also, does that mean you are the equivalent, in my understanding of, say, an Oversoul, a supervising guide overseeing a group of people?"

"You could say that."

"The others you are working with, are they in this reality, or are they in a different reality?"

"There are some in your own, and others in different realities."

"To help us understand this more, could you explain the different realities?" I invited.

"How do you wish these other realities to be explained?"

"What realities are they? Can you can explain in a way that we could understand?"

"You are very much aware of several realities, whether it's the physical reality that you are in—in human life form—or the reality of spirit. Another reality is the extraterrestrial. There is a reality within the earth, within the air, within each planet. There are different realities within the time/space continuum. Many realities exist within each dimension," was the succinct answer.

"Am I correct in assuming that each one of us has at least one guide from the spiritual reality working with us, and also one from the extraterrestrial reality, a cosmic guide?" I asked.

"You have several guides and assistants from both."

"If we have several from both of those realities, how is it decided who works with us?"

"Prior to incarnating, each soul chooses what it wishes to experience in a given lifetime. If one chooses, say, to become an instrument through which information or healing energies are to be channeled, then certain agreements are made at that time. At some time during the earthly or physical lifespan, the soul who has chosen to channel these energies will seek out ways to develop abilities that will enable it to do so.

"Some do this in order to teach others, either through writing about their experiences, talking about them, or teaching in a classroom or group situation. At these times, many different guides may come through to handle the different forms of energies during the different stages of development and growth.

"This gives the guides, and those wishing to channel, the opportunity to work together. After a period of time, when a person's vibratory rate has been raised considerably, other higher energies or guides may take over because the person's energy has become more compatible with the finer vibrations. Each has to become accustomed to the vibrations of the other; their vibrations must match up for compatibility."

"So our guides are constantly changing, as we constantly change our vibratory level?"

"This is part of the reason."

"One reads of people who seemingly haven't studied metaphysics and all of a sudden they see an illuminated entity or being manifest that begins dictating material for a book. Are these people more clairvoyant than others?"

"It may appear as if they are newcomers to the experience, but they may have done this in several incarnations. When a soul is ready to take on a chosen task for this lifetime, an opportunity presents itself for the awakening to occur without due hardship for that person; that is the time for the being to manifest," came another clarification.

"Each soul is guided, but is allowed to make its own decisions. Sometimes, because decisions are made on a level other than the conscious one, this could cause a person to be

amazed at what transpires when a being appears. One may feel one never consciously asked for such a thing to occur."

"Have Derek and I done this type of work before?"

"Several times."

"So, what we are attempting to do now is...?"

"Remembering, and fine tuning the instruments to raise your awareness, not only of the reality in which you are presently observing and participating, but also the several other realities that are going on within the same time and space," the guide answered quickly and with clarity. *"As your awareness grows and you become familiar with how to handle these other realities, you will be able to pass this information on to others.*

"You have skills that you are unaware of at this moment, ones that you are developing and fine-tuning. As each new experience comes your way, you have the opportunity to assimilate, put it into practice and record the results. You are using your own intuition and feelings to discern if the energies are safe to work with, or if you should close off the session and start over. And you are aware of the inspiration as it is given to you, such as how to place your hands when healing, changing the arrangement of the crystals you are using, and discerning when it is appropriate to pass on information you receive at that time."

"You say we have both been writers before. It seems we are using quite a long-winded process. Am I suffering from delusions thinking that one day the writing is just going to flow? At the moment it seems that we are just talking to someone we can't see, who won't give a name, and as a result a book is to be published. It seems like more should be occurring than this. What we're struggling to do, so far, hasn't given us anything that's any different from what umpteen other people out there already seem to have received, and with apparent relative ease," I complained with candor, I thought.

"On the surface it may appear simple for others if you are comparing what you are doing to what others have written, but some of these people took three to five years, if not longer, to complete their works. They have gone through learning to hone their skills, or they may have expended considerable effort doing research. Those who seem to write book after book may have taken years acquiring the background, in order for them to write on their chosen subjects."

"Isn't that when one is writing on a purely one-reality, physical level and doing it without consciously asking for assistance? This isn't what we are doing."

I realized I must have sounded like a whining child fussing because someone else was getting a larger piece of cake, and decided I'd better change my approach. "I guess, in fairness to ourselves, comparing the years others may take with their first book and what we have accomplished in little more than three months, we're perhaps ahead of schedule."

In the words that followed, there were absolutely no changes of pace in delivery, no hint of reaction to my complaints, no offence taken, no attempt to placate. I was impressed.

"You have developed skills you are unaware of, sensitivity, an inner-knowingness, and the trust that you are developing as the inspiration is coming through will build until the greater part of what is to be put down is received. Yes, there is some information that is superfluous. But it is there for a reason, so you may fine-tune your skills and judge for yourselves whether information that is given, and about which you have written, is worthy of being placed in a book or is just to fill up the page."

"We were not just wanting to fill up the page," I said hastily, "we were hoping for 'new' information that other people will find very interesting, things to assist others in their search. If we write about all the hardships or difficulties we've had whilst writing, how will that give others any inspiration to persevere?"

"This is the side of writing very few see. Some authors do give the impression that they woke up one morning and wonderful information and inspiration just came to them and now they are successful writers—just by waking up. Some have awakened, but don't know the source of the information, whether it's from one in another reality who's playing a game, or one who's actually bringing out the highest potential for the assistance of all."

"When writing before, I just assumed I had a gift for writing, and yet, what I'm doing now is so far removed from that other way."

"It is best to learn how to saddle a horse before you ride the animal, so that you do not slip off when it is in full stride. All the jobs you've had, the previous training, all is assisting you now, even though, at times, you wonder why you are doing things this way; it seems so far removed."

"When I first began working at a newspaper, I had been a freelance writer; I didn't have any formal training in that area, but I was able to bluff my way through. It's as if the words were magically given to me and I became competent and very successful. I guess it was all training for now. I have now learned there are different ways of writing, whether by just allowing words to flow, or recording information this way and transcribing it into the written word."

"You are aware of the intuition and guidance that is given, and you now realize that this guidance has always been with you, even though when you received that first job as a newspaper reporter you were oblivious to guidance that led you there," the guide pointed out.

"That was how I wanted to earn my living. If I was a writer in previous lifetimes, then surely that would explain my ability to write," I retorted, with a twinge of impatience.

"Because of imprinting and commonly passed judgments, sometimes the overall picture is not seen. If you look at, say, becoming a writer, a pilot, or a doctor, these careers or avenues cause you to realize that this is the goal, this is where you are at now, and that is where you wish to be. And at the end of all the studying or training, that is all you need to see.

"But look at the overall picture of your own life; there are skills and qualities that have been honed besides that of the writer. You have raised a family, taken care of other people. You are also a healer, taking in people and assisting them; you have a profession to work with people in another way. And you are teaching others through your classes, meditations and writings. All of this has assisted in creating what you are today, well rounded and balanced. You're not just laboriously working at a desk day after day, processing paper. Far more is going on behind the scenes, and you are reaching many people at different levels.

"This is just to show that a bigger picture is being created; while you are now taking care of only a handful of people at a time, through the writing you may reach thousands, even millions."

"Say someone has an ambition and wishes to follow a certain profession or trade in a specific area. He's convinced he has a gift or calling, believing he's a 'naturally born pilot' or whatever, like the ten year old kid who can fly a plane whilst standing on his head viewing the control panels from upside down. Doesn't it mean that the 'natural gift' was in fact because he learned those skills in a previous lifetime?" I challenged, still flogging the same horse.

"A person may acquire skills in this lifetime in order to establish self-confidence or independence, to be able to handle decisions, the operation of a machine, whether an airplane or a printing press. It may seem the person carries the skills from one lifetime or another; that is possible. It is also possible that the person needs to hone certain skills or develop a trust in his or her ability to use the machine, and it appears to come easily."

"Then what about those born into certain families where they are encouraged to carry on the family tradition because of the parents' wishes? They may end up with a trade, skill, or profession they don't even like. What would be the reason for that?" I asked, almost belligerently.

"There are several reasons this may occur. It may just be an issue between parent and child. One may choose an existence with certain people and with certain conditions to overcome in order for the soul's growth. It may be to understand that one does not have to con-

tinue with choices that were selected, that one does, in fact, have the freedom to choose or to change. Or it may be that the soul chose the parents who would provide the best background for following family tradition."

I marveled again that the guide hadn't taken umbrage at my tone of voice, and decided I'd better continue on a more reasonable note. "Am I right, then, in thinking we don't choose our incarnations in a linear fashion, one after the other with each following, say, in chronological order? And is it true that this lifetime we are living now may have been chosen many lifetimes ago to experience these lessons at this time?" I asked.

"They are all chosen at the same time. When the soul decides it is going to experience all things, at that time the pattern for the experiences is already set, as if within the blinking of an eye. Imagine a spinning top as it begins to pick up speed, if a drop of moisture falls onto that spinning top, it is sent out in all directions in fine particles. In the same way, when the choice is made, liken it to that one drop that is sent out and spins off as all the lifetimes, all incarnations and experiences are chosen at the one time."

I thanked the guide for being so patient with me and brought the session to a close. But I felt glum. I was disappointed at myself. And nothing was going the way I expected or wanted. Sure, we were getting some good responses here and there, yet delivery was slow, and sometimes rather bland; the proceedings had lost a certain flamboyance. I felt shortchanged.

Breakfast didn't help my mood at all, and later, as I transcribed the tape, I felt even worse. I walked into Derek's room and, without saying a word, flopped onto a chair. Derek knew at once it was time to check in with Kalindras, the guide I had been told would be with me for the duration of the book.

Kalindras, bless his soul, quickly put things in perspective: long hours at the office were taking their toll and it was time for a break. Derek agreed. A fleeting weekend trip to the West Coast would provide a welcome change, and to really cheer me up, he'd take me to visit an importer of crystals to look at the latest acquisitions from Brazil. And with that, a snap decision was made for a pre-dawn start for the twelve-hour drive to Vancouver.

Although our long drive was eventful and tiring, our arrival in Vancouver left us with ample time to visit Derek's favorite crystal merchant. Within moments Derek carefully placed in my arms a large hunk of dark green geode; I staggered under the rock's weight, its hollow interior richly lined with large amethyst crystals of deep purple hue. It was 'love at first hold.' This grotto-shaped eye-catcher would look good in our healing room, I hinted. My man agreed. I love him....

The sun had already set as we finished our transaction, but Derek had another surprise in store. He wanted to take me to an energy vortex near Third Beach in Stanley Park. My anticipation heightened as Derek parked our jalopy. He reached for a large flashlight and then indicated the direction of an old concession building.

The moon above escorted us to a path between the trees and several minutes later we were off the beaten track, on our own with Mother Nature. We inched our way along a trail lined by leviathan trees. I wished we could have been there whilst it was still daylight, as I would have loved to feast my eyes upon the colors and textures of bark and foliage.

There was an ethereal quality to the scene as Derek carefully guided me over enormous roots, some as thick as the trunks of their neighboring cousins. Lacy fingers of pale moonlight reached way down through the tall evergreens and deciduous trees, pointing to ghostly silhouettes of ferns and shrubs.

I shivered as Derek led me to a circular clearing hugged by seven mighty trees. As I walked within their embrace, I held out my arms; I could actually 'feel' a tall column or pillar of energy in front of me and when I stepped further into the vortex, I felt an invisible force pushing me gently backwards. Standing there, swaying, I momentarily closed my eyes, overcome by a feeling of deep respect for the majesty of nature. Then I leaned against a tree for support; I'm not sure how long I was there, but I was aware of fully imbibing nature's smorgasbord through all the physical senses as I breathed in damp forest smells laced with salty air from the sea.

After a while, Derek guided me gently down through the trees and onto the beach. I mentally tuned in and invited Kalindras to be with me to witness this timeless harmonic convergence of ocean and shore, and then I followed Derek to the water's edge. The restless waves of the incoming tide raced to within inches of our toes as we faced the horizon. I could hear the ocean talking to me as I acknowledged her roar, and the white tips danced back and forth in front of us in the wild ebb and flow of a stormy quadrille. The wind whispered a message in my ears and then it wrapped itself around me, holding me in a long caress.

Then I understood. Because Kalindras was with me, all of my senses had swung into high gear; all sounds, smells, taste, even the touch of the wind as it caressed my cheeks; all were highly magnified. The physical sensation of feeling nature so intensely anchored me to the surroundings, and as I gazed out over the ocean and up into a sky adorned with stars, I detected traces of distant memories paused at the edge of time and space. Then I heard Kalindras saying that this 'energy of renewal' would prepare me for the next part of my 'journey.' I sensed that both Derek and I were being prepared for something major ahead.

* * *

Back home again, revived by our break in routine, Derek, bless his heart, began another session. Either we're slow learners, our hearing needs some adjustment, or we're just plain optimists. He began by stating, "We would like to know who we are channeling. It seems we are having difficulty obtaining a name."

"Giving a name would make it so easy for you."

"It's either that, or we might call upon that energy to work too much!" Derek joked, and added quickly, "No, I'm just making light of the situation."

"If continually called upon, we would deem it a great honor to be working with you both."

"Thank you. We enjoy the process."

"You don't have to go through this process, [to acquire the information or to channel] *but it is one that you have chosen to go through."*

"Some people seem to be able to just sit down and channel and they have a whole book in no time, yet I often feel we are plodding away and not really getting anywhere. Why is this?"

"Those you refer to may see the same vision or being manifest frequently, they are certain of the energy and they know where it is coming from. In time, you also may do the same and be given information that way, but, as you have chosen to work for it, you are being guided and encouraged to do that."

"Who would choose to make things difficult when it would be so easy just to have everything given to us?" Derek laughed; he was enjoying this conversation.

"Someone who wishes to show others how to do it. Does that sound familiar?"

"Yes," Derek beamed. "All too familiar."

"Not only do you understand what is meant when we say you create your own reality, you are also endeavoring to create another reality for others, by showing that this is possible for them, too," the guide continued in a more serious tone. *"They may believe that this can only be done by certain individuals who wake up one morning and find they have this wonderful ability, and the information just flows, or they have a brilliant, luminous being who manifests and dictates everything to be written down. This isn't the norm for*

most people. Yet most people have within self several wonderful books that could be written to assist others like themselves.

"And when your readers realize that these gifts are their own inheritance, as are their other psychic gifts, they, too, will become willing to explore the possibilities and seek out those who can assist in doing exactly as you are doing, in a safe way, so that they, too, can learn to sift through the information they may be given and use their own judgment as to whether it is valid or invalid.

"What you have written will be published as it sets out the guidelines and the warnings, the care that must be taken," the guide assured us with cryptic conviction. "Drawing upon your own experiences, you not only give precautions and safe procedures, you also show others how to set up their own protection and why it is necessary.

"You will also show the importance of recognizing and acting upon one's own inner responses and signals. In this lifetime, although somebody brings you into this world, you are on your own and you go out of this world alone. And everything that happens to you, from beginning to end, revolves around your decisions, the lessons you learn and how you learn them. And when you need help and advice, the greatest and truest help and advice you can rely upon is that which comes from within. So it is important to teach how to discern what information can be trusted, in the way you teach your students.

"Continually seeking help and guidance outside of self is part and parcel of the learned behavior of giving away your own power to others. If you begin to go within, to trust, to rely on self for answers, beginning with the instinctual responses and later by consulting with the Higher Self, you will find that lessons become a lot easier. Conditions that are initially seen as problems are recognized as being learning situations or challenges.

"Answers or solutions to challenges are much more quickly found and applied when you have reliable advice and assistance. But where is that going to come from? Are you going to follow what other people think is best for you, or do you wish to follow that which you know is right for you? The only way to know that which is right for you is to find it from within."

Derek told me afterwards his body 'felt' that these were very important truths; he gets a fine tingling sensation across his shoulders whenever he receives 'truths,' sort of a 'confirmation' that it's something he should pay attention to. He sat on the edge of his seat as the guide continued:

"To the beginner, this may seem to be an insurmountable problem. Some may say: 'That's alright for those who know how to do this.' You all know. Some of you have simply forgotten this.

"You will find that, frequently, people you endeavor to assist or teach will come running to you for answers, because, out of habit, that is what they have learned to do, but it is not in their best interests," the guide cautioned. "It is time for them to learn again how to be able to stand on their own feet, and the only way to do that is by becoming reliant on self. This is not implying relying upon one's ego. We refer to the true self, the inner-self, the all-knowing self, the Higher Self or soul essence that was created and is still connected with the Universal Oneness you call God, as you have been reminding your students."

The following day, I could tell from the enthusiasm in Derek's voice that he was hoping I had tuned in to the same energy. After exchanging greetings he spoke in a lighthearted tone. "I know we've talked before." He paused expectantly, hoping for a response. Undaunted when nothing was said, he continued, "We've spoken about how we would like the information to flow smoother and faster. We do recognize we've chosen this way so we could show others all the ups and downs, the ins and outs, but I still think Diana would wish to have a faster delivery."

"Your choice was not necessarily made on a conscious level. When you have known something, when words have flowed easily and you have tasted success, you become familiar with a certain format or routine. When one who is experienced at writing chooses to change the format or routine, perhaps it is to assist others who have not had similar experience but could be enticed to try for themselves and who would indeed find this book to be a learning tool.

"The book that you are writing will give others encouragement and inspiration to seek for self. Even if it gives only a single person inspiration, it will bear fruit. If that person goes forward and becomes reacquainted with nature, say, and within that new awareness finds the true meaning of his or her own spirituality, it is a wonderful accomplishment. That one person will become an example to others and pass on the knowledge to others so they, too, may follow suit."

By the tone of voice and the slow, precise manner of delivery, Derek was convinced he had communicated with this 'guide' before, and it's not in his nature to let an opportunity slip by if he feels he's on to something. He asked, boldly, "Have we spoken before?"

"Yes."

"Then may I know to whom I am speaking?"

"You may."

"Do you have a name we can use?"

"Yes."

"Then to whom am I speaking?" Derek laughed; he suspected someone really wanted him to work for an answer.

"Kajuni."

"Kajuni? Hi! It's an honor to be speaking with you again. I remember now...we were 'introduced' at one of our Channeling Workshops. Does this mean I may ask for you by name every day from now on, to assist?"

"On your quest for the information you seek, this is not what you have chosen. But there will be other occasions for us to talk. It is appropriate for us to talk today because both of you have been thinking about fragmentation of the soul, more particularly, different aspects of the soul."

"That's right!" Derek said with surprise. "But it wasn't exactly on the agenda today."

"Desiring to experience all things," Kajuni began, *"the soul may choose to fragment itself so that different aspects of self may experience and learn simultaneously, not linearly as you use time measurement; much learning can be experienced in the now."*

"As we are speaking, as something is presented to you, there is a knowingness coming from deep within." Kajuni paused for emphasis. *"And when people are prepared to accept that indeed there are many aspects of themselves in different realities and dimensions, then it will come as no surprise as they awaken to this understanding and see another aspect of self.*

"They may not like that which they see, but if they have reached the stage where there is acceptance of all others, where they acknowledge and respect the divinity, the soul-essence within all of creation, then it will be easier to accept aspects of self with which they were unfamiliar.

"Now, when there is acceptance that each other human being is also an aspect of self, and has been since the conception of All-Life, it will be easier for the individual to understand and accept that all other species, here and elsewhere, are also aspects of self."

"I understand this," Derek acknowledged, "but isn't it possible that fragments of our own soul may have become earthbound and did not return to the Light to carry on?"

"There is always a possibility for everything. But there are some things that it seems almost best, shall we say, to ignore for the present, things that are remote possibilities. If you start putting energy to words, to something that may be a possibility, it could distract you from what is more appropriate for you to be pursuing at this time. Singleness of purpose in following one's set goal will take one to a destination far more quickly than when making many detours.

"There are many different planets and many different life forms which also have multiple aspects of themselves in that experience. If you are going to include all of those possibilities, I am afraid, my friend, much confusion may occur. It is better to direct your energy into what you are seeking at the moment, otherwise you may be going merrily around in

circles like the animal trying to catch its tail and never quite succeeding," Kajuni continued, somewhat humorously.

Derek told me afterwards he felt like saying, 'Hang on here! Slow the horses down,' as he wanted to digest what had been said, but not wanting interrupt a response of this depth, he kept his mouth shut and inched further back in his chair.

"There is such a vastness, more than an ocean, more than a universe, of possibilities," Kajuni went on. *"In your training you have learned that you are limited only by your imagination. Everything you could possibly conceive, or dream to conceive, is a possibility. The human mind is an incredible phenomenon of creativity but most of you have absolutely no concept of its capabilities.*

"But regarding other realities and possibilities, know this: when an issue requires particular attention, and you have found this already, energy is created to bring that issue to the forefront. If it is not attended to, energy will be generated to recreate the scenario again and again. When necessary for you, or appropriate for you to explore the many other diversions—shall we call them the many other aspects of All-self that are out there—they will crop up in your reality one by one, to be dealt with at that particular time, to allow the natural sequence of things to occur. Know, too," Kajuni emphasized, *"that nothing is ever brought into your reality or awareness before you are ready to deal with it."*

That, to Derek, seemed to be another, more profound way of saying, 'When the student is ready the teacher will appear,' and so, if those other aspects of self are us, we are actually our own teachers! Ironic, isn't it?

There had been a pause in the dialogue as if Kajuni was giving Derek time to think, and then he answered Derek's unspoken question, *"It is important to work on accepting oneself first. It is important to love oneself, although, when a person has been taught to believe poorly of self, this may seem hard at first, as it may be in that person's perception that he or she is unworthy. Very often self is the last one to be accepted."*

"That is an understatement," Derek threw in.

"One of the first steps is to recognize the divinity of spirit, the Divine Essence, within everything, within all creation, to recognize the divinity within every person whose skin may be a different color, or one who speaks a different language yet his skin is the same, one who is being referred to as a foreigner, meaning something that is foreign to oneself. Begin by acknowledging that we are all indeed brothers and sisters," Kajuni stressed.

"The next step is recognizing the divinity within all the animals, all the creatures upon and in the earth and bodies of water, recognizing the divinity within all the plant life and the mineral kingdom, and also recognizing the divinity within the elements. When

people are able to do this honestly, being truly honest with themselves, their progress really takes leaps and bounds."

"Is there any particular order, or which step should be taken first?" Derek inquired.

"The order in which this is done does not have to be a hard and fast rule, but it is good to recognize the divinity within all people, because it is with other humankind that your greater learning takes place. With continued persistence, it does become easier, even if there is dislike or intolerance towards someone, or a type of person, or thing, or type of species. It is not just necessary to love and recognize the divinity within people whose skin is a different color, whose race, religion, creed are different; it is also necessary to recognize that divinity within those persons judged to be, say, fat or thin, or beautiful, ugly, or deformed, or those viewed as living a life of deprivation or embracing a lifestyle condemned as not conforming to certain moral codes, or one that is considered to be unattainable, out of our reach." Kajuni added, pausing again for emphasis.

"For many of us, that will be quite a tall order to fill," Derek responded.

"There are so many intolerances towards each other, yet each and every human being is a mirror image of an aspect of self. Some believe in the supremacy of one group or race, religion or belief. These are the ones who will have most difficulty accepting the different realities, for they are blinded by their own prejudices; they have chosen the hardest lessons to learn.

"Enlightenment begins with the decision to start and continue to radiate love and light towards all, and that includes self. But it is important for all to understand that telling people to love and respect themselves is not telling them to puff out their own egos," Kajuni reminded us.

"People with the strongest opinions, the strongest dislikes, the strongest aversions and prejudices, have a most difficult path to walk. And all, including those displaying the greatest amount of intolerance towards other people, whether those of a sect or a group or a race, they have indeed chosen to learn that way. The impact is powerful, however, when the true realization dawns that we are all One; and as that realization sets in, then there is much rejoicing, above."

There was softness in tone as Kajuni continued. "There is a uniqueness about being human and the human condition, because of the emotions. Earth is the planet of emotions. There is beauty and purpose in all things, including emotion. It is for each to find that beauty and that purpose. But it is necessary to find that purpose and that beauty from the heart, not from the head, not by rationalizing but by becoming aware of the pure emotion of unconditional love.

"We are all here to assist each other," Kajuni stressed, quietly, "even those condemned for living a certain way or criticized for the way they behave or do things, each in their own way assists. Whether it is by being the example of fairness and perfection personified, or reflecting to us perhaps an undesirable aspect of ourselves we do not wish to see, it is all for a specific purpose, each person acting out a specific role for our mutual learning.

"The ones we despise the most, those who appear to hurt us the most, the ones who frustrate us the most, or those who really test our patience might be the ones from whom we have the most to learn. And perhaps they are showing us what it is we need to recognize in ourselves and work upon for our progress, the progress of our soul.

"Within all this, man is learning. A great orchestration brings everything together, one family, one community, one nation, one planet within one universe within many universes. Each has its rightful place. Even the minutest speck of sand upon a beach, or particle of air or water, each has its own appropriate place, and each is dependent upon the other for its existence, in being part of the One Whole."

"Thank you, Kajuni," Derek whispered, as he brought the session to a close.

Wow, what an excellent assimilation of the aspects of the human condition, good and bad.

* * *

I guess we really are creatures of habit. In the middle of January 1995, we were still plodding along with the same old questions. Derek began: "It seems we're experiencing difficulty arranging for the appropriate guides to assist us. Can you suggest the types of questions we should ask?"

"Any perceived difficulties are just scenarios that you are creating for yourselves. What you are seeking is so simple to achieve, but you are overlooking the trust factor."

"Because of the fears we have?"

"It is because of not wanting to be misled; you are seeking the truth. There have been several suggestions made, each one equally valid. They were given merely for you to become more comfortable with what you are doing. You may find one more to your liking than another.

"There is a need to feel confident that what you are doing and what you are asking is correct. However, know that all questions are correct, because there is a reason for you asking each one. You might question why it is being asked, but there is a purpose."

"Are our reasons for not trusting because we do not trust ourselves?" Derek asked.

"Very much so. As much as doubting yourself."

"It has great impact when, as children, we are told we don't know anything."

"Or when it is suggested that you are telling untruths. All children seek approval; like children, you are still seeking approval. You are trying your best to receive information in the most perfect way, so that there will be no recriminations, no chastisements, no criticisms; and at the back of your minds you are also concerned that it must meet the approval of the other."

"That's true," Derek agreed. "Have you been reading my mind again?"

The guide passed over Derek's question and continued: *"But you also have to be prepared for the unusual and the unexpected. Don't be too hasty in dismissing what you receive. At least allow it to go through the process of being put into written form for you to read, and later, you might find that within the transmission there is surprising information that either strikes a chord or a remembrance. After that point, if anything appears to be highly suspect, you may discard it.*

"Many seeds are being sown as the words are given," the guide offered, *"but when words are first read, often those seeds are not obvious; that may be because one reads what one is expecting to read. Sometimes, certain phrases and passages are glossed over, because that is not what the eye of the reader is wishing to receive at that time, or maybe, is not ready to receive. Yet the seeds are there and will grow at the appropriate time."*

"Many people buy books and skip through them quickly, missing a lot," Derek threw in.

"If they are to receive information contained within a book and they have not already gleaned it from the first reading, when they are ready, they will go back to it."

"That is so true," Derek exclaimed. "Just recently, Di randomly opened a book she read ages ago and we found some very valuable information neither of us realized was there before."

"This is because, as you learn new things, understanding and awareness increases. What is read and interpreted initially is in accordance with the understanding of that time, but when passages or whole books are re-read, your attention is drawn back to words that now contain new meaning. The information was there beforehand, but you were not ready to receive it earlier."

Derek finally realized he was speaking to Kalindras, my writing companion. "I knew that," he grinned, pleased at recognizing the 'speaker,' and he nodded acknowledgment. "Even information we have written or recorded ourselves," he continued on track, "once it goes through the process of being entered into the computer and printed out, the message somehow seems different, more profound. There's something about the written word when you see it in front of you, as opposed to hearing the information; it can be the same, word for word, but often when we listen, we don't listen closely because we're too busy processing what we are hearing."

"You listen carefully to something that has specific meaning for you, but whilst attention is focused upon that, however, other words sometimes creep on by and you are not aware of what they have to say; you were too preoccupied with words that preceded them. Or information doesn't touch upon what you wish to know, so, as the questioner, you are formulating the next question, thinking how you can turn the conversation around so that your question is answered.

"Liken yourself to the prospector," Kalindras explained, painting a vivid picture. "You are panning for gold, and finding semi-precious gemstones in the process. You bypass the gemstones because you are specifically looking for gold. Later, when you find you haven't panned any gold in that day's work, you reflect back over what you did. And then, you remember. Somewhere there were gemstones that might be worth something! And so, you go back to retrieve them."

"I love these analogies; they put the point across so effectively," Derek enthused. "I am sure we will be looking for more than gold when we read the printout of today's session."

"Analogies sometimes create colorful pictures which prevent dialogue from becoming too dull; a splash of color makes the message more palatable."

"I was advised not to try mounting an old horse by climbing over its head," Derek laughed as he shared a recent analogy, "it was suggested I try mounting it from the side instead. It created a lot of amusement. The symbology was quite witty."

"Humor gets a message across quickly without taxing the brain," Kalindras offered, "and as you found, laughter goes a long way in assisting understanding."

Chapter 14

We finally tried out one of the procedures suggested to access information. Before going to bed one night, we both meditated briefly, and at that time I asked for the highest of my spiritual guides to be with me next morning to ask the correct questions; I also asked for another high spiritual guide to answer whatever questions Derek may ask.

The following morning, Derek took his place in the recliner in my office, holding Intensity, and after a few moments I welcomed the guide who greeted us. I don't remember my opening question, but I do know I had the onyx egg on my mind; at least I was trying to make sure I didn't ask the same old question again.

Something prompted me to ask about how all life started, how creation occurred. I was so taken by the very beautiful and humble words which came through that I failed to realize our recording equipment was still on pause, and so I lost the first part of the session. I remember being told that there are many books that explain 'creation' and I was impressed by the reverence with which things were being expressed, although I noted there were fairly long pauses in between my questions and the answers, as if the responses were being relayed from a distance.

The answers seemed so plausible and understandable, but it became obvious Derek was uncomfortable with what was coming through and he stopped the transmission.

With conscious voice channeling, the instrument or vehicle—the person whose body or voice is being used for the transmission, namely the person who is doing the channeling—remains fully conscious whilst in the altered state, in just the same way as a person in a light trance or under hypnosis. So, being conscious of what is going on, the vehicle is in control and can stop the transmission at any time. There's no pre-requisite to be 'unconscious' for this type of channeling.

I was really disappointed when Derek stopped the session. He explained he felt it wasn't an 'appropriate' question I had asked, because he didn't want to get involved with any Creation versus Darwin's theory of evolution, and, as there were long pauses in between the answers, he doubted their validity.

Although I understood where Derek was coming from and respected his decision to stop the session, I couldn't help thinking that perhaps his reluctance to continue had something to do with not feeling worthy enough to receive such information. 'Hey, that's too lofty a subject for an ordinary Joe like me to channel information about.'

We do know that the higher the guide, the finer the energy, and sometimes during transmissions the waves of energy do appear to fluctuate between statements; the energy literally comes in waves. The whole scenario may have been a test in trust. But if it was, we scored a big, fat zero, for as soon as Derek got out of the chair and we traded places, he rewound the tape and recorded over it as I began channeling; I was so disappointed when I found out later.

Of course, Derek had to ask the same question I had asked his guide. Now I could really feel my own hesitation. No wonder Derek chickened out. This was such a biggie, would my guide be able to respond? I had asked that question for his guides to answer, not mine! But here I was, in a rapid 'what goes around comes around' scenario, and I could sense my own stunned reaction.

"On the questions already raised this morning, could you give some information on the breaking away from Source, where we have come from, how we are endeavoring to return?" Derek asked my guide.

'It was anticipated that sooner or later you would arrive at this question; however, if your conscious intentions had been voiced earlier, we would have suggested you ask for those that we feel are more qualified to answer. As was stated earlier, it is in many of your books; however, the desire to ask for the information to be repeated in current day language and in a way that can be accepted by all is understood," my guide responded.

"I was unsure about the information I was receiving, so I decided that it would be more appropriate to have Diana try it," Derek admitted.

'Now you see, the moment you begin to doubt any information, it makes it difficult for the responses to come through because that doubt creates a barrier. The Creative Force, as you described it earlier [in our discussion after he had stopped the channeling, Derek had referred to this Force] *are the words that were given to you. It is almost impossible and extremely limiting using words to attempt to give a fitting description of the Creative Force. However, we will attempt to communicate a brief picture.*

"The Creative Force is the living expression of That Which Is, sometimes called God, or The Oneness, The Great Spirit, God-Goddess-All-That-Is, The Source," the guide began. *"It is a force, an energy, forever expanding and is an expression of Itself.*

"Life, as you would term it, was given as an immense outpouring of the love vibration, which It Is. And during this outpouring, minute particles of the Creative Force were expelled outwards in the way that a volcano bursts forth and erupts. Words are inadequate to describe the magnitude of what occurred.

"In the outpouring, many stars and universes were created, and many souls, minute replicas of Itself, were generated outwards. Large clusters of energy were formed. Each of these particles of energy, teeming with the creative properties as expressions of Oneness, took many forms, and they began to drift further away from the Creative Force. As the energy moved, there was a settling in the cosmos, and many different life forms grew."

At this point the words stopped. As they were being spoken, I was experiencing a combination of intense impressions, sensations and feelings that my heart was exploding outwards, and I had fleeting pictures crossing my inner vision as if I were witnessing some long dormant memory. I began describing what I was feeling and seeing:

"I am sensing a massive activity going on, like an explosion; I can feel energy bursting outwards; there are particles which seem to come together like gaseous combinations of different elements. It is like certain molecules attracting certain molecules in the ebb and flow of a current. It's similar to the energy that's created when something is thrown into a body of water, yet it isn't water, and concentric circles are formed and expand outwards; they go in all directions. I am seeing the vastness, as if one were out in the universe, in the sky, or the area we call the sky, which is endless, and it's like I can see, or I can sense bodies of energy. Some collapse and return, like they are drawn back to the Source. I just have a sensation of downward motion of what's like a shower of dust; then particles go off in different directions. Inexplicable activity is occurring.

"I can sense a set pattern and yet it seems quite random, but it is part of a motion of energy, and what appears to be just falling downwards is actually falling outwards and upward, in all directions. It's very hard to put into words what it is I am seeing here and what I am sensing. I see what looks like a land mass, where something has formed, like a planet and gasses...it's hard to see because of the stuff that's around the energies."

At this point I finished the description as the vision I was seeing and sensing faded and Derek continued directing the session again. "It was explained in an appropriate way so that Diana will be able to write about it using her own words," he stated.

"*If the vehicle had a scientific understanding it would be explained differently; but we know she would challenge any scientific information or reject it; however, she will be assisted with the remembering. In all the early teachings and in the holy books and writings, there is an explanation of what occurred that now seems so far-fetched for the 'logical' or 'scientific' mind to accept. Yet, it was once accepted on faith. The accounts were told or written by those who had received similar visions, and were explained in wording that was appropriate for man's understanding at the time.*

"*That which you call God, the Oneness, God-Goddess-All-That-Is, the Creative Force, is not an old man who sits on a cloud surrounded by angels. But man, wishing to explain what he felt his creative 'Father' must be like, created the benevolent father figure to explain to others in a way they could understand.*

"*Everything throughout the whole of the universe contains all the information of the beginning. And it is within each particle of life, each mineral, or gas, everything that has come to grow on the earth, everything that is on and above or in the earth, all contains the information of the beginning.*"

There was a slight pause, but Derek kept quiet. Then the words continued:

"*As people's awareness is increased, as their own sensing of what life is expands, as they become fully cognizant of and recognize and accept their part, there will come the knowingness and understanding of who and what they really are, in their part of this cycle of life, in just the same way that you are experiencing a new understanding.*

"*In the soul's search to complete its journey, there is that inbred desire to return to the Oneness. When all the experiences have brought the awareness and the total acceptance of self, and the total acceptance of all that is, as part of the whole, as being part of the Oneness, All-That-Is, then the soul is able, in its physical expression, to understand the many realities. And the soul then has learned and experienced all that it possibly can in this dimension and will eventually return 'home,'*" the guide concluded.

I was seeing an energy being drawn up into a larger energy.

Derek's voice took on an unusual softness as he said, "That is a very good description of breaking away from and returning to Source."

As the session concluded and I returned my conscious awareness to the room once more, I could feel my eyes were aching, my forehead was throbbing and everything seemed to be surrounded with a yellowish light.

"I guess a lot of energy was generated to give you the pictures and the information," Derek suggested, yet in his tone I could detect coolness, like disbelief.

As ache and throbbing gradually dissipated, I felt elated, as though I had just struck a mother lode. What a powerful experience to have just 'witnessed' and felt. I even sensed that vast outpouring of love. Believe me, nothing, but nothing, could top this experience for me, the magnitude of which there are literally no words to appropriately express or describe. The memory of that vision, I am sure, will remain with me for the rest of my life.

No matter how skeptical Derek may have been, my experience was, after all, my experience, and I will treasure it forever.

But I can really understand Derek's reluctance to tackle the subject of creation. Six weeks previous we had done a session as Derek held Intensity and I directed him to connect with the Onyx Deva. I had asked whether the planet and everything on it was created, or did all life just evolve, and I could tell Derek didn't feel comfortable with either the topic or the answers. The response was:

"*There is but One Source, but of creation, all that was created has taken millions of years to reach the stage it is at now. Much of what was created has changed form many times in its evolution.*

"*Each lifetime there are lessons added upon lessons, experiences added upon experiences, to assist the soul to where it is now, and each experience has helped it to adapt. As it adapts it goes on to another set of changes. Other life forms have done the same.*

"*All life-forms have not come to the same place* [Earth], *as there are other universes and planets that have experienced creation in their own way. Some destroyed themselves, others added to their forms, some took away from their forms in order to adapt. Each of these life forms is unique in the way in which it evolved. At the time when some were first created, owing to the few 'materials' available for adaptation to their environment, existence was such that their form was very simple. Others developed into highly evolved beings. Some of them wished only for experiences of their own light and took on no form.*

"*All life evolves. Mountains choose a stationary experience, whereas your plants undergo seasonal experiences. Other life forms have chosen similar situations and adapted their bodies or forms according to survival needs. Some of these life forms evolved without certain aspects, such as emotions or feelings, but each has its own experience. Many species, animals and other creatures on the planet that have been around a long time, lack emotion. This is because it was necessary for them to be able to kill and consume others in order to survive; surviving through basic instinct is all they understand.*

"*Life, as you know it in this physical plane, is experienced through limited perceptions; you have been taught not to use those faculties that would enable you to do a great many things. This was not intended. It was intended for everyone to have these special abilities and to use them, but by not allowing or not reawakening these abilities, many remain ignorant of their natural gifts. Many are like mechanical toys that only move when wound; there is no understanding as to what they are really capable of doing.*

"Many life forms on other planets are aware of their abilities and have developed them to their fullest potential. Humans had incredible creative abilities once, but now don't remember how to use them; they have lost the ability of being able to create with the mind. Yet those beings from other planets, other galaxies, travel looking for different areas in which to expand their growth, their understanding, in their search."

Afterwards, Derek had described what he had been shown during the communication:

"Some of the pictures I was getting were of beings adapting to different planetary conditions; those living underground would have big eyes, because of the lack of light. Some are similar to us because of the same conditions that we have here on the earth."

Although I had felt incredibly elated when I had been shown a 'vision' to help me understand about creation, I wondered if perhaps Derek was right about it not being a suitable topic for us to go into. However, a few days later, without previously letting Derek know what I would be asking, I decided to 'take the bull by the horns' again. This time I directed Derek to connect with one of his highest spiritual guides and, after our formal introduction and welcome, began asking questions:

"Recently I asked about creation and Derek felt that may have been an inappropriate topic. Is it inappropriate to be asking about creation?"

"You may ask whatever question you wish, however the responses may not match your expectations if the particular guide you question is not versed in the area of the question asked. Guides endeavor to communicate to you according to the extent of their understanding, and their perception of what is asked."

"Would it be best to ask the same question several times to see if one receives more from one guide than from another?" I wanted to know.

"It would be best to ask for the appropriate guide for the particular subject you wish to discuss. During the type of channeling you are doing at the moment, conscious-channeling, you are aware of the questions asked, you are also aware of the energy, judging whether or not you should continue or dismiss it and start over. You feel or sense if the energy is expressing unconditional love or being judgmental. It may seem to you that you are filtering, censoring, what is coming through, or expressing your own point of view. It is for you to judge whether the information that is channeled through you is valid or invalid, whether received through conscious-voice or deep-trance channeling.

"A deep-trance channel cannot guarantee that the information being channeled is indeed coming from the highest spiritual entity or guide either. That person may have, at

some time, decided to leave his or her body and unknowingly allowed a lower astral form to take over, one that may like the performance and attention it is receiving by expressing itself now in the guise of a high spiritual guide or master. Nor should the information taken from a conscious-voice channel, or from anyone else, be taken as the truth—unless the ring of truth is felt within self and it sits comfortably as a truth; if it doesn't, you may dismiss it."

"Some people believe a channeler is given information at a level corresponding to his or her educational background or intelligence; if that were so, would it preclude us asking questions like ones on creation?"

"There are no rules precluding what you may or may not ask; ask whatever question you wish. With all of the responses that you receive, it is for you to feel for the truth within you as to whether they feel right or wrong."

"Whatever questions we do ask, are we being inspired to ask them?"

"Inspiration is given to you in various ways. The exact question may or may not be given to you, as you may in your own way consciously interpret what has been given to you, depending upon what you feel or think of the 'inspiration' you received. If you were to think, or be inspired to think, say, of a key, you may feel you've just been given the answer to the question, although the inspiration may have had a different meaning. And if you were inspired to ask a certain question, the question may be rephrased in such a way that the meaning is inadvertently changed by the addition or omission of a word or two. Whichever happens, there is no harm done; the process of lessons and understanding is there."

"Since the onyx egg was first placed in my hands, the greater majority of the questions I ask are centered around the information from the beginning of time, as we know time. So it shouldn't really come as any surprise to any of the guides if I ask questions about creation and how we came to be here. Guides, from what I can determine, are highly telepathic and aware of what's going on at all times, so there are no secrets. Therefore, why is it necessary to ask for a specific guide?" I asked.

"This was suggested for the two of you, in case you wished to have a more appropriate guide assist you with your questions. At this time you are going through a learning process. Frustrations that you may be feeling over this process may be due to other influences, and not the channeling or questions. As to whether the questions are appropriate, they are all appropriate and so are the responses. The process provides lessons, of learning to trust both yourselves and your guides, and judging the validity of information you receive, so you may determine whether to accept it as a 'truth' for yourselves."

"Last night, I asked for an appropriate guide to be present today to answer questions on creation. Is there an appropriate guide with us to answer questions on creation this morning?"

There was a long pause. Apparently the guide I had been speaking with was not putting the response into words at this time; instead, Derek was given his own 'vision.' "I am seeing picture images."

"Could you describe them?" I asked.

"Some of them are quite alien in form. I see a lot of stars and space. I'm seeing a mass of energy, like a ball or cluster, radiating like a sun. It becomes larger, almost like a cloud that is coming nearer, getting bigger and bigger, until I seem to be in the middle of it. It's spreading out in all directions. I just got the words "Creative Force," forcing out in all directions, expanding, going out, passing through everything. It fills up the entire universe."

"Does that mean that the universe was already there when the Creative Force came through?"

"I got that this Creative Force was expanding outwards. I'm now being shown small life forms on various planets."

"Did they come about because of the Creative Force?" I asked.

"It's like they were created to serve a particular purpose."

"Can you see who's creating them?"

"It's like they are just being created," Derek replied.

"Just materializing?"

"No, not just materializing. It is like a trial and error process they went through so they would be able to adapt to the environment on this planet. I'm getting a picture of a monkey right now. I'm being told that this monkey was created, not for the evolution of mankind, but for man to see himself within all life. It's not to show that he evolved and became better and more intelligent. It is for man to respect each animal and recognize that it is also a life form equal in importance to his own. Man is also aware of other life forms that have intelligence and are able to communicate with him. Even the domesticated cat and dog know how to communicate, reflecting back to him unconditional love and trust. They were all created equal. Man only has a superior intellect.

"I'm being told that what I'm seeing about the animals is later on, not at the origin of creation," Derek continued. "There were species that were on the face of the earth that are now extinct, some were unable to survive and others were used until they became extinct. Some of these earlier life forms served a purpose but due to earth changes and other reasons, became extinct. The earth seemed to go through a phase of growth and then went on to the next stage."

"Were the new life forms created, or was it actually an evolutionary process?" I asked.

"I am being shown that both processes were involved. They were created elsewhere and then brought here to this planet, and then, as they adapted, it became an evolutionary process. When they were created and brought here, it was not known if they would be able to adapt. Some species were unable to survive due to the extremes in temperature," Derek explained.

"At what point in earth's history, in linear time as we understand it, was man first created?"

"It's not quite that way, as other planets had life-forms on them. Earth became inhabited after life forms were brought here to see if they would be able to adapt to the earth plane. As they adapted in order to survive, they changed. Some were not compatible. There were different species of man; some that were brought here were at a particular stage in their development."

"Who was it that created these species?" I asked.

"Other life-forms that have been around for countless millennia. They created mankind, even before the earth was formed. They came from different planets. The different races were developed to help the species adapt to the earth's atmosphere and environment. Many underwent experimental procedures."

"Like mutations?

When I realized the conversation was being spoken again in the third person, I knew Derek's guide was answering the questions:

"Yes. These are still going on with your scientists."

"You mean, by genetic engineering?"

"This is a form of some of the experimenting."

"There are remains of dinosaur bones and prehistoric animals that existed on earth several million years ago, but I understand that, as yet, there haven't been any remains of human life forms that date to such early periods. Why would that be? Is it that there weren't any human beings around at that time?" I inquired.

"During its many changes, land masses have expanded, continents have risen and fallen, adding layers upon layers to the earth's surface since those times. The human remains are there, but are buried within the earth itself and beneath the ocean floors."

"What happened to those mutations? In mythology, there were beings that were half man and half animal. Were they just myths or fables?" I questioned.

"Beings of this sort existed, but became extinct, as did various other species, either from being unable to reproduce themselves, or being killed because they were the type of creature that others feared."

At that point, I decided we'd gone into enough. I needed time to rethink what the next questions would be. This was getting to be a little heavier than I had bargained for. Anyway, it was time for us to trade places. Maybe Derek would change the topic of questioning, too.

I settled into The Chair and took a back seat, as it were, while Derek began speaking with my guide: "I was wondering why, when I'm channeling, I feel reluctant when questions are asked about Creation."

"This is a delicate area. What has already been said about the slightest shred of doubt applies. Sometimes, when there is doubt in your mind, the answer that would flow is unable to do so because it is impeded by that doubt, and so you close off the transmission.

"As you have already learned, when you are consciously aware, as in the conscious voice channeling, if the nature of the questions causes you discomfort, if you feel you are not worthy enough for the answer to come through, or that it is, say, too lofty a question, if you are uncomfortable in the least little bit, the information will not flow. And, although the attempt is made, the response may be felt as unsatisfactory, because, as that is what you anticipate, that is what you create in your perception."

"Is there a particular reason why we are asking questions on Creation?"

"Yes. If you ask questions on what you feel are the most difficult of topics, or ones that would seem to be the most challenging, and you receive answers that feel appropriate, plausible, understandable, and the answers come through to your satisfaction, after that, you would never doubt any questions you may wish to ask. If you can ask or receive answers on a topic of that magnitude, then there would be no fears of touching upon any other areas. The trust that you are seeking, the wanting to believe, would be satisfied and formed in that one instance. The answers would serve more than one purpose if you felt that they were 'right,' and were a truth that you could accept for yourself."

"If there is hostility in the voice when questions are being asked, would that have an effect on the person being used as the channel?" Derek asked.

"Most definitely," my guide was quick to respond. *"It could cause a shutdown of the receptivity on the conscious level. That does not mean an answer would not be given, but there would be a barrier there at your level."*

"If the guides were asked the same questions over and over, would they not become tired or annoyed, as answers have already been given?"

"We do not mind what questions are asked because emotions are not a factor; there are no egos to be bruised; there is simply the total acceptance that comes with unconditional love. So, do not fear of asking the wrong or improper question or the impolite question, or even asking the same question several times.

"Where questions are asked aggressively," my guide continued, *"the perception of the aggression is only felt with the physical, the mental, and the emotional aspects of self. It does not go further.*

"If it is that answers are sought from higher energies, but if the conditions are not right, those higher energies would not come through to answer the questions. If it were a situation where the higher energies were present and already answering, the questions would not disturb, although the session may be brought to an abrupt conclusion by the person through whom the information is being channeled," my guide concluded, perhaps from the power of suggestion.

In all, though, we found this and all other sessions had been very fruitful for the varying ways we received the information, whether from visions, during a meditation, thoughts and words upon awakening, or the guide speaking directly and formally through the channeler. This made our journey and the whole process of seeking answers all the more exciting, not knowing always just how or when the information would be channeled.

Chapter 15

As our session at the office began one morning, my body was vibrating; it had been since I was awakened during the night by a sensation akin to having received some kind of high voltage shock treatment; any more and I would have lit up like a Christmas tree! Once we started, though, the 'buzzing' sensation did not feel quite so overbearing; perhaps I was becoming more used to it. When I tuned in, however, there was a subtle difference: before Derek asked each question, I *knew* exactly what he was going to ask, yet, because I had been so abuzz with my own physical sensations, we had not previously discussed the topics we hoped to touch upon!

Although from time to time we had noticed some slight telepathic exchange when we both said the same thing at the same time, there had been nothing quite like this. Was this new mental insight tied in with the raised energy vibrations within my own body?

With my attention focused upon the energy flowing through my body I heard myself saying, "I'm being given the name Darginak. Whoever is here says it's the name of a Lord of the Universe. An appointment was made and it will soon be time for us all to talk. We're being told that it is getting close to the time of major earth changes. Everything is speeding up. We must be prepared."

That was all that was said and then I felt the energy leave. I opened my eyes and looked at Derek. "Lord of the universe, indeed," I said, beginning to shiver again. "We've either got one helluva trickster on our hands, here, or else something really big is going to happen."

Derek looked very subdued and took hold of my hands. "That was no trickster," he said, gently. "I think it's what all this preparation and channeling is for." He wrote down the name we had been given.

Returning to our Center after breakfast, we began our set daily ritual, mentally filling the whole place with light and then making our way into our

Reiki room, where we do any distance healing that has been requested for others, and then taking turns giving each other a hands-on healing. This day, it was Derek's turn to be first on the healing table.

To start off the session, as always, I said a short prayer and raised my arms to receive the energy. Immediately, I became aware of a strong pulsating in my hands. Still standing in the same manner, I sent out a mental prayer asking to be a clear and perfect channel for the healing energies. This time, however, I did something I hadn't done before, I also asked for my highest 'cosmic' healing guides that were working with the Light to be with me.

Quicker than the blinking of an eye, I felt the energy in my hands really intensify, and I lowered them onto Derek's chest. 'Derek's sure gonna be cooking today,' I said to myself, smiling, but my thoughts seemed to get put on hold. At that moment, it felt like I was entering some type of time warp. I knew I was channeling a powerful healing guide.

Then the proverbial penny dropped again, as I was filled with a sense of knowing...and I knew...I KNEW! Here I was, doing what I had done before, on countless hundreds of occasions in numerous lifetimes, performing a 'laying on of hands.'

Because I am normally so engrossed with the spiritual aspect of things during a hands-on session, I had always simply assumed that the healing guides were spiritual guides. Just call me Old Faith-full. What I hadn't realized until now was that, it was done long ago with the assistance of the cosmic guides, too. But then, I had no reason to believe differently before my present knowingness; that must be it. What a revelation! The cosmic energies or guides assisted all those incredible healers of times past. I was thrilled with my new piece of knowledge, my new inner knowing, my new truth, and equally thrilled with the session as it progressed.

After a few minutes, with my hands resting lightly on Derek's chest, in my inner vision I began to 'see' a young oriental man, sitting cross legged with a bowl of prepared rice on the floor a short distance in front of him. Beyond the rice there was burning incense of some sort in a small container surrounded by grains of uncooked rice and dried leaves and grasses. The young man prayed for a few moments to thank the Universe and God for his life on this planet, then he bent forward, touching the ground with his brow to salute Mother Earth, the sustainer of all life, and the elements. Next, he addressed the rice, giving thanks and asking it to strengthen and nourish his body; this was done very reverently, as he was communicating with it on a spiritual level, recognizing the God-spark or divinity that is within all life forms. Then he blessed his physical body and asked it to accept the rice for the nourishment and strength it would give.

As I looked into the young man's eyes, I recognized that it was Derek as he had been in a previous lifetime. I told Derek what I was seeing and he acknowledged that he understood the message being conveyed to him.

I couldn't help thinking that if everyone carried out a similar spiritual and heartfelt preliminary before eating, their bodies would perhaps accept the food more readily and their digestive systems find it more agreeable. Most people nowadays rarely say grace, and if they do so, it's a perfunctory, hurried formality so they can dig into the food quickly. I felt a little guilty knowing I fell into that category. Not any more, though, I told myself; I was actually impatient to try out the ancient 'procedure.' From now on, I will be putting more meaning into what I say before eating.

I realized how pretty darned privileged we are, learning like this from what we do each day, and I thanked our guides, both spiritual and cosmic, for bringing us one more piece of the puzzle.

* * *

It had been said one morning that cosmic guides will 'communicate' when we least expect it. They were certainly right on that score.

Normally, with the set format we employ to tune in, there is no mistaking where we get our information from, but one day, Derek's vision was obscured by a large, ovoid-shaped, white light. He aborted the procedure, but when he tried a second time, the light was still there. It was obvious that we were to communicate.

I greeted the 'light' and asked whom I was addressing. Normally, we're not given a name, but there was a slight pause, and then a faltering "Shum...Shumbala," as Derek cleared his throat to allow communication to flow. I asked Shumbala what was the purpose of this communication.

"It is to let you know that there are several of us here at this time. When it is appropriate, our assistance will be given. At this time things are not being actively pursued by us because of the other work that you have chosen to do first; once that has been completed, we will talk again, at a different level than now.

"Although to you your progress may seem slow, know that great strides are made when things are diligently done."

Little more was said. After exchanging blessings our guest departed. I looked forward to renewing our acquaintance, although I felt it was a pity we probably wouldn't be communicating until we had finished working on the book.

From time to time, when we least expect it, these cosmic guides 'pop in' briefly to see us, sort of a quick reassurance just to let us know they are still around, to tell us things are going according to plan; and then they 'pop out' again. On another occasion Derek asked what we should be doing to prepare ourselves to receive the information we sought.

"The physical vehicle has to be made strong before you receive information from certain higher frequencies," the response came, *"and the sooner your vehicles are prepared, the sooner other information will flow. As toxins are removed from your bodies, your energy will be brighter, attitudes and feelings will be clearer. Once this has been accomplished, your awareness will be heightened. We will be here to assist as you move forward into a new understanding."*

"Would you care to give us some clarification about distance and thoughts?" Derek asked. "Other planets, other galaxies are light years away, yet if I were to mention a word or name, calling a cosmic being here, it seems as soon as I say the name, the being is here."

"The cosmic being you refer to is here with you at all times. Although there may seem to be an enigma of contradiction, things are, as you perceive them, in whatever reality you perceive them to be. If you perceive them to be a distance away, they are a distance away. If you perceive them to be in the here and now, it will be the here and now.

"It is appropriate that humankind adopts realities that fit in, realities of conformity. If you were to introduce everything into your reality in this dimension here and now, you would find it difficult to cope; you also would find it extremely confusing. For now, it is perhaps better to invite into your reality maybe one thing at a time until you have a clearer view, or a new perspective has been acquired. Do you understand?"

"Yes, and I'm still amazed that thoughts seem to be able to travel faster than light."

"Your thoughts, your imagination, can transcend all things, can pass all time barriers, all time zones, as you know them. You may momentarily draw to you at the speed of thought whatever it is you wish to focus upon. You may indeed focus upon all realities at once if you have reached a certain level. The juggler begins with one ball, adding another and then another. With practice he can add many more and becomes quite proficient at handling all of them at once.

"As your own knowledge increases, and as memories of other incarnations are recalled with a random thought, the understanding, the knowingness that is within you will release a little more at a time. Your comprehension on this level, in this reality, will grow," our 'guest' continued. "The human being, as you well know, is not at this stage ready to

acknowledge, accommodate all the information and knowledge available to him; this is why the average human brain is operating at only one tenth of its capacity. However, there is a gradual expansion, a change, taking place. You have tools that have been made available to you, to increase, shall we say, the activity, the working capacity of your brain.

"There is a lot going on behind the scenes at this time. Much has been made available to you without you being aware of it yet. You are only aware of a fraction of what it is that you have been given. Just trust. Know that you are progressing at a rate which is appropriate for you at this time."

Was the guide referring to the crystal caps that Derek had fashioned, one for me, and one for him? I rarely used mine any more, possibly because I felt a little silly when unexpected people arrived at the office and smiled at my unusual head adornment; perhaps this was our cue to wear them again. Or was something else being referred to? I decided it was time to wear my crystal cap again and at the same time re-read what I'd written. Maybe if I 'panned for gold' I would find the right clues.... I couldn't wait to get started.

Chapter 16

The benefits of meditation and visualization became the topic one morning as Derek began asking questions of our unseen guest. "With the guided visualizations we facilitate, are we actually assisting participants to increase their own power of awareness by having them use their own minds and imagination, putting them to work?" Derek inquired.

"*Most definitely. And you are doing it in a way that is palatable. Those who don't find it palatable are not ready for the next stage in their development,*" my guide responded.

"Is there anything you can share about 'correct breathing' and meditation?"

"*Concentrating upon one's breathing is a way of freeing the mind from wandering thoughts. While the mind focuses on taking deep breaths, visualize or feel the waves of relaxation flowing through the body as each breath is exhaled; this helps relax the body and at the same time assists to disassociate self from all the daily preoccupations.*

"*Breathing in deeply through the nose and exhaling slowly through the mouth is a good preliminary, not only to get one into the relaxed state, but assisting in aligning the body's energies.*

"*Holding the breath for a few seconds after inhaling and exhaling is also beneficial for those seeking to expand psychic experiences. At those precise moments of holding the breath, an opportunity is created for psychic centers to open as other processes occur...within the subtle bodies...because of that slight pause in the normal breathing function.*" The guide paused as if to stress the importance of what had just been said.

"*Different disciplines teach different breathing techniques. Certain breathing techniques are sometimes combined with physical movements that assist with the flow of energies, such as are found in the Hatha Yoga, Tai Chi, and other disciplines. Deep and rhythmic breathing is also encouraged in the more vigorous forms of meditation embracing specific dancing or motion, the swaying of the body, the spinning of the body. All of these will take one into a deep meditative or trance state. Different cultures have different ways of inducing meditative or deep trance states."*

"If I were to spin around in circles, would this assist me in achieving a deeper trance state?" Derek asked.

"It may, if continued for a sufficient length of time, and depending upon balance, pace, intent and certain other factors. It would take considerable practice."

"There are breathing techniques which involve tilting and rolling the head as one exhales, or using various body movements whilst inhaling and exhaling, allowing deeper breathing. Is the main purpose of these exercises just to bring oxygen into the system?"

"All forms of breathing bring oxygen into the system. Deep breathing takes full advantage of the capacity of the lungs, but it is not necessary to contort the body to allow deeper breathing," the guide replied succinctly. *"Many books set out good meditative and breathing practices."*

"What would be the most beneficial time to meditate?"

"The early-morning hours are good, but there is no hard and fast rule; it is a matter of personal preference. If one is serious about meditating, one will feel moved or inspired to meditate at a specific time or times each day."

"Could you explain the difference between closed-eye and open-eye meditations? Are there more advantages to one or the other?" Derek asked.

"One form of meditation is done with the eyes open, the other with the eyes closed. Both methods are equally advantageous in the experiences they provide.

"With the open-eye meditation, as one learns to 'see,' in the same way that one learns to see and read auras, there can occur what appears to be a clearing of the mind, but it is a clearing of the inner 'vision.' As the eyes become unfocused, and when this method of meditation is practiced on a regular basis, one may begin to see certain aspects of different realities which one has not seen before. Furnishings within a room, even the walls may disappear as one learns to see beyond the physical or material reality normally perceived; one may see past the third dimension into other dimensions. This is an inherent ability that may be mastered with practice.

"If the eyes remain closed during a meditation, one may view from the inner creative mind center; this is particularly helpful when following a guided visualization. While using a different sense, one may be aware of these other realities and dimensions with the eyes closed; however, the experience is quite different than when the eyes are open."

"For an open-eye meditation, would it be best to concentrate upon deep breathing and view an object at a certain distance away?"

"Concentrating upon a pattern of slow, gentle, and rhythmic deep breathing is always a good way to start any meditation. Keeping to the chosen pattern of breathing, you may

focus upon any object. It doesn't have to be off in the distance; it can be a picture or mark upon the wall, or furnishings a few feet ahead, or a spot upon the floor. Some people choose to gaze at the flame of a candle as it burns. Some choose to look into a mirror, however, caution is recommended," my guide offered, "although if one experiments with the different methods, one will find that which is most appropriate."

"People who do scrying or crystal ball gazing, aren't they actually doing an open-eye meditation?"

"It is somewhat similar, as the person scrying or gazing is using the crystal ball or mirror as a point of focus to enter a trance, an altered state of awareness or different 'reality.' There are advantages to using a quartz crystal ball, as its energies may assist in the process."

"I'm assuming that, as glass balls don't have the same properties or energy as quartz crystal balls, they wouldn't have the same benefits for scrying."

"The energy is different, but they may be used as a point of focus. A bowl of pure water may be used in the same way. At first the light reflections may be distracting; however, one will learn to look past or through the distractions and see beyond, not consciously looking beyond, but allowing the eyes to relax, unfocus and therefore 'see' beyond."

"The first time I took part in an open-eye form of meditation, I could sense my conscious awareness of the physical world out in front of me, and it was being drawn inward as I focused on being a spark of energy within the physical body," Derek volunteered.

"It is a good method for meditation. You frequently use a closed-eye meditation in which you extend your awareness to the energies in the room, becoming one with them. It is another version, except you are experiencing another aspect of your sense of touch or 'sensing' in one, whereas in the other you are using the visual sense, directing attention to that which is focused upon or seen rather than felt, to begin the meditation.

"When one sees that self is a speck of energy or a ball of energy, one develops a different understanding of the physical form which houses the soul. The human being is so used to viewing itself as a physical being that it frequently forgets to look for, or see, the spirituality within self or others. The human being sees only another human being rather than spirit housed within a human form.

"If one is to consciously look out, project awareness out of self, and, as you say, look back at self, viewing self as a speck of energy or light within the physical, with practice it becomes much easier to see the energy or light within others at all times. It brings an awareness of what you are, rather than what you see or think you are, so that when you would look at another human being, you would recognize the spirituality that is there also.

"When meditating with eyes closed—the method you most frequently use—you become aware of others by sensing their energy, and as you allow your own energy to merge with other energies, you feel the connectedness of spirit in that way."

"Certain sects in the world believe people can only reach spiritual heights through sexual denial; is that something that would be recommended?" Derek asked.

"Celibacy is encouraged by certain sects. Conforming to that particular belief system may be required, in order for them to belong."

"Is it true that by abstaining from sex, the vital energy or bodily fluids normally expended or used up during the sexual act could be redirected by the celibate to provide a superior energy for his spiritual communion, or is that merely fallacy?"

"There is a difference, a considerable difference," my guide stressed, *"during the sexual union of two energies joining together; it is a combination in which one adds to, or complements, the energy of the other, and this can generate or create a higher energy. They are not burning up or depleting the energy by partaking in the physical union. The celibate, then, does not have the added energy of another to assist in reaching certain heights. The beliefs of some are that by totally abstaining from sex they will retain specific strengths or powers which they may choose to utilize in a different manner."*

"I suppose there are many different roads, different avenues one may take to reach spiritual heights. But why do certain groups feel it necessary to separate themselves by making celibacy a criterion for practicing their beliefs?" Derek questioned on this new tack.

"Each has free will to search out for self what feels right. If people wish to follow a belief system calling for celibacy, that is a choice they may make. For some, it may be a means, a way to seek communion with their spirituality or higher aspects of self. By practicing celibacy, by denying their own sexuality or sexual urges, they may be attempting to redirect the energies that would normally be expended during the sexual union, believing that these energies should be directed towards the spiritual aspect of self.

"Some believe that when a man ejaculates seminal fluid he is losing part of his vital life force energy. There is a tendency to overlook the fact that the creative part of man is able to create and recreate on all levels, and that his ability to create never diminishes, even when he feels he has passed the age of sexual desire and expression on the physical level. He is doing himself a sad injustice if he remains oblivious to the co-creative mental, emotional, and spiritual bodies. It is not necessary to deny one or another of the aspects of self. But, you see, the belief system originated, as did many belief systems, at a time when man was not as sophisticated in his approach to learning and understanding as he is now.

"There are many groups or sects that deny their own sexuality," the guide continued. "But one must not fall into criticizing different belief systems, as the soul has chosen to learn through certain lessons. If lessons are chosen for learning to occur through celibacy, or through practicing certain rituals, then that is why the soul is attracted to, or drawn into, those areas. While one aspect of a human being, or the soul, is choosing to incarnate and experience celibacy, another aspect of that same soul may be choosing to be overly sexually active, so that both ends of the scale, as it were, are experienced."

"What about homosexuality?" Derek asked. "I've come to understand there are many reasons why someone would choose to experience this lifestyle, either for their own soul lessons, or for others to learn from."

"Sexuality is an aspect of the human condition. For some, the sexual act may be a basal set of motions embarked upon in order to achieve nothing more than a physical release. For others, it provides a gateway for procreation to occur. For heterosexual beings, and for partners of the same gender, within a significant relationship, the sexual act presents a means of physical expression through which the emotions of love and affection may be conveyed. When choosing to associate with others of the same or another gender, there may be an internal compulsion, a driving force.

"The reasons why one may choose to experience homosexuality are varied. There may be a certain chemical make-up within the physical body that causes this desire. In seeking for experiences of the same gender, sometimes there are also those external influences, the unseen influences, which can cause an attraction towards someone of the same sex.

"The choice to experience homosexuality may have been made at a soul level. There may be a soul choice of experiencing discrimination, and this is sought through the physical expression, through the sexual expression. It may be that one soul is choosing to learn about the male and female aspects of self, wishing to learn about both at once."

"How can those people or groups placing judgment on this type of lifestyle come to a different level of understanding?" Derek asked.

"Their judgments are part of their learning." the guide stressed. "You see, one's judgments are rarely one's own. It is, for some, a frame of mind that one has bought into; it is a belief system that has been adopted as one's own. If it is believed that something is bad or something is good, this judgment is not necessarily arrived at through one's own experiences in life. It may be arrived at through someone else's verbalized or written dictates, or edict."

"I can understand some people feel they may be affected by those [homosexuals] if they are associated with them; they fear that they may be judged as being of the same persuasion."

"That can stem from fear of being classified alongside others. When one is wishing to draw attention away from self, that fear may be focused or appear to be directed towards those others. The topic, homosexuality, presents many different facets, it is not straightforward. Nothing is. It is part of the experiences of life.

"Let us take love, for instance. How do you learn about love? There is the word 'love.' There is an emotion that accompanies it. There may be an experience that accompanies it. But, you see, all emotions and experiences have their own facets, their own levels, their own depths, as it is with everything," my guide was careful to explain.

"Every single experience that man can experience, or that woman can experience, is part of each soul's learning. If one wishes to experience love, how does one know how to experience love? Is it a physical thing? Is it a mental thing? Is it something that's emotional, or is it merely a concept, an idea, a word? What are the shades or degrees of it? Every experience of it, whether heterosexual or homosexual, is but a choice that has been made. How does one understand unless one has undergone the experience, but what part, what aspect? Each plane or level has its highs and its lows, its ascents and descents.

"In order for the soul to reach the true level of the perfection it seeks, it is necessary for the soul to undergo every experience. And this is why it is, perhaps, most unwise to criticize others, to judge others. Because, without realizing it, each soul himself or herself has experienced those things, whether in this lifetime or another, and done those things that perhaps may seem offensive in one incarnation, yet acceptable in another."

"This life we are experiencing is so intricately interwoven, as one experience affects another, creating yet another."

"Each experience is as valid as another, each experience is right. Yet this is so difficult for many people to understand. You see, even those discriminating and condemning, they may dream of certain things occurring, and indeed be shocked and horrified at the depths to which they sank or the heights to which they may have risen in their dreams. They keep it a secret from others that they have indeed indulged in this and that when asleep. It was all a dream; and they were ashamed of their dreams on those occasions. But are they to be judged for dreaming those dreams, in the same way that they themselves judge how others live their lives? Yet they themselves have already lived those experiences, albeit in a different incarnation, or in a different dimension, or different state of awareness such as the dream state.

"This is all part of the soul's chosen learning and it applies to all of us; it is so we may learn to function from the heart. And it is for those still judging and discriminating to learn every facet of the word 'love,' to learn every facet of the state that is love, to learn every facet of the words 'unconditional love' and to explore them from every possible angle. When they learn to live those words and become one with the full meaning of those words, then there is nothing more for them to learn on this earth plane and the need to be here no longer exists. The soul will have reached a sufficiently high level or grown in wisdom sufficiently to *have attained that state of perfection it sought; by that time, it will be ready to return to God."*

"During sexual union between two people, there is an energy that is created at the time of climax. At that point, whilst using their own visualization or creativity, can they then redirect this energy to certain parts of the body that may require healing?" Derek asked.

"This is possible. It is also possible to use the energy created at the time of mutual climax for an out-of-body experience; sometimes this can occur spontaneously without attempting to direct the energies. Through the union of consenting partners mutually sharing the highest expression of the love emotion, certain conditions may be generated that afford each soul the opportunity to experience another dimension or spiritual state."

"In order for that to occur, would both partners have to be fairly open and receptive to experience self and the other partner?"

"It can occur when there is a manifestation of the pure love energy being experienced by both partners. You see, there is not just a communion on the physical level during such intimacy; there is the possibility of mutual communion on the mental, emotional, and the spiritual levels, too. For some people, all these aspects of self are in perfect harmony and so the right conditions may be created for this experience to occur. However, generally speaking, although the physical bodies may both be enjoying the physical communion, this does not necessarily mean there is going to be an out-of-body experience, or any experience other than the physical climax that can be attained."

"Would it help if they meditated first?" Derek asked

"If a couple were to join together in meditation first, extending their light to envelop each other and then consciously jointly connecting at the base chakra, and the other major chakras, this could set the scene for generating the right conditions for a mutually rewarding spiritual experience."

"This brings us to a point of understanding that if people were to be become more aware of themselves physically, mentally, emotionally, and spiritually, through meditation, say, then it would have quite a beneficial affect on them," Derek stated.

I smiled to myself as I was transcribing the tape. Only Derek could start off asking about meditation, bring the whole conversation around to celibacy, then sex and then slide back into the meditation theme again without batting an eyelid.

All the topics were very interesting, I told myself as I continued transcribing the tape, but I'd never have guessed there could be such a connection between them.

"Is there something you could suggest that would assist a beginner in meditating?" Derek continued with his questions.

"*Yes. Something you yourselves have learned and taught many times, and that is extending one's own inner light, to begin. It is very beneficial to start by consciously focusing upon the inner light that is seated at the very center of one's being, then, mentally and consciously, expand it outwards into the aura.* [See figures 1, 2, and 3.]

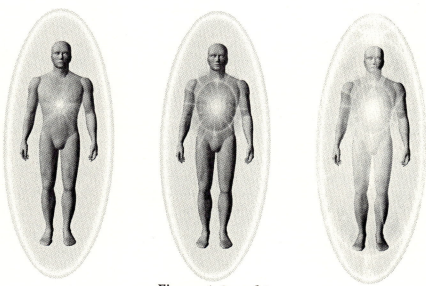

Figures 1, 2, and 3
Expanding the inner light to permeate body and aura.

"*This may be done quite simply by visualizing or imagining a small spark of light in the area between the heart and solar plexus. Mentally, see, feel, and sense that spark;* **know** *it is there—pretend if necessary. Concentrate on that inner light. It is the very essence of one's being. You see, this spark of light is the real you. It is that creative spark of God-energy you bring with you into each incarnation and which remains within the physical until the transition you term 'death.' Now, imagine that spark of light becoming stronger, growing larger, expanding, until it permeates every atom of the physical body. Still concentrating on that light, mentally increase its size, expanding it even further outwards until it is at least three feet or more beyond the body in every direction, until it com-*

*pletely encompasses the whole of the energy field, the aura. See self as being within the center of a sphere or cocoon of **inner** light. Then, make an affirmation that this is one's own domain.*

"This procedure helps keep away negative energies, creating a protected space in which one may learn to operate at the highest possible vibratory rate. The process of expanding the inner light also causes the aura to expand and strengthen. With repeated use, it can bring about a healing and strengthening of body and aura. Also, there are additional benefits; the exercise helps one to become more of who one truly is, which in turn assists one to reclaim latent gifts of one's divine inheritance.

"It is also suggested that, until one becomes accustomed to meditating, this should be done at a time and place in which there is least likelihood of being interrupted by sudden noises or someone entering the room.

"Also important is to be as comfortable as possible wherever and whenever one meditates; if one is not accustomed to sitting on the floor with legs crossed, this should not be considered a prerequisite. Sitting in a way that is most comfortable is recommended, preferably with the spine as straight as possible. There are reasons for this, but if sitting is not feasible, due to certain health conditions, one may also meditate lying down.

"However, it is beneficial to remain flexible regarding preferred methods of meditation, so as to not become locked into just one particular method, one particular piece of music if music is used, or one set format. If one becomes too rigid in one's ways, by using only one format, there is a danger of meditation becoming master of the experience rather than the tool for the experience," the guide concluded on a very interesting note.

* * *

Radiating outside the human body is the aura. This auric field is an energy field, made up of several layers of energy comprising the mental, emotional, and spiritual 'bodies' and the inter-relating 'spaces' between. Universal life-force energy is drawn into the body through seven main chakras. [See figure 4.]

This life-force energy is drawn in to adjacent nerves, glands, and organs via each chakra, to 'nourish' and sustain the physical being. It is also vital to the auric field. Sometimes these chakras are referred to as 'spinning' energy centers.

As a person mentally generates light from within, expanding it outwards and extending it in all directions, he or she is giving it intent to embrace or encompass the physical body and all seven inner layers or energy bands of the aura, filling them with light.

On several occasions we have been reminded to generate our own light to strengthen our energy fields before meditating or entering different states of awareness, such as immediately upon awakening or prior to going to sleep. It is equally important and beneficial to do so before entering anyone else's home—in fact, before going anywhere, whether to a church, place of business, workshop, class, and especially shopping malls, movie theatres, or any place where other people gather.

Figure 4
The seven main chakras.

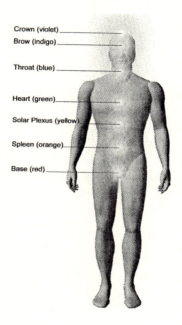

As we begin to raise our vibration and awareness, it follows that we will become more aware of different energies, hence, we may become super-sensitive to the conditions of other people around us. We may begin to feel aches and pains for no apparent reason. Instead of accepting or laying claim to these physical discomforts, we may mentally instruct our guide or angel to 'take this away' and ask that healing light and love immediately be directed to the person to whom it belongs.

Becoming proficient at working with and projecting our own light, to the point that we could say it is operating on 'high beam,' not only strengthens our auric field, it is also good for our peace of mind, knowing it offers a certain amount of protection from psychic and other forms of mental 'attack.'

The responsibility for our 'protection' rests with self. Our guardian angels or guides are here with us always, but they do not intervene, even though they know what is about to happen, *unless we first request their help.* Even then, just asking for their help is not enough to take us out of a situation that we may have already chosen consciously, or on another level, to experience. Yes, divine intervention occurs when our life may be threatened and we haven't yet completed the tasks or lessons we have set for self. But our guides will not intervene if we are consciously and openly courting and inviting in energies that are not working for our highest good—they will allow us to have the experience and 'learn the hard way.'

There are a number of ways to assist the strengthening process to protect us from negative energies. These include eating a healthy diet, ensuring we get adequate rest, increasing the vibratory rate of our energy fields on a daily basis and making sure our consciousness is not anesthetized through the use of drugs and alcohol, which bring about a natural fatigue and lowering of vibration. It is also advisable to avoid pushing self to extremes that cause fatigue. The same applies to lowering our energy field through venting or being exposed to uncontrollable anger.

Most importantly, we should become masters at using the imagination, so our inner light may be used to create a strong, protective energy field quickly and spontaneously.

Everyone will find his or her own way of doing this. I had the dickens of a time trying to visualize my inner light at first, until I saw a figure-skater doing a spin, crouching down then reaching her arms upwards to regain her full height. This gave my imagination a wonderful tool. From then on I simply pretended I was a spinning figure-skater holding my inner light which grew and expanded further outwards each time I crouched and drew myself up again. Eventually, it became second nature for me to not only 'see' my inner light, but to 'sense' and 'feel' it, too. Derek told me he found it a challenge until he imagined his inner light to be like a tiny balloon that expanded each time he took a deep breath and exhaled. One of our students says he imagines his inner light to be a golf ball, which gets bigger when he changes it to a tennis ball, then a soccer ball, and finally a giant beach ball. Another student says she imagines she is using sweeping arm movements and at the same time uses physical gestures to push her inner light in all directions.

With practice and a little imagination, everyone will find something that works.

However, I give a wide berth to misleading information that says it's not necessary to protect yourself, that you can just visualize a column of light coming from above down into you and you're okay. If we do that, we are opening ourselves up to any 'light' that may be there, whether extra-terrestrial, spirit, or entity of a similar or slightly higher vibration than ourselves. Once we open ourselves up to that 'column of light,' we might inadvertently be giving permission for anything from other dimensions to come into our own space. Not only that, it keeps us locked into the old belief that everything of a high spiritual or god-like nature can only be accessed 'out' there or 'up' there, namely, outside of ourselves, instead of from within.

Because most of us do not know or cannot see what we are dealing with, it's so advisable to wait and practice expanding our inner light and strengthening our energy field until we become proficient at working with our own inner light and energy. Also, it's important to reclaim dominion or take control of our personal 'area.' *Knowing* our light is there is equally important, whether we can see, feel, or sense it or not. By *knowing*, as we concentrate upon that light of ours, we immediately expand it outwards throughout our whole body and aura. At that point we may claim dominion by affirming the following words either verbally or mentally:

> "This is my energy field, this is my domain,
> Only God's purest light may come to me,
> I radiate pure light.
> This is my light,
> This is my energy field,
> This is my domain."

Practice doing this until it becomes automatic, like breathing If you are uncomfortable with the word 'God' in the above affirmation, you may substitute 'The Creator,' 'Great Spirit,' 'God-Goddess-All-That-Is' or the name by which you address your Higher Power or Divinity.

By getting into the habit of generating our light in this way several times throughout the day, it will eventually become second nature, and we will be able to do it as fast as a thought; by that time, it will be *more* than a form of 'protection.' We will have reclaimed an ability and possibly developed sufficiently to the point where we are really operating from the presence of our true light.

Whilst walking up a hill one day, using slow, steady physical movement as a form of meditation, consciously strengthening my light at every step, (which, incidentally, carried me higher and higher with a degree of ease to which I was not normally accustomed on uphill walks) the thought struck me that generating light this way must also serve as an additional form of 'protection.' But what?

As I finished my climb, a sense of elation seemed to flow through my body. At that point I received an 'answer' in the form of a sense of knowing: the Israelites, in Biblical times, escaped the hand of death by painting a sign in lamb's blood upon the doors of their homes. Our spheres of light around our physical houses, our bodies, could be the 'sign' for deliverance, to keep us safe during predicted earth changes! What an interesting concept.

***

It has already been explained that by frequently repeating the process of generating our light, we strengthen our aura or energy field. By making this a regular practice, and re-generating the light several times throughout the day, our light may eventually become 'switched on' at all times. After practicing on a daily basis several times a day over a period of several months, we will not only have created a strong energy field, but our vibratory rate should have become sufficiently raised to create the perfect environment, like a well-lit sanctuary, into which to invite our Higher Self.

Viewing Higher Self from within our sphere of light, this highest aspect of our soul is generally located within the eighth chakra zone; its color is generally seen as silver-white and is in one's energy field a distance above the top of the head at the outer edge of the aura and in line with the crown chakra. There is also a ninth chakra; its color is generally seen as gold and is located a further distance away, above the eighth chakra [see figure 5].

Before a formal invitation is extended to Higher Self, it is suggested that one's inner light be consciously extended outwards to embrace and encompass the eighth chakra location. A mental request or invitation at this point may be made for Higher Self to join with the physical body, and when the energy of Higher Self is felt, sensed, or 'seen' (it radiates an effulgent silver-white light), we may consciously draw it downwards and further inwards until it completely infuses our sphere, totally filling and surrounding us with its light. When the energy is felt, extend a mental greeting and acknowledge any telepathic thoughts that may be received.

Do not be surprised or alarmed if, at first, it seems that your heart is perhaps beating slightly faster than normal; this sensation will pass. But should it continue or any physical discomfort occur, such as a headache, or feeling of restriction in the throat area, it is an indication that one's energy field (aura and expanded inner-light) needs to be extended further outwards in all directions, to give Higher Self a little more 'room.' If the discomfort persists after expanding the aura and inner light even further outwards, either we are not ready, or we are insufficiently prepared for this communication, or, this is not the energy of Higher Self and the session should be terminated immediately.

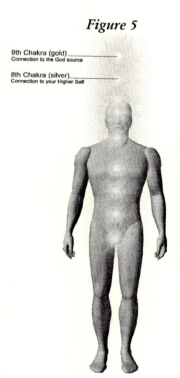

The Eighth and Ninth Chakras.

As a way of becoming acquainted with Higher Self, if one is in the practice of saying prayers or meditating in the mornings or evenings, this would be a most appropriate time and reason to 'invite' Higher Self to join the proceedings.

After a mutual rapport is established, helpful suggestions or answers to questions may be received, but a person will never be told what to do by Higher Self. When communicating with Higher Self, all telepathic thoughts received will be positive, loving, and uplifting. Should negative thoughts of a controlling, critical, judgmental, or deprecating nature be received, then dismiss the energy at once by mentally and physically pushing it out of the auric field, and terminate the session—this is not Higher Self. It is inadvisable to re-attempt contacting Higher Self without first beginning the procedure over again.

We can't stress it strongly enough: beware of attempting to communicate with Higher Self before you are operating from within your own sphere of inner light. Refrain from making any invitation to have anyone or anything use you as a channel—and that includes saying to yourself 'I open myself to receive' or 'I open myself up.' In your enthusiasm to reach out and connect, you could be naively extending an invitation to be deceived by those claiming they wish to be of help. Of help to whom? Another species or ours?

Everything is not what it may at first seem to be, as Derek and I found out shortly after we began channeling. Most of us cannot see into other dimensions. But this doesn't mean that there are not those amongst us from different dimensions that are quite capable of operating not only in their own dimension but within ours also.

Only the naive would be fooled into believing that everything 'out there,' or even while one is endeavoring to 'go within,' is of a high spiritual or holy level. Unless you are an advanced student of metaphysics you may not know the difference, and even then, you may be fooled; there are many energies from different realities with abilities far superior to ours waiting for an unwitting invitation to join you. Divine intervention may keep you from harm's way physically, as at one level or perspective you are protected. But if you extend an invitation for others to use your physical vehicle (body) for channeling or other purposes, then that experience, because of the free will factor, will not be taken away from you or prevented. Any permission given to use your body is in effect an open contract heavily weighted in favor of those unseen forces whose real motives may be concealed.

Chapter 17

I believe that Biblical references to people being possessed were what Derek and I would call cases of entity-attachment. 'Possession' was a known and accepted fact back then. It's unfortunate that today very few people either know of or would give credence to the fact that there are disembodied 'hitchhikers' everywhere. I would even go so far as to state that countless numbers of people have them aboard, but are blissfully unaware of their presence. And many people who believe they are immune to this because of automatic protection from their guardian angels and 'gate-keepers,' as many clairvoyants or psychics claim, or because they lead 'good' lives following the middle path or the Good Book, may be deluding themselves.

Let's get a few things straight here. Not all entity attachments are demons. They are the disembodied spirits or souls of ordinary people who died and, for one reason or another, never went on to the Light, or Heaven, or whatever name we use for the celestial haven or dimension to which most of us hope to go after death. And whether it was through fear, ignorance, remorse, a reluctance to give up material possessions, unfinished business, not being prepared for death, or simply not wanting to leave family members behind, doesn't matter. They were ordinary people when they were here, with ordinary failings and foibles, aches and pains, just like you and me.

After drifting around for a while after death, often because they don't know where else to go, or because they are too afraid to move on, they attach themselves to living people. Some do it simply to be of help, some to learn by observing.

If a person didn't learn his or her 'lessons' while alive, he or she can be attracted to someone still living who is going through a similar scenario in order to work through the problem or situation until the lesson is learned or a new understanding reached.

It's wise to remember the old adage, 'Like attracts like.' It happens. But whatever their reasons for hanging around this earth plane, when given a new perspective and direction, and a reason to go forward, they frequently choose to continue their soul journey on a higher plane of existence.

Through our own personal research from the many sessions we've done, it seems apparent that these entities are often attracted to young children, who are able to see and communicate with them. Young children are incredibly clairvoyant until they shut down their psychic gifts, and this often occurs when they become very scared of what they see, or when they find their unseen 'friends' cause too much trouble, as is the case when mom and dad don't believe what the child says.

A child may have been physically or emotionally hurt, or is sad or angry, generating emotions wholeheartedly, in the way that children do, when a 'friend' who is invisible to anyone but the child, may appear to offer comfort and support. A rapport is set up and the entity, wanting to be of help (or hindrance) may attach itself either to the outer aura, or more deeply within the magnetic energy field of the child, and needs help to be released. People who ridicule this theory had better start looking within, literally, as it isn't just children who attract entities—whether they can see them or not. No one is immune.

We are all surrounded by our own unique energy field, or aura, which fluctuates and changes, depending upon our moods, emotions, and state of health. In times of distress, anger, grief, physical exhaustion, and particularly when the body's energies are run down or out of sync, due to consumption of drugs or alcohol or for other reasons, the protective aura may shrink for a while, leaving the body vulnerable.

Have you ever known someone who, when sober, is a perfectly wonderful human being, but after a few drinks becomes a 'different' person, acting totally out of character, with a complete personality change, and later claims he or she doesn't remember anything that happened? Or a person who's feeding an addiction while trying to quit so is not successful? Whose addiction is it—that person's, or an invisible hitchhiker or two that really latched on and are freely enjoying the habit at someone else's expense?

It certainly is a good reason to be less judgmental of other folks. When people claim they can't help what they are doing, it just may be that they really can't help it, and won't be able to change their behavior until they seek help. Attached entities can and do make their presence felt, frequently through their aches and pains, although they may not necessarily be aware that they are affecting their host with 'symptoms' of conditions present at the time of their death. And they also express their own anger and frustration through the emotions of their 'host.'

Have you ever wondered why you were attracted to the most unlikely person, or surprised yourself by going out with somebody you knew you didn't like? It could have been an entity at work that fancied the other person.

Maybe you're in a relationship and the two of you keep breaking up. Life is intolerable when you are together, so you split; then you can't understand why you get drawn back into the relationship again and wish you'd stuck to your guns. It could just be an attachment influencing your decisions.

The abusive person could very well be living out an entity's hatred-driven desire to get even because of its own unfinished business.

But I really do find it sad when a client learns of an attached entity and doesn't want to let it go, for whatever reason. It could be a relative or friend who passed on. When an entity is discovered and the client wants to hang on for dear life, through nothing short of selfishness, then that person is actually holding up the entity's spiritual evolution by preventing his or her progress. And into the bargain, the client keeps whatever aches, pains, personal idiosyncrasies, and shortcomings belong to the entity.

The lonely person who feels unloved is less likely to let go of an entity if he or she feels it is the only 'person' around offering love. Artistic or musically inclined people sometimes are reluctant to let go just in case their talents also go. We knew an excellent medium who was very clairvoyant, but she was scared that if she let her attachment go, she would lose her psychic abilities and so lose her income! Fortunately, that didn't happen; in fact, after undergoing a spirit-releasement, she was more in tune than before the session; even her psychic readings became more reliable once she finally ended up using her own psychic abilities and not information given to her by an invisible 'hanger-on.'

Unfortunately, many psychics, because they 'open themselves up' a lot, often haven't a clue that they may have any number of entities aboard. Naively assuming automatic protection, they become very defensive or angry if it is suggested they may have some entity attachments. "My gatekeeper wouldn't allow that to happen to me" is the indignant comment I've heard more than once. Little is it realized that the indignation may stem from an entity, alarmed at being discovered, that is attempting to chase away someone who might expedite his or her departure from the scene!

What these psychics don't want to believe is that they are no different from anyone else and are subject to the same dangers. If they fly into a rage, become physically exhausted from over-exerting themselves, get sick or run down, their auras shrink and they are wide open to being 'jumped.'

One doesn't even need to be a psychic to be 'jumped.' One morning, a young couple contacted us wanting to know if we could do a 'ghost-busting' session at their apartment. A few days earlier, the woman had awoken gasping for breath. She had felt a pair of hands gripping her throat and when she opened her eyes she had seen a 'horrible face' right up close. As she wrestled with her attacker she frantically repeated the 23rd Psalm and eventually managed to free herself from the vise-like grip. To her amazement, when she looked around, there was no one else in the room except the husband who was sleeping soundly beside her.

The wife immediately woke her husband and told him of her terrible ordeal. He was enraged and leapt out of bed, looking around for the now invisible assailant. With exaggerated movements suggesting an invitation to come close, he gestured to whoever was there, saying aloud that the attacker should leave his wife alone in future and try picking on someone more his own size, namely, himself. Three days later, the husband awoke in the early hours literally fighting for breath—it was his turn to feel hands tightening around his throat as he wrestled with the steely grip, desperately trying to remember the words that had helped his wife. It was obvious that his 'invitation' had been accepted.

We willingly 'cleared' the apartment for them. After that, neither of them was bothered by any other invisible assailants, although over the weeks, as spooks came and went—the young woman could now see them—it was necessary for us to repeat the procedure. Finally, we cleared the whole apartment building; then we instructed the couple how to keep their suite clear of the wandering earthbound spirits and how to dispatch them to the Light.

There began to be a change in the husband, however, and at one point he told us that he felt it wrong for us to 'play God.' He knew it was possible for these earthbound spirits to get drawn into a person's energy field, but so what? If people wanted to try the experience of having someone with them, then that was their own business, he said, and nobody had the right to interfere or command any entities to leave. What harm could there be, he asked? He'd done it recently and felt quite okay, he emphasized. Was this the husband speaking or was it an entity that had taken over?

We warned the young man that once invited in, these entities could stay and eventually take over the body. He was adamant that would never happen. Naively, he believed he would always be in control in such a situation. We recognized that he didn't want to listen to anything further and it would be futile to try and change his mind.... This is, after all, a free will zone.

It really saddened us, though, at a later date, when the wife expressed concern because she had discovered that her husband had begun carrying on three or four-sided conversations, some in different dialects, whenever he thought he was alone. She confided in me one day that, she didn't even know any more who was making love to her and she didn't know how much more she could take of her husband's behavior. Had he begun to pay the price or had she? We suggested that a surrogate session could be done 'in absentia' to free him of the entities. We recommended that this be done for him immediately. But she declined our offer. She chose to honor his decision as he'd already said that he didn't want any help and made her promise she wouldn't seek help on his behalf. She said a surrogate session would break that promise.

I've often been asked why our guardian angels or guides don't keep us safe from such situations. I always respond that our angels or guides are nearby the whole day through, but they are distanced from us (they cannot impose their will on ours). And they can only assist us from that distance, when requested, although they do try to guide or steer us away from certain conditions. But if we have actually invited an entity in, consciously or unconsciously, through our own thoughts and actions, our guides can't intervene; because of our free will choice, they must allow us to go through the experience.

I suppose it was because of my own silliness that I became a sitting duck for a discarnate entity that attached itself to me one early morning. Perhaps I had to go through the experience in order to learn from it. Maybe it was a reminder for me to always connect with my inner light upon awakening and to expand it outwards to completely fill my energy field. We call the process 'setting up our Light.' Whatever I'd done to cause the situation to occur, I'm in no hurry to repeat the experience. But I will share it just to illustrate how easily we can be affected by the presence of those we can't see.

One evening we'd made a snap decision to take a trip to Vancouver. But we couldn't leave until early the following morning. It's fair to say that Derek and I always seem to be doing things on the spur of the moment, at least when it comes to going any place on our days off.

We had been unable to get to bed early that night because the evening's class finished after ten, and by the time our students had left and we reached home, it wasn't much short of midnight before I got any shut-eye. Nevertheless, Derek wanted to leave around 2:30 AM. I was still very tired when he woke me and would have been happier with a much later start. Dragging my feet didn't assist in slowing our departure, and so I reluctantly climbed into the car.

After only a short while on the road I began to feel nauseous. I told myself it was just because I was traveling on an empty stomach. So I searched out the cookies I'd hastily packed for the trip and nibbled on one. Bad move. Searing heartburn became nausea's companion. So did thirst. But the mere thought of the coffee substitute in Derek's thermos turned my stomach even more. I'd have to suffer it out until our first pit stop.

Four and a half miserable hours later Derek pulled into a gas station. While he refuelled the car, I staggered out of the vehicle and steered my body towards the cafeteria. Perhaps a drink of water and some dry toast would appease my stomach. No such luck. One mouthful of my meager breakfast and my stomach immediately felt as if it had gone into a violent spasm.

Derek had joined me in the cafeteria and ordered a man-sized breakfast. He munched happily whilst my imagination worked overtime as I watched him eat. I blamed the car for the way I was feeling. After all, it was probably the smallest one in which I had ridden any distance. And I'd never experienced carsickness before. That must be it; the size of the car was obviously the cause of my nausea. Or maybe, without us knowing it, poisonous exhaust fumes were seeping into the vehicle. But why was Derek unaffected?

I moaned to Derek about how sick I felt. With fork still poised in mid air he began to speak to me in hypnotherapy mode and I willingly submitted to his questions.

"And if this burning feeling of nausea could talk, what would it say?" Derek asked. The impassioned response was, "I want to get out of here." As Derek elicited more responses he discovered I had picked up a 'hitchhiker.' That's right, the invisible kind.

Apparently, my intruder was in the car when we got in. It had been easy to invade my space because I was so tired and peeved at having to be up so soon when there seemed to be no logical reason for us to leave that early. I was annoyed at myself. I had allowed my physical body to be pushed to its limits by not getting adequate rest. And we had been on the road for some time before we thought to fill the car with light so as to clear out any negative energies. We should have done that before climbing aboard. But, by the time I remembered to generate light around and inside the car, it was too late.

When Derek regressed me back to the moment when I got into the car, at a subconscious level, yes, I was aware of the other energy in the vehicle. There was no doubt about it, a discarnate entity was 'on board' and soon after, the old cowboy had quickly attached himself to my aura. After all, I had literally sat in his 'lap' or space. And my energy level was quite low due to the lack of sleep. On a conscious level at that early hour, I was too tired, disgruntled and preoccupied to notice his presence and therefore my aura had shrunk and my extra-sensory perception or alert sensors were turned off.

As Derek asked more questions, we quickly learned that the entity, whose name was Jake, disliked traveling with us and wanted out. The motion of the car and sight of roadside grass verges whizzing by were making him feel deadly sick. His preferred mode of travel was horseback.

Derek made the appropriate suggestions and directed my unwelcome traveling companion to leave, telling the old man to take his conditions and sickness with him.

At least I'd learned my lesson. Never again would I stagger into a vehicle at 2:30 AM after little or no sleep without having taken proper precautions. I'd either make sure the vehicle was cleared before getting in, or I'd get enough sleep so that I could function properly and remember our safety routine.

I know this entity stuff really does happen. I know, too, that once they've gone, all their 'symptoms' of aches, pains, sickness, etc. go at the same time. I do believe in the spirit-releasement process, and above all, I do believe in Derek's ability, and my own for that matter if I am the facilitator, to get rid of earthbound entities once and for all...providing there is no unfinished business on the entity's part!

Back on the highway again, however, I still felt sick. Because our little session had taken up more time than we expected, I knew it would be a while before Derek decided to make another stop. When he did, I got out of the vehicle to stretch my legs. We'd covered over 600 miles since setting out from Edmonton and I was literally gasping for something to drink. I purchased a couple of cans of soda for the next leg of our journey and then climbed back into the car, comforted by the knowledge that the soda pop would settle my queasy stomach.

I didn't want to be a nuisance, and I was trying not to complain. But as I was still feeling so very nauseous, I began to doubt the validity of the whole releasement or depossession process. I told myself perhaps it was only in my imagination that there had been an entity 'on board'. Maybe I had been making up all the responses in my head. If Derek had dispatched some kind of earthbound entity or spirit, why didn't I feel better? Once they are dispatched, their 'symptoms' go with them.

Derek climbed aboard and started the vehicle once more. As it roared to life and began to pick up speed, I took a few sips of soda before realizing this, too, was a bad move. The sight of trees, more grass verges and road whizzing by made me feel worse.

Out of the blue I asked Derek how much further we had to go. He said we still had another 400 miles or more ahead of us. He estimated it should only take about four or five more hours to reach Vancouver, depending on traffic and driving conditions.

At this point I felt a tremendous sense of panic. I blurted out that would be equivalent to two weeks with horse and buggy. That was strange. I still felt sick and demanded that Derek stop the car immediately.

Realizing that the 'hitchhiker' was still with me, Derek began his hypnosis jargonese again. I wanted to tell him to get off the bandwagon and leave me alone, but instead the words came out, "STOP THE VEHICLE, NOW!"

By the time Derek pulled over to the shoulder of the road and stopped I already had the seat belt unfastened and the door open. I quickly leaned over and willingly parted company with what little I'd consumed that day. I carried on and on, heaving, the bitterness of bile burning my throat. Derek came round to the passenger door and assisted me to the front of the car.

He began questioning Jake again as to why he hadn't left when he'd had the opportunity during the first impromptu session. Derek reminded Jake that he had asked him whom he would like see again and Jake had responded that he'd like to see his wife. When Derek had asked the Beings of Light to bring her down, Jake was aware of her presence. He even made like he was going to leave with her. So why didn't he go? Derek asked. And why wasn't I aware that he hadn't left?

It dawned on me that as I had been feeling too sick and tired to follow the proceedings closely. I'd simply assumed Jake had gone.

Again, Derek asked the old man why he had not left with his wife when the opportunity presented itself. Jake responded that he only wanted to see her again to know if she was sorry for what she had done. But, he added, she was the last person he'd go anywhere with...she had poisoned him!

Bingo! So that was why I was 'picking up' or feeling his stomach's burning 'nausea.' And why did Jake's wife poison him? A little probing revealed that Jake had been heavy-handed over the years and she couldn't take it any more.

Derek's tone was kind as he asked if the old cowboy had learned anything from what had happened. The answer was "yes." Jake knew he had driven his wife to murder. He said he now realized he had deserved what he got. But, although he now felt remorse for the way he'd treated his wife, he didn't want go to the same place she had gone.

Derek used the opportunity to explain how each soul chooses to learn its lessons and suggested that if Jake had learned something from the whole experience, then it was time for him to progress to the next stage of his soul's journey. Jake listened to some more explanations about life after death and was reassured by Derek that there wouldn't be some white-bearded man on a throne 'Up There' pointing an accusing finger or sitting in judgment. The old cowboy finally realized that he was, in fact, his own judge and jury. Shortly after that change in his perception, Jake really did leave me to go on to the Light, taking his own baggage with him, sickness, heartburn, shooting pains in the stomach and all.

Miraculously, I felt better instantly. I was ravenous and tackled the munchies Derek had bought at the previous pit stop. In fact, I really enjoyed the rest of the journey. Apart from the gentle reminder of tender stomach muscles complaining they had been jerked into exercise earlier, I felt absolutely fine. It was as if someone had flicked a switch and I had gone immediately from feeling painfully sick to feeling incredibly healthy again. Small car theory be darned! Ditto for carsickness.

I would say that the only people perhaps immune to entity attachment would be those whose conscious awareness and vibrations are raised to such a high level that entities operating at a lesser frequency cannot penetrate their auras; they would only gain entry should those people become sick. The strange thing is, when a person has reached those higher vibratory levels, they rarely become ill because their thoughts and actions no longer attract such conditions.

Hypnotherapy or surrogate sessions for a spirit-releasement to be performed, whether done for ourselves or others, will not change a person's normal personality; however, such sessions can and frequently do help us to become more at peace with ourselves and with the world around us. Also, it is strongly recommended that we become seriously committed to pursuing and maintaining a healthy lifestyle, so as to avoid leaving ourselves wide open for an influx of unwanted 'guests.' Once we understand this, what greater incentive do we need to take responsibility for our lives?

But to deny that any one of us could be the target for entity attachment is the most foolish stance to take; it ranks alongside the ostrich sticking its head into the sand, the 'if I can't see it, it's not there' scenario. We can't see the air we breathe, and we can't always smell it, but that doesn't mean it isn't there.

* * *

During one of our channeling sessions, Derek began asking questions about entity attachments and what we can do to protect ourselves from their influence.

"There is a very bright light created here as you are working," my guide responded, *"and so you attract those entities that are seeking assistance. They are attracted to your light as moths to a flame. Each day, if you mentally create a column of light a short distance from the building to attract those who are 'lost,' and if you make a request that there is someone within that column of light whom they recognize and trust, they will perhaps proceed to the light unaided. This will take care of some that are attracted to your light.*

"If either of you feel a little under the weather, shall we say, it would be advisable to refrain from attempting to channel," my guide cautioned, *"because at those times you are at your most vulnerable, even though you are wise enough to take precautions every time you seek to enter an altered state of awareness.*

"Warnings given by many religious organizations were given for a good reason. A person may be playing with fire when attempting to communicate with those existing in another dimension, which includes the earthbound entities; that is why it is necessary to 'test the spirits from whence they come,' as recommended in your Bible. All who seek to communicate with 'spirit,' not only those who work with Ouija boards, can be attracting the lower astral forms. There are exceptions, of course; sometimes a person comes in contact with a being that brings much enlightenment."

"Is it true that sometimes entities remain earthbound in order to create more chaos upon the earth, or because other beings prevent them from carrying on with their spiritual progression?" Derek asked.

"Some such influences may be present. However, prior to the state of transition you call death, there may have been a condition or belief held that would deter the soul from going to higher dimensions. There are not armies of other beings standing there to frighten those souls away from the Light after 'death.'

"Souls may remain earthbound because of low self-esteem in one form or another; fear caused by religious beliefs is one factor, or conditions of chaos may have been present at the occasion you term 'death.' Strong ties to family members can also hold them bound to the earth plane. Even self-judgment could cause this attachment if the soul feels remorse at having misjudged or harmed another, or not loved sufficiently, or not expressed sufficient love; a sense of failure and its own emotions may be holding it here. If that soul does not believe in 'life after death' and is convinced death is a journey that will take him no further than the graveyard, then that is where he will remain until circumstances occur for him to realize differently. There are many factors why the entities do not return to the light," the guide explained.

"Through my work, I've come across mischievous entities that seem quite capable of driving people to their death," Derek remarked.

"You see, all souls, whether embodied within the physical or not, are very powerful; they have abilities which may only be discovered after the passing over," the guide explained. "This is why certain disembodied spirits may delight in discovering they can influence those who cannot see them; their influence may be felt more after 'death' than when they were 'alive.' Some may have been quite ingenious while living on the earth plane, in ways you would term as not good, such as the criminal being highly creative in a manner that society deems unacceptable; this creativity does not necessarily stop after 'death.'

"At birth, each soul arriving upon the earth plane starts with the same advantages. Actual life itself is the same for everyone; we each color, or set a course, with certain limitations we place on ourselves either before birth, during birth, or after birth. Some are impeded by physical or mental conditions, but all of these restrictions are placed by self through one's choice or perception. Yet all souls are equal, all have the same advantages.

"In spite of trials which are all self-imposed before commencing life upon earth, their purpose will be revealed, will be perceived, will be followed, because each person is not alone. Each person may have one, may have many guides, coaxing and attempting to lead self to achieve the full potential of progression open to self in that life-experience.

"And so, if upon transition after physical 'death,' the person or soul has reached a sufficient level of understanding and is ready to go on to the next higher level or dimension, then that will occur. However, it will not occur if he or she did not reach that level or has entertained free will choices or beliefs that impeded his or her progress. But know this, the deceased has to come to certain realizations after 'transition,' and eventually, when ready *and willing, and wishing to progress to a higher level, the opportunity will be provided for the journey to continue,"* the guide concluded on a reassuring note.

* * *

During another conversation with one of my guides, Derek again touched on the subject of entities and how they could be assisted. "There appear to be millions of disembodied spirits, entities stuck or held for hundreds of years within the earth plane or astral plane. Is this the reality they have created because of their beliefs?" Derek asked.

"Yes, in most instances. Soul Workers such as yourselves, and all others teaching ways to achieve enlightenment, attract them in the way honeycombs attract bears. You have been shown a way to assist the discarnate beings by mentally setting up a column of light a short distance away from yourselves that contain many types of things that will attract their attention. There are those who would only be attracted to certain individuals, but if you were to use your imaginations and create something in that column of light to attract attention, such as a cathedral or a carnival—whatever you feel inspired to create—that is where they would be drawn. If you create more than one column of light, there will be a variety of conditions for the confused ones to go to where loved ones can be seen waiting. It is preferable to create these columns of light outdoors.

"Many disembodied souls learn in a manner similar to osmosis through those into whose energy field they have been drawn. Because of people such as you, many of these souls will be dispatched before certain earth changes occur. If anyone wishes to assist those suspected of being present in a house or building, the person wishing to help may mentally 'project' a column of light outside the house or building, and then mentally direct the discarnate soul into it. 'Pretending' a column of light is there will also create that column of light, because of the thought and intent. One may ask for a Being of Light, an angel, or a guide to assist the 'soul' into the light where a deceased family member or some trusted friend is waiting. Also, when these words are read, if there are those present for learning purposes, they too get the message, and as the reader becomes aware of their presence, he or she will know what to do," my guide concluded.

* * *

Derek was seeking advice one day about the advisability of assisting a friend clearly plagued by entities. My guide was very quick to respond to Derek's inquiry:

"It is beneficial to examine your motives before assisting a friend, or deciding what may be appropriate for other persons. When expressing love and concern for others, in your desire to assist, it is preferable you do not take away their challenges; it is not always in their best interests to remove the very things they have chosen as the instrument through which learning may occur. Sometimes it is appropriate to intervene as an agreement or contract to do so may have been made on another level."

"Another Catch-22 situation," Derek exclaimed. "But I wasn't planning to be the knight on his white horse charging down the street to save everybody from themselves. I do realize people must arrive at their own choices; when ready, they will ask for help."

"Very often the greatest way to assist another is by allowing your own light to shine," my guide suggested, "showing the way by example with love and compassion, sharing that which is yours to share. Very often being the example is of more assistance than the gallant deeds of the knight in shining armor, though both do, in effect, achieve the same purpose, because of the intent."

"I suspect part of helping is to just let others know that we're here if needed."

"This is wise. If choosing to seek help, they [the entities] will be guided to where they will receive assistance, just as you are guided by those guardians or guides assisting you in this type of work [spirit releasement]; however those guardians or guides must be asked for specifically."

"Do they have a particular name or designation?"

"You may call upon the Beings of Light, and they will assist you in dispatching the unwanted energies. You will be inspired to say the right words."

"We have been trying to do releasements in a 'humane' way, although we do know of people in our line of work who use a more callous approach, like a traditional exorcism."

"It is wise to treat all entities with respect, but if they do not wish to leave, remember the old adage, 'All's fair in love and war.' But first, offer a choice. If necessary, use every means at your disposal—whichever method you feel is best."

"We've encountered many uncooperative entities. Is it fitting to ask the Beings of Light to take them away?"

"You are guided during each individual set of circumstances. If it is felt that an energy is so angry or destructive that it cannot be reasoned with, or would prolong the session, or even invade the facilitator or surrogate, you have the liberty, the discretion, and the choice to do as you see fit."

"If asking for a 'container' in which to restrain an 'uncooperative' energy, should we be more specific?"

"As you use the words, you create a thought form or image of what you are requesting. If you think of a canister or sphere, whatever you are thinking of, you create. If you are vague in your thoughts, the 'container' will be rather vague. If, as you are talking about a container, you are thinking iron-clad thoughts, then you will have an iron-clad container."

"We don't want to create something that would cause alarm for the entity."

"All your words, telepathic or spoken, are energy created and are simply governed by thought. If, in your communication, you are indecisive as to the form of the container, the indecisiveness is already created and you would have no faith in what you are communicating, and therefore you would create an unstable or ineffective container," the guide cautioned *"and the session would be unsuccessful. When working with these energies, always keep your thoughts decisive, precise and strong."*

These conversations with our guides certainly gave us much to think about and subsequently proved to be of great help in our surrogate and spirit-releasement work.

Chapter 18

I've come to the firm conclusion that nothing ever occurs randomly in this life we live; everything follows a set plan, and we are tied into 'past' lives in ways we rarely get an opportunity to know about or understand. Sound inconceivable? Earlier in this book I did say fact could be stranger than fiction. Now is my chance to relate one or two incidents.

Why would a 'chance' encounter enable a small item, given to me over thirty years ago, to be delivered to its rightful owner as a gift, in a scene re-enacted for the second time in almost two thousand years? How could acute pain, suffered for years, disappear after a past-life regression? And what about channeling information from higher energies like Derek did centuries ago before he died for his labors?

I'd had problems with my lower back since the late 1960s; a disc in my spine would 'slip' or rupture periodically. I'd be completely laid up with excruciating pain for several weeks at a time. Over the years the condition deteriorated.

By about 1975, I was re-diagnosed as having a degenerative disc disease. It reached the stage where the severe pain remained constant because, with the slightest movement of my body, vertebra rubbed against vertebra. My doctor had suggested possible surgery to remove what was left of the disc and fuse the adjacent vertebrae.

But I didn't want to undergo surgery. I was a single mom with four kids still at home and I had no other relatives they could go to for the duration of a hospital stay. I didn't want my children to have to go into foster care for a month or two whilst I recuperated from surgery. I just couldn't do that to them. Also, I knew a woman who claimed her son had undergone exactly the same surgical procedure on his spine and afterwards he was left paralyzed from the waist down. No thanks. So I stuck with the pain.

At first, to handle the agony, I was relying on prescribed painkillers. But when I learned that these inoffensive looking capsules contained narcotics, I was so shocked I had fifty fits about where I could end up. That discovery changed my life. There was no way I would knowingly continue taking narcotics. I quit cold-turkey.

Immediately, I started seeking other ways to handle pain and began practicing self-healing meditations and guided visualizations. Eventually, by utilizing a special visualization that caused my brain to release endorphins, I did learn how to control the pain so that I could get to sleep at night. Of course, my movements during sleep would cause pain that woke me several times during the night, so I had to repeat the process again and again. And I realized I was only 'treating' the symptom, not the cause.

I remember on one occasion when I was in bed and the pain was just too intense to bear, I had literally cried out to God, saying I couldn't take it any more, and I begged for help. I was no stranger to prayer, but on that particular occasion, as I opened my eyes I saw a brilliant oval light 'standing' at the foot of my bed; as it radiated outwards and lit the whole room I realized that my pain was abating. I began pinching my arms to find out if this vision was 'real' or if I was somehow hallucinating. I was most certainly wide-awake and it sure hurt when I pinched myself. And then I realized there was no discomfort in my back at all as I moved! Exhausted from fighting pain for so long, I laid there for a while, just gazing at the beautiful light, and eventually I dozed off to sleep. When I awoke in the early hours the light had gone, but so had the pain...for the time being.

About three years before I met Derek, my degenerative disc condition had reduced me to walking in a way my sainted father would have described as a 'here's-me-head-and-me-arse-is-coming' gait, like I was leaning head-long into a gale force wind. I could stay on my feet for only a few minutes at a time. Then I heard from a psychic to whom I'd gone for a reading. She told me of an upcoming three-day past-life regression workshop that was to be held out of town. I would find it very beneficial to attend, she said.

I had never heard of past-life regression before, and I idea no idea how attending a workshop could help me. Besides, my shoestring budget would not stretch that far. So attending any workshop was out of the question.

A few days later a neighbor came to visit me and as we sipped coffee I shared details of my visit to the psychic and her suggestion. My youngest son, Karl, hovered restlessly nearby as we visited, and later, after I escorted my neighbor to the door, my boy disappeared into his bedroom. When he reappeared he walked over to me and thrust a bundle of dollar bills into my hands. He insisted I should put the money towards the cost of the workshop. I was choked with emotion. My child had just given me all of his paper route savings that had been earmarked for a new bicycle. On hearing of Karl's gesture, my older sons, who already had left home, donated the balance so that I could attend. Talk about divine providence giving me a helping hand through my sons. I guess I was literally intended to be there.

Towards the end of the workshop, I was regressed to a lifetime that would have most bearing on my present one. The incarnation I accessed was one in the early 1800s in France. My mother had died during childbirth. As an orphan, I was living with about five other motherless children of different ages, in a dirt-floored dwelling. But there was no real mother figure on hand, although different women came to bring bread and a type of watery gruel for us to eat.

Even though we were really poorly clothed and seemed to lack proper nutrition in that life experience, we all survived childhood. At age sixteen I married a peasant boy and we raised our own family. We lived a simple life but we were very happy. I recognized the peasant boy. He's now my youngest son, Karl.

When the regressionist told me to review that former lifetime to see how it related to my present life, I realized that this time around I had chosen to be the mother figure. But in doing so, I had taken things to the opposite extreme. In trying to be Super Mom for my kids whilst fighting excruciating pain, I was baking bread, sewing, making clothes, being overprotective and supportive, my life revolving around my offspring even to the point of refusing the surgery so I could be there for them all the time.

Then the sirens and whistles blew and the realization hit home. I could still be a good parent and do a good job without being so rigid and sacrificing myself to my children. More importantly, I recognized that it was now time to lighten up the load I'd created for myself and had been carrying around for so long.

When I was asked how that insight made me feel, I responded, "Like a big weight has been lifted from my shoulders." At that point, I was brought out of the regression and told to go and join the other participants.

As I began walking away, the regressionist called out to me, "And how do you feel now, Diana?" I spun around to respond. Immediately, I was totally overcome with joy as I realized that not only was I standing erect, my lower back was totally free of any pain. I began running across the room kicking my heels in the air like a rodeo horse intent on bucking its rider. Friends told me later that I had walked around with a silly grin on my face for a full two weeks after that past life regression. And I'm still smiling. Miraculously, I've been pain-free in that area ever since.

I vowed then that, somehow, some way, I would learn how help others in similar situations. I guess that decision helped create my present reality.

* * *

Just over thirty years ago, during the late sixties, I was traveling the 'overland route' by mini-van with my two sons, aged four and two, and my then husband. Our exciting and unforgettable trip started in Australia (where I had lived on and off for nine years) and carried on through southeast Asia and the Middle East, finishing some 30,000 miles and thirteen months later in Britain. The trip of a lifetime, you might say. I believe I've since learned the real reason why I undertook that sometimes hair-raising adventure with two youngsters in tow.

Whilst in Jordan, we considered ourselves to be very blessed when a local university student volunteered to accompany us to Petra, to act as our guide and interpreter at the ancient ruins described in tourist literature as "the Rose Red City of Nabatean times."

Before arriving at Petra, our young guide explained the inadvisability of purchasing any relics, should we be approached, because he had heard that there were some unscrupulous merchants in the area selling backyard-manufactured 'antiques' to unsuspecting tourists.

We were busy exploring the ruins when my sons became extremely distressed; a very wizened old woman, dressed totally in black, had begun following us. I assumed she was just fascinated by my very blond-haired fair-skinned boys, and I offered her some money so that she would go away. She left just as soon as our guide explained to her that both boys were scared because other women had approached and then pinched them on their arms and cheeks.

Later, when we were on the point of leaving Petra, the old woman appeared again. She came right up to me and held out a fragment of pottery and a small earthenware bottle about three inches long with a bulbous bottom and narrow neck. She looked over at the boys and then said something as she looked at me again. I hadn't a clue as to what she was trying to convey. Our guide hurried over to shoo her away. He thought she was after some more money. But the old woman apparently just wanted me to choose one of the items she was holding. I picked the little bottle. When I tried to offer her more money, she refused. I wasn't really sure what our interpreter had said, but I smiled and thanked her.

Although I believed the little earthenware bottle was just some backyard piece of pottery produced by locals for the tourist trade, I treasured my souvenir. I had been tempted to let the boys use it in their games a couple of times, but later decided to keep the little bottle wrapped in cotton inside an empty tobacco tin. I wanted my souvenir to survive the journey.

A couple of years later I was working in England as a newspaper reporter for *The Northern Echo* at their Middlesbrough regional office. While covering an event in that city, I met the Curator of the Dorman Long Museum. At a later meeting I told him about my interesting little piece of earthenware pottery. On a hunch, he asked me to bring it to the museum; he would like to take a look at it, he said.

Several days later I complied with the Curator's request and handed him my Petra souvenir. Still acting on a hunch, he took detailed measurements of the bottle and sent a sketch of it to the British Museum's Department of Antiquities in London. Their interest, too, was sparked, and so the lowly little earthenware bottle made its way to London, where it was carbon-tested to determine its age. The British Museum subsequently reported that my souvenir dated back to the first century AD. It was, they said, typical of pottery used in the Middle East at that time period and they presumed it was an unguent bottle that had been used for holding ointment or sweet-smelling oil. Of course, I wrote a feature article about my 'souvenir' for my newspaper, and the story, together with a photo of my boys holding the ancient bottle, appeared in print shortly afterwards.

After that, for almost thirty years, I still kept the little unguent bottle swaddled in cotton, hidden away in its tobacco tin, with a yellowing copy of the newspaper article also carefully tucked inside, rarely taking them out to handle or show anyone.

And then, just before Christmas of 1992, after completing one of a series of hypnotherapy courses, I told Derek I felt a strange compulsion to show the tiny earthenware bottle to Anny Slegten, the Director of the Hypnotism Training Institute of Alberta. And, depending upon her reaction when she saw it, I just might give it to her.

The following morning we gave Anny a call and made arrangements to stop by. I simply said we had something she might like to see, but, apart from that, I didn't tell her anything. I made the decision on the way over that I would say nothing of what was on my mind, although for some reason unknown to me then, I knew deep down inside that my Petra souvenir really belonged to her.

I wanted to see how Anny would react when I placed the little bottle into her hands. If there were any signs of recognition, I'd give it to her. If not, I'd keep it myself. Secretly, I was hoping she would just see it as an interesting souvenir of mine.

When we arrived, we were ushered straight into Anny's office. First, I took the newspaper article out of the can for her to see, and then I gently unwrapped the miniature earthenware bottle and placed it into her hand.

Immediately, Anny was moved to tears. She already knew of a previous lifetime she'd lived during the first century AD, and had already experienced a few fleeting memories of it. But as soon as she took hold of the little bottle, a host of memories began flowing to her like scenes in a movie, filling in the details of that past lifetime.

Seeing how Anny had been so moved by the little earthenware bottle, I told her I wanted her to have it as a gift...but, as it turned out, this wasn't the first time I gave it to her. Apparently, it was one of a set of four that I had made and given to her as a gift in that lifetime, too!

And, surprise, surprise, Derek also was my husband in that incarnation. Whoever said that history repeats itself certainly knew what he, or she, was talking about.

* * *

One day a friend of mine came to see me. She's very psychic and equally forthright. Derek had never met or spoken to her before. I took her into his office to introduce him. She took one look at him and blurted out vehemently, "You'd never be able to hypnotize me!" Taken aback, Derek asked if she was challenging him in order to prove that he couldn't do just that. Her response was an immediate "yes." So, unwilling to bypass a challenge, Derek began facilitating a session with her. Little did she realize that he would use her own resistance to take her into a deep hypnotic trance. It worked.

Almost immediately she regressed into a former incarnation in which she was a monk. Then Derek guided her to an important event in that lifetime. It took Derek quite by surprise when she opened her eyes, sat bolt upright, pointed a finger at him, and then began accusing him of abandoning her. However, Derek skillfully led her into a deep trance again to find out more of that lifetime. She had apparently recognized Derek as being another monk in that incarnation. His name then was Brother Job; she was Brother Matthew. In that life, they began, in secret, to write down what was being said as they heard the 'voice of God' speaking to them during the middle of the night. It was something to do with the 'Law of One.' While still in an altered state of awareness, my friend passionately complained that she was 'left' on her own to 'face the music.' She was killed after church officials, following exposure of the nocturnal exploits, summoned Derek and the Abbot.

I was present during the whole session. To say the least, we were all amazed by what had transpired. But I wanted to find out more, so I offered to facilitate a dual past-life regression. My intention was to regress them both at the same time, to see if they could simultaneously access that lifetime together. This was successfully done the following day, with each of them taking turns describing their clandestine, candlelight channeling sessions in a cellar at a secluded monastery. Then I directed Brother Matthew to retrieve one of the handwritten parchment documents they had apparently hidden in a recess behind a rock in the wall. Next, I suggested she read it aloud. Right on cue, my friend began reading the words...and then I was astounded again as Derek completed the sentence! Wow, what a session that proved to be.

Later, when I asked Derek to tell me what Brother Job was like, he described him as a "Friar Tuck type of guy, rather on the chubby side."

Some time after that experience, our guides suggested we look into the origins of our current abundance issue, or lack of funds; it could stem from past vows of poverty in which we relinquished all worldly goods, they said. And so we decided it just might prove profitable to explore past life scenarios where we may have made such vows. It might also help us find out why we seemed to be attracting people to us who couldn't pay for our professional services, we reasoned. Our motives were good, but it didn't pay the rent and overheads. Business couldn't go on much longer at this rate.

As Derek sat in The Chair, I guided him into a deep relaxation and made the suggestion he access another lifetime in which he had vowed to relinquish all worldly possessions. At once, he began to experience a pinching, tweaking sensation in his throat. Then he started describing a scene in which he was wearing a beige robe; he was nervously pacing up and down in a small, sparsely furnished room, back in a lifetime as a monk, wondering how to plan the next move. He wasn't too sure what was going to happen next, except he knew there was definitely something wrong; he was experiencing a deep sense of foreboding.

I directed him to move ahead to an important event. He began describing another scene in which he was looking at symbols in a book, and he spoke of a triangle superimposed upon a half-circle. He knew the symbol was pretty important, and began talking as if there was someone else with him.

When I asked Derek what his name was in that lifetime, he said, "Job." Although I didn't make the connection right away, Derek had re-accessed the same past-lifetime that he and my friend had both accessed together during the dual regression I'd facilitated for them recently. What I found most interesting was that, apparently, I was the Abbot at the small, remote abbey or monastery in Wales where they (Brothers Job and Matthew) had been sent.

It seems the two young monks had been up to some aberrant behavior not normally condoned, and they had been 'banished' from their previous monastery and dispatched to a smaller, more secluded one.

Derek stressed that the Abbot also knew the significance of the symbol. I advanced Derek to another important occasion in that incarnation. He was waiting in an office that hinted opulence. Among the gold and green office paraphernalia on a desk standing at one end of the room lay a golden paper knife with a jade handle. This was the office of some high official. Brother Job and the Abbot had been summoned for an audience with officials and were anxiously waiting for their arrival.

I instructed Derek to take a close look at whoever entered into the room and to give me a description. Derek began to describe the person as wearing a long white robe and a type of skullcap. He also recognized that person as someone else known to us today. I asked Derek why he, a humble monk, and the Abbot were there.

Derek became very agitated, saying, "It's important. They want it, and I know it's not right. I know it isn't going to be used properly. We have to be careful. As soon as they found out about it we were in a lot of danger. We are a threat to them because we know what is going on within the Church."

I advanced Derek to another important event in that lifetime. It occurred at nightfall, very shortly after Brother Job and the Abbot had met with the high-ranking church officials. The two were in a room at an inn, discussing the journey home. Then the door burst open. Four men, with hoods obscuring their faces, immediately overpowered the Abbott and

Brother Job. After being murdered, the bodies of Brother Job and the Abbot were dragged outside and thrown into a thicket.

What was so important? Why were they killed? Was it because of information within the 'book' that Brothers Job and Matthew were writing? When I asked where the book was, Derek said it was back at the monastery, hidden inside the cellar walls, as Brother Matthew had taken the precaution of hiding it.

Derek said he knew he received the divine information directly from God. He then added, "The information channeled was always given with love. However, because of the situation and the Church's position of control, carrying out crimes in the name of God, he, Brother Job, at the scene of his death, vowed, 'I want nothing more to do with the God who created all this.'"

He also made a vow to never again trust the Church or the source from which the information came. Derek was, of course, referring to the sacred information Brothers Job and Matthew were channeling during the night.

"The same precautions must be taken again, so that the information doesn't fall into the wrong hands," Derek cautioned. "We must keep separate what we learn and what we have done together (in that past life). If we can take some of the information now and join it up, then we will do so. The work, the book that was so closely guarded, will be rewritten so that it is understandable. The truths will be in what is said, although the wording will not be as archaic as before; it will be more 'palatable.' It will be incorporated into a book in much the same way that information is being channeled to us now. Within our story there are a lot of truths being revealed. Truths are always truths," Derek finished in a hushed tone.

What did it all mean? Would Derek and I re-channel the information he and Brother Matthew received during that lifetime, and perhaps write another book? I didn't have time to find out or even bring Derek out of the past-life regression properly as there was a knock on the office door. It was time for his appointment with a client. The gentle knock rocketed him back into our present reality.

At our next channeling session, I used the opportunity to ask about Brothers Job and Matthew and the 'sacred book.' "The book that Derek and our friend wrote lifetimes ago—will that be written again, and if so, will I be assisting in that writing?" I asked.

The response came quickly from Derek's guide Robert. "*Yes. The Word will be given again, some time after your present manuscript is completed. It may be a joint effort by the three of you, as you were all connected with the work before.*"

EPILOGUE

By September of 1995, I was still plodding along working on the book, although it was becoming a chore. The fun part was over. I had sort of written a book, but there was so much editing work needed before I could submit it to any publishers, and deep down inside, I knew that to really finish the job I needed isolation. More than anything else, I wanted seclusion within sight of the mountains, where there would be no pressures, no obligations, and no interruptions -- so I could just submerge myself in working on the book.

It's amazing how energy is created so that we will fulfill our obligations or do whatever it is we have chosen to do. Equally surprising is how the thoughts we put out certainly do create our future and what becomes our 'reality.' Three months later, clear out of the blue, a young man phoned us. He was a former student of ours and we hadn't heard from him in a long time. He said he had been thinking of us a lot and felt indebted to us for having helped him so much during one of our workshops. He felt compelled to do something for us in return. Then he asked if we still had 'the pioneer spirit.' I laughed as I asked him why. That's when he offered us the use of a cottage in British Columbia. He'd rented it for six months, he said, but had just been offered a job at Mount Baldy, so the cottage was available for four months if we wished. We would find the mountain view to be very refreshing, he threw in. You bet we've got the pioneer spirit, I thought to myself. Without drawing breath I told him we'd jump at the opportunity.

So, without any planning on my part, I got what I had wished for. And in the process, I found out just how quickly and completely that reality can manifest. I longed to be near the mountains. I'd asked for isolation. I got them both. And into the bargain, no pressures, no obligations, no interruptions...and just the barest of essentials!

So, on what best could be described as little more than a whim, we brought classes and workshops to a halt, and closed the office. On New Year's Eve, we packed Intensity, Sanctuary, all our crystals, our computer, two cockatiels plus cage and a few belongings. We gave away most of our furniture and other possessions, including our old jalopy that had refused to crank over in the minus-30 degree temperature. And then, some very dear friends chauffeured us to the mountains.

As we settled in for the ride, I couldn't help wondering what else was afoot. Although I cried like a baby when at the last minute I had to part with my new electric frying pan because there was no more room available in the vehicle, I did know there is a positive side to all this moving house. This was the tenth occasion in our five years together. Each time we move, more junk is discarded as what was once considered a necessity becomes redundant. 'If we keep going at this rate,' I reckoned, 'we'll eventually be down to one suitcase.' I can't help wondering if there is an underlying logic to this moving that we're not yet aware of. Are we being 'prepared' for 'traveling light'?

We certainly seemed to be poised at the edge of a new threshold. And then our extra-ordinary adventures in learning began all over again as the book was nearing completion.

Tired, and almost penniless, with typing becoming painful from blue knuckles protesting the cold (our little cottage had heating in only one room), I wrote a letter to friends, epitomizing our voluntary 'exile' and chilly sojourn. The following excerpt from that letter speaks volumes:

I'm not sure why we're here except to be near mountains to finish the book. But what a delightful method of self-punishment as we freeze our buns off while gazing out at the beautiful mountains.

I know we laughed about the place having running water—about us not having to go running for it, that is. Well, yesterday, we awoke to frozen water pipes and did have to go running for some! During the night the temperature dropped to a record low for here. They say it reached minus-24 degrees.

Due to the cold, we've had to abandon the bedroom, but we've hung sheets over the doorways to keep the heat in the 'living' room (we literally live, eat, and sleep in the one room) and we've been burning candles everywhere else to take the chill out of the air. In every room except the living room we can see our breath when we speak.

In spite of the fact that it's been so frigid in this little abode, we're truly grateful, it houses a need, although I haven't got too much done on the book these past few days—my fingers get so stiff with the cold they complain and refuse to work.

But you've got to see the funny side of things. Derek quite literally winds our down-filled sleeping bag liner around me to keep me warm so I can type, whilst he wears a pair of ladies large and luminous orange bell-bottom ski pants with a bib front that he paid five dollars for at a thrift shop. Yep, it's that cold!

I think there's comedy here that could be called 'Diana's folly'! You see, it's been a wonderful lesson to remind us that in all of this creating our own reality stuff, we must be very specific when we ask the universe for help. I guess I should have asked for good heating in the place and everything in working order and doors on every room...there are no inside doors and you can see straight into the bathroom from the front entrance! And talking about the bathroom, the water goes cold as soon as it hits the bathtub, so ablutions are over and done with very quickly, as you can guess.

And if I didn't laugh so much at the ramshackle electric stove being a joke, I'd get too angry to use it. The large element only works on maximum and no other setting, the left rear ring only works on medium, the right rear seems, um, okay on most, and the right front only on low. But I can't complain about the oven, even though the door doesn't close too well, as the interior, bless its little workings, labors zealously to provide us with homemade bread, which I bake just to warm up the kitchen every second or third day! There's no shortage of running water when I use the oven...the kitchen is so cold that heat from the oven causes rivers of condensation to roll down the walls. Of course, I always keep veggie stew or soup on a slow simmer all day and that doesn't help the condensation situation...but we have to keep warm some way!

* * *

One night, when I was feeling rather tired of our hardships, I cried out to the Universe, asking why on earth were we doing all this. I got my answer through a vivid dream. And in the morning, while we were both still huddled under our down-filled sleeping bag liner, Derek regressed me back into the dream:

"We're riding on a bus and are asked to get off and give a message to a woman who'll be sitting at the stop, waiting. We get off, deliver the message and then get back on the bus again. Someone yells that Mrs. So-n-so has just given birth and her baby was delivered by a little girl. We're asked to deliver another message, but the next time we get off, there's no one waiting."

Then, whilst I was still in that altered state of awareness, Derek asked me what was the meaning of the dream. My interpretation came easily: "We're on a journey. But we have a message to give to the world, which is symbolized by the woman waiting at the bus stop. The baby is the 'book.'

The baby being delivered by a little girl means that when the book is ready for birth, it will be published quickly by a relatively young publishing-house. Getting off the bus the second time and finding no one there means that the second 'message' or second book is already taken care of, and is also going to be published by the same publishers." I was thrilled with my interpretation. Looking for a 'relatively young' publishing house could certainly narrow our search.

Although isolated in our own way—the place was without a phone—I knew we weren't really alone. We were so comforted in the realization that our guides also came for the change of scene.

* * *

On those final days of putting the book together, we realized that in all our seeking for answers about Intensity and Sanctuary, we had essentially undergone an extensive initiation into soul consciousness that had raised our level of conscious awareness to heights and dimensions formerly undreamt of by either of us. Although not apparent to us then, we had actually been supping at the fountain of knowledge many times. I guess we were so engrossed in looking for the proverbial woods that we had been unable to see the trees around us.

Our guides told us to prepare for an avalanche of mail as a chord will be struck within the hearts of many who read "The Awakening Time" poem over again. For some readers, from deep within their being, like the echo of a distant cry, they will feel the remembrance of the promise and the vow. For them, this indeed will become the awakening time!

What the guides hadn't told me was that my book had grown out of all proportions to well over one hundred thousand words, and I was faced again with more pruning.

It was Good Friday 1996, and I was busy adding the finishing touches, I thought to the book. However, the computer completely shut down. Derek recognized the cue that our guides were wishing to communicate. Now, I wonder, how could he have guessed that?

As he clipped a microphone to my sweater, I heard the opening words of "The Awakening Time" poem, "The time is now to listen." I began seeing the vision of a young man, and at that point it was as if I had a sense of 'knowing.'

I said to Derek: "I don't want to put an interpretation on this, but I see a young man carrying a cross, the crowds are parting as he walks through, and there is much sadness on his face. The people who wish to help him are being held back, and there are those who know that if they do help him they will be put to death. This man believes differently. There were those watching from above. It need not have happened this way, but it did, because of the choices he had made. It did not need to be such a dreadful death with humiliation in public."

I heard the words again as my guide began speaking:

"*The time is now to listen. These words can be applied to everyone today to give an opportunity for the ego to take a back seat and listen. Much is occurring at this time. It is time for all egos to sit back. That is not to say, remove the ego, just give it a well-earned rest. On a day such as today there are many memories that have been amassed. It is an awakening time in many ways, an opportunity to remember events that took place a long time ago.*

"*Those appointed by Rome needed the support of the Jewish people and the Jewish leaders at that time. For Jewish leaders, it was bad enough that there was trouble between the different sects, but it was worse that there were those amongst their numbers within a sect who were causing trouble also. All three groups had their own beliefs.*

"*Those that cannot be seen were assisting a man to carry a cross. He was perceived by Rome to be only a vague threat. But it had to be shown by people in control that they were doing something. It was intended to make an example of him. He was taken, as accounts reported, cruelly nailed. This man had the ability, if he wished, to take himself right out of the scene physically, but he chose not to. And his fears at the last moment—'Father why hast thou forsaken me'—caused by a weakened state, prevented this. But his 'death' served a purpose, showing others that there is no death. And those who were with him saw him again. They were playing with fire,*" my guide continued ominously.

"*During this occurrence and the one alluded to in ' the promise and the vow'* [referred to in "The Awakening Time" poem], *both sacrificed were honoring their beliefs, what they believed in.*

"*The Christ energies will return and the people through whom the Christ energies will be returning are already here. There are many through whom the energies will be working, but it is befitting that they become cleansed and humbled, not in a subservient way, but with a humility that comes with knowing one is in one's rightful place, along with everyone else in their rightful place.*

"*When the time is right, the returning Christ energies will manifest through certain people, as changes occur and as it is necessary. This time there is a group energy that is required. It will arise like a flame and it will spread throughout the planet. You will take* a very active role at a later stage. There are those whom you know, and you will recognize the others. Some you have met and others you will meet.

"As you become less concerned with who is right and who is wrong, as you become as you really are, you will find a power will manifest, not just in your hands or in your hearts, but in your whole beings.

"You will see that you are illuminated from within all the way out. And as others look at you they will see their own origin; you will reflect to them what they were, what they are and what they will be—which is what you are—and they will be it; your very presence will do this for them. And blessed shall they be that will come into your presence and the presence of the others who will assist you. Your path is long but you will be given more assistance than you realize possible.

"You will know that there are others working for the chosen task. And you will know that the power and the glory come from the highest. It is with you, but it soars at a higher level, and it will manifest through you. And you see, by that time, people will be ready to receive and understand.

"There are things that you cannot say, or you must not say. It is best to say nothing and be the example, and there will be a lot more that is said when words are not spoken. The people will receive the energy by being in proximity, and as they receive the energy, and as they speak of what they have received, when they are with others, those also will be filled with the energy.

"And it will be as if the people are taking each other's hands and reaching right around the world; the energy will be spread like that. The healing energy has to go through the human vehicles in the same way; it will pass from one to the other. They will not realize what they are doing; they will be conduits of Light until the planet is filled with new energy that will uplift. The whole of the planet will be raised into a higher dimension, and it is only with the assistance of the Lords of Light that this can occur. They will be the ones directing the energy to those such as you. These Lords of the Universe are ready and waiting, and know they have your full cooperation.

"If everyone realized the significance of the undertaking, of what is occurring during these times, you wouldn't all be locked into your little power struggles to prove who is right and who is wrong! Look for the light within each other. Look for the light within everyone. You see it in their eyes.

"Those who avert their eyes are afraid, that is all. There are those who feel shame and regret. There will be many unable to hold the gaze for more than a second or two; for others, it will be less than that. They, too, will be affected by the presence, by the Light.

"There is much for you to do yet. We will be with you as we will be with the others. You are blessed," the guide concluded on an encouraging note.

What is one supposed to do after receiving a message like this on a Good Friday? Sit in stunned silence? Go for coffee? Transcribe the proceedings or hide the tape and then ignore the whole thing? All of the above! Derek did in fact transcribe the session and put the document away in a folder, where it remained for seven months. At the end of that time, when I thought I'd finished editing the book before submitting it to a publisher, Derek was thumbing through the folder and found the document. As we read it again, at the last minute, there was what can only be described as a driving compulsion to include it in the book. We couldn't ignore it any more.

* * *

Before putting the book to bed, or at least in the hands of a publisher, Derek and I pondered if, perhaps, *The Awakening Time* was incomplete in some way. We questioned whether there had been too much talk of mutual bickering rather than writing of the unusually deep bond that developed between us. The bond was our bonus, you could say, an extraordinarily special end result of our disputes, yet a bonus of which we were blissfully unaware at the time those disagreements occurred.

We now understood that whenever our differences had arisen, they also created the energy required for us to investigate the matter and find the hidden, underlying cause. Even our constant self-questioning always included the phrase, "What am I to learn from this situation?" And we always delved deep for answers.

Now, when we look back upon our journey, we realize that each hurdle miraculously became a stepping stone to take us closer to our mutual destination and each other. Was this because not only did both of us recognize the divinity within the other, but we began to embrace it also?

We remembered words of wisdom Kajuni had shared with us after one of our tempests. *"You have found as you continue to work together towards your common goals that your love grows stronger. If you feel, as you look back upon the times you have spent together, that there has been a deep underlying bond of love inspiring you, then share this with others. It may give them reassurance and encouragement.*

"When there is strife occurring within a relationship, although their mutual expressions may not on the surface appear to be ones of love, the participants may recognize the underlying motivation. Who, other than someone operating from love, would be prepared to assist the other, or be assisted, in that mutual learning process...unless that bond was

there?" Kajuni asked gently. *"Even with no remembrance of that initial attraction which drew the two of them together, there is still hope. Because of the purity of love that was in the heart as one met the other, the knowing was there, the understanding was there, and the joy and the anticipation were there.*

"And for them it can be the same again, just as soon as they recognize that all of life's trials are self-imposed so that the soul may truly learn its lessons through the full expression of each facet of love. Know, too, that each participant within a relationship has chosen the most perfect partner with whom to join for those mutual learning experiences."

We both felt truly blessed by our relationship and our journey. Our sincere wish is for others to witness the blessings within all of their own relationships and so recognize the glimmer of love-light from which a higher understanding emerges. Our experiences have taught us that everything happens exactly as it should. And we look forward to the remainder of the journey.

As I included those final words, the room resounded with the cry: "Derek, I've finished the book!" And from the kitchen, I heard my funny man yell, "Save it!" You bet!

But there is one more thing of which I am quite certain. Derek and I will still enjoy our early morning sessions working with Intensity and Sanctuary as we continue in our attempts to discover the secrets held within those green onyx eggs!

And although I know the winds of change are about to blow once again, I sense Derek and I, like two restless tumbleweeds, will welcome its embrace. I guess time alone will tell whether there really are such things as spirit balls, spiritual and cosmic guides, or guardian angels, onyx eggs with sacred information, devas and crystals that tell of a promise and a vow, or major earth changes that will come to pass. But until anyone can prove differently, we will cherish our own beliefs and allow others to have theirs.

Derek's Postscript

Foresight is a wonderful tool. But if we have the ability to see what is to happen, would we go through the experience? Hindsight, on the other hand, comes after the experience, so, looking back at the journey Diana and I embarked upon, I'm now able to understand why the front of this book cover includes the words "Initiation into Soul Consciousness."

It is easy to get so caught up in the mainstream of life around us that we become accustomed to believing what we see and hear and experience with our five senses is 'the whole truth.' We only use ten percent of our brains and those five senses…yet there's so much more to us than that…if only we dare reach further to become all that we are, if only we're prepared to take the next step and open our eyes, our real eyes—and use our inner vision.

During my 'awakening time' I found that within the process I changed many of my truths (with a lot of protest and fighting) along the way. You've probably heard the saying, "Behind every good man there's a woman telling him how to do things or that he's wrong." It's true. But I can now see that, for me, this was a blessing in disguise. My beautiful lady ranks high among the most wonderful blessings of my life.

I now understand that the person pushing our buttons, the one who has an opposing view evoking an emotional reaction within us, is actually assisting us to search within. It's telling us there is something within us that requires attention. That person is simply being a catalyst in presenting us an opportunity to move beyond our present level of understanding, thereby testing our willingness to be personally challenged. It also gives the opportunity to check if our truths are valid and to see if we are open to the truths of others. If we are not open to expanding our truths about self and life and learning from such an opportunity being presented, we may stagnate and limit our growth.

Part of my "Initiation into Soul Consciousness," I believe, is this… "The Awakening Time" is to recognize what my personal truths are so that I can consciously begin to accept myself, to see the divinity within, and then to see the divinity within others (all life forms). At times I had to place my beliefs aside and allow my feelings to let me know if things that I was experiencing were true for me, or if I was being influenced by prior programming or imprinting. I now know it is important to focus inwardly to seek our own truths. Otherwise, how are we able to know what is really true for us? Accepting only what we feel comfortable with and leaving behind what doesn't feel right helps bring us to the point where we're ready to raise our level of understanding, which then becomes our new truth. And our new truth assists in our awakening.

I'm still working on two of the toughest lessons that are a big part of the initiation: 'patience' and 'tolerance' with self. I would like to share a short passage from these pages that helps me remember why we are here:

"The soul yearns for reunion with the God Essence and undergoes certain experiences through the physical body, to bring it closer to the state of perfection it seeks before it can be reunited. These experiences provide the soul with an opportunity, whilst in the physical, to express unconditional love, through patience, tolerance, and love of self and others.

"In the process of striving to attain a higher level, or the level of perfection it seeks, conditions are sometimes induced that promote dislike of self. You strive to receive recognition and acceptance from others, yet you reject yourselves, your physical bodies, for whatever reason. Although unaware of it, you project that rejection outwards to others and in turn, this rejection is projected back, reflected back to you. As you think, so you create; if you think negatively of self, so you create more about which to be negative. If you think of self positively, others respond positively to those thoughts by recognizing the positive energy being projected. Your thoughts are your greatest tools."

See the beauty within your life, as everything has meaning. When you least expect it, you may find your truth…between the lines you read…or between the words you hear…in those small places where only your heart knows the truth. It's up to you to look for it.

Derek

Printed in the United States
1496300002B/70